Advance ~~praise for~~
Surviving a Mass Killer Rampage

Chris Bird has artfully challenged citizens to prepare themselves to survive a mass killer incident. It's a challenge that may save your life! Chris Bird effectively recounts real life incidents to show the power that citizens have to react and respond to criminal incidents before law enforcement can arrive. Citizens have a right to not become a victim or crime statistic. Fifty-five years ago my father-in-law, Bud Zielny, protected his family by shooting an intruder. Rather than discourage, law enforcement should encourage citizens to own and be trained in the use of firearms with which they can respond when required to save their life or the life of another.

— **Sheriff John Whetsel**, Oklahoma County, Oklahoma, Past President, International Assoc. of Chiefs of Police

Every few years a true expert comes along and delivers to America a seminal work on the insidious problem of mass-murder in our schools. With this book, Chris Bird has revealed the problem — and the answer. The threats to our children come in many shapes and sizes: from single and multiple student shooters, to adults and even terrorists. Yet the solution is, in most cases, the same. It is a simple and common sense approach that unfortunately takes the painstakingly expansive research and analysis that Mr. Bird has offered. This book is not only critically important and compelling reading for anyone with children in school or who works in our schools, but for anyone who cares about keeping our most innocent safe from the most vile harm imaginable.

— **John Giduck**, J.D., M.S.S., PH.D., CHS-V, Author of *Terror at Beslan*, *When Terror Returns*, and *Shooter Down! The Dramatic Untold Story of the Police Response to the Virginia Tech Massacre*

For over twenty years, the unthinkable has occurred over and over: the killings of innocent victims simply to achieve a high body count. Sick, deranged, and inexcusable are but a few identifiers. *Surviving a Mass Killer Rampage*, by noted author Chris Bird, provides historical analyses of these phenomena, as well as pragmatic approaches [to prevent them]. This book is a "must read" if you are at all interested in a factual, well-documented understanding of mass shootings.

— **Dr. Richard Caster**, former Executive Director, National Association of School Resource Officers

The stories in *Surviving a Mass Killer Rampage* are well-written and factual. Overall it is a good book for the general public to read and heed. We still have no solution to the problem of mass killers other than trained firearms carriers on the scene, as well as informed and vigilant members of society who are willing and able to fight back.

— **Jack Dean**, retired Texas Ranger Captain and former U.S. Marshal, Western District of Texas

This is a fantastic piece of work! The time you spent interviewing those involved in each incident has produced a very clear picture of both the killers and their victims' actions throughout the ordeal. Other than training I have attended wherein the investigating agency presented the incident from start to finish, never before have I been privy to such detail.

— **Wayne Rausch**, Sheriff, Latah County, home of the University of Idaho

This is a very important, must-read work. It is extremely well researched and will prove invaluable to those charged with determining how to deal with the active-killer issue in their school or place of business. For what it's worth, I think the new training model should involve the Benner-style training, as well as the ALICE program. Then the people responsible for the security training would be able to develop a combined plan for the armed as well as the unarmed participants.

— **Ed Lovette**, retired CIA officer and firearms instructor for the New Mexico State Police

Having read both of his previous books, it is quite evident that Chris Bird is an excellent in-depth researcher. *Surviving a Mass Killer Rampage* confirms this. It was my honor to contribute some of my work to the book. In *Surviving a Mass Killer Rampage*, readers should enjoy interesting factual information, conclusions, and valid advice woven into stories in a way that only Chris Bird can do. Readers may easily visualize being present at these scenes as Chris unweaves each incident. Speaking of being there, in today's perilous world, armed or unarmed, readers could very well become what Chris Bird terms as "Irregular First Responders" in such locations and predicaments that he recounts. Chris Bird makes a perfect case for the freedom envisioned by our forefathers when they gave us "Liberty's Teeth," the Second Amendment to the U.S. Constitution. In *Surviving a Mass Killer Rampage* Chris shares numerous tips, concepts, and principles that will give readers reality-based, practical ideas about how to survive a mass killer rampage.

— **Ron Borsch**, PACT Consultant Group and retired police trainer

Bird compiles data from many killings and collates them with comments from topic experts. He outlines the training in Texas, Utah, and Ohio, where armed staff have been part of school response plans for years. The reader is presented with details to really understand what happens and knowledge to formulate a plan that will make those around them safer.

— **Alan Gottlieb**, author and Founder
of the Second Amendment Foundation

Chris Bird is a journalist's journalist! His ability to make sense of today's rampant violence is amazing indeed! This book should be studied by all who are concerned about current trends in world history!

— **John S. Farnam**, author of *The Farnam Method
of Defensive Handgunning* and President
of Defense Training International

Chris Bird offers many examples of how murderers and terrorists work. They all like unarmed victims. "Don't be one" is an inescapable lesson of Bird's research.

— **Larry Pratt**, Executive Director Emeritus,
Gun Owners of America

A book about mass violence, written for the general public. Bird brings the victims' stories to life, allowing the reader to grasp the personal cost of mass killings. It is an informative book for anyone and a compelling study for school board, school administrators, church leaders, employers, and managers who care about their employees.

— **Jim Irvine**, President,
Buckeye Firearms Association

SURVIVING
A MASS KILLER RAMPAGE

When Seconds Count,
Police Are Still Minutes Away

SURVIVING
A MASS KILLER RAMPAGE

When Seconds Count,
Police Are Still Minutes Away

Chris Bird

Privateer Publications
San Antonio, Texas

Published by: Privateer Publications • (210) 308-8191
Post Office Box 29427 • San Antonio, TX 78229

Printed in the United States of America.
Impression 10 9 8 7 6 5 4 3 2 1

Publisher's Cataloging-in-Publication
(Provided by Quality Books, Inc.)

Bird, Chris, author.
    Surviving a mass murder rampage: when seconds count, police are still minutes away/ Chris Bird.
    pages cm
    Includes bibliographical references and index.
    ISBN: 978-0-9835901-9-4

    1. Mass murder--United States. 2. Emergency management--United States. 3. Victims of violent crimes --United States--Case studies. 4. Self-defense--United States. 5. Crime prevention--United States--Citizen participation. I. Title.

HV6529.B527 2015   364.152'340973
                         QBI15-600211

Library of Congress Control Number: 2016937024

To my editor and friend Susan Hughes, who has supported my publishing efforts from the beginning, and her husband Bruce Hughes, also my friend and IT supporter.

"In a moment of decision,
the best thing you can do is the right thing.
The next best thing is the wrong thing.
The worst thing you can do is nothing."

— Theodore Roosevelt

"The only thing that stops a bad guy with a gun
is a good guy with a gun."

— Wayne LaPierre, National Rifle Association

"Hiding under desks and praying for rescue
from professionals is not a recipe for survival."

— Greg Crane, ALICE Training Institute

CONTENTS

FOREWORD
by
Massad Ayoob

It is an honor to write the foreword for Chris Bird's excellent book on surviving mass murder rampages. Over the years, Chris has done substantial primary research — that is, debriefing the participants and survivors, not just cutting and pasting news stories — on incidents of self-defense and defense of others. The result has been an exemplary series of "you are there" books, analyzing not only what happened, but the lessons that were learned.

The book you're holding in your hands addresses a topic that has terrorized our nation and the rest of the world, and yes, the word "terrorized" is used advisedly. The attacks seem to come primarily from three sources. One is the politically motivated and/or religious fanatic whom we associate with the term terrorist. Another is the sick narcissist who wants to become famous for murdering the innocent in large numbers, inflicting terror, death, and maiming to somehow feel more powerful. Finally, there is the thwarted loser who seeks personal revenge on schoolmates and teachers, or bosses and employees, for being more successful and more likable people than he (or she). Terror is the goal of each category. They follow the lead of Niccolo Machiavelli and Benito Mussolini — they would rather be feared than loved.

We humans are the dominant species on the planet. There are only two things we fear: that which we do not understand, and that which we cannot control. Here, in the book you hold in your hands, my old friend Chris Bird addresses both. He allows the reader to *understand* how these things happen, and he advocates the methods and equipment known to *control* them and stop the killing, giving example after proven example.

In, say, the year 1950, only firefighters seemed wise enough to have fire extinguishers in their homes. If you went to the family physician and asked him to teach you closed chest cardiac massage, as cardiopulmonary resuscitation was called then, he would have looked at you as if you were nuts and told you to go to medical school if you wanted to learn that stuff. And if you had asked your local police chief about deadly force against criminals, he might have told you to go to the police academy and become a cop, because that was *their* province.

Today, things have changed. The homeowner who *doesn't* have a fire extinguisher in the kitchen and the person who doesn't know CPR and other basic first aid is seen as somewhat derelict in their responsibilities to their family and indeed to society. Self-defense is the last bastion of the "let the professionals take care of it" canard, but that too is changing rapidly, and all of this is true for a very good reason.

At this writing, there are an estimated 765,000 full-time, sworn (i.e., armed and invested with arrest powers) police officers in the United States...345,950 full-time firefighters... and 241,200 full-time paramedics and emergency medical technicians. *This in a country populated by approximately 320,000,000 people who at any moment may need those emergency services.*

Each of those full-time emergency-service professionals is scheduled for a 40-hour work week, in a week that contains 168 hours. Some of those weeks each professional is on vacation, or on sick leave (often hurt in the line of duty), or in mandatory in-service training. *Do the math!*

This means there is going to be a response-time factor. As Chris Bird and his blue ribbon experts point out in this book, response time covers only the period between when the first call comes in to emergency dispatch and the first of the professional responders arrive...*but there is also the time it takes the terrified victims to make that call in the first place.*

The fire extinguisher and the smoke alarm became standard when Americans "did the math" and realized that in the time it took them to make the call and for the fire service to respond when flames flared up on the stove, the entire house could "become involved" and perhaps burn to the ground and kill everyone still inside. But a smoke alarm and a fire extinguisher allowed the victim to be the first responder and limit the damage to scorched wallpaper and a smoke-darkened kitchen ceiling. In the time it took for the emergency medical personnel to be summoned and travel to the scene, the ordinary citizen with first-responder emergency-medical skills could be the difference between a live trauma patient or one who had bled to death, a live heart-attack victim instead of a dead one.

It is exactly the same in mass-murder situations. Those there on the ground — what has now become the killing ground — can stop the murders and save lives. But that's true only *if* they know what to do…and are equipped to stop the killing.

A couple of years ago, I joined Chris Bird and our mutual friend Dr. John Edeen on a panel at the annual Gun Rights Policy Conference. I said then, and have said before, and will say again: "So-called 'Gun-Free Zones' are simply hunting preserves for mass murderers who wish to kill helpless humans." John and Chris, and so many more professionals in this field, have come to the same conclusion.

We already have armed security made up of parishioners at many houses of worship…and that concept is spreading. We are already seeing armed school staff, such as the Texas School Marshals…and that concept is spreading, too. It worked quite successfully in Israel since the Maalot Massacre, and though it has come late to America, well…better late than never. When Israel went in that direction, we heard the same weak cries of political correctness raised here: "Moral victory, blah blah! Educators don't carry guns, blah blah!" And to her great credit, then-Prime Minister of Israel Golda Meir authorized the armed-school-personnel program with a cold, hard statement of reality: "We will not make politics on the backs of our children!"

The book you now hold in your hand speaks The Truth. Read it. Spread it and its message.

Because that truth, the truth Chris Bird has delivered to you, will save lives in the future.

Massad Ayoob has been a firearms/deadly force instructor since 1972, performing that function full-time since 1982, and served nineteen years as chair of the firearms committee for the American Society of Law Enforcement Trainers and thirteen on the advisory board of the International Association of Law Enforcement Firearms Instructors. He is the author of twenty-one books, including two authoritative texts in the armed self-defense field: **In the Gravest Extreme** *(Police Bookshelf, 1980) and* **Deadly Force** *(FW Media, 2014), along with thousands of articles. He has also served as an expert witness for the courts in weapons/homicide cases since 1979 and has served as a part-time, fully sworn police officer for forty-two years.*

Introduction

In 2011 when I was putting together the sixth edition of *The Concealed Handgun Manual*, I dealt with what police call "active shooter" incidents in the first chapter entitled "Mass Shootings." Since that time there has been increased interest in these multiple shootings where groups of people congregate.

As I write this, the coordinated attacks in Paris are still making headlines. I felt these incidents and how ordinary people can deal with them and survive deserve a book-length examination. I have expanded that first chapter into *Surviving a Mass Murder Rampage: When Seconds Count, Police Are Still Minutes Away*.

I should point out that no one can guarantee that you will survive a mass shooting incident, but this book provides accounts of many such events and suggestions for training and tactics that will increase survivability. The best precaution is to have a gun, but in most cases active killers choose venues that are "gun-free zones." In the same way that in the military "friendly fire" isn't, "gun-free zones" aren't. They are only free of law-abiding citizens with guns.

The incident that shocked the American public more than any other happened at Sandy Hook Elementary School in Connecticut, where twenty children six- and seven-years-old were murdered along with six adult school employees. This shooting, like other mass shootings, predictably resulted in calls from the usual anti-self-defense suspects for more gun-control laws. None of the proposed laws would have prevented that shooting or any other school shooting. Fortunately, some people realized that a different approach was needed. This has led some schools, notably in Utah, Texas, and Ohio, to allow staff members who have concealed-handgun licenses to carry their guns in schools.

It is mostly the school and college shootings that have resulted in changes to law-enforcement practices to cope with these active killers. There is also a growing recognition that law-enforcement officers are not the first responders in these incidents — ordinary people on the scene are. I have dubbed these folks "Irregular First Responders."

This book could not have been written without the support and cooperation of John Benner and his crew at Tactical Defense Institute. John allowed me free access to several of his classes teaching educators and ordinary citizens how to cope with active killers. He was one of the first to realize that time is the enemy and that armed people on the scene trump waiting for law enforcement.

Benner's classes train civilians who are assumed to be armed. However, the vast majority of active-killer attacks take place in "gun-free zones" where all but the killers are unarmed. Greg Crane's ALICE program addresses the unarmed response. Greg was kind enough to allow me to take an ALICE instructor course, as well as to share his thoughts with me. Chapter 8 is the result.

My coverage of mass killings is organized in four parts. First are shootings in schools and colleges, from the University of Texas Tower incident at Austin in 1966, through Columbine and Virginia Tech, to the Sandy Hook shooting in 2012.

Second are mass shootings in other places — Luby's Cafeteria, Killeen, Texas, 1991; New Life Church, Colorado Springs, 2007; and Pinelake Health and Rehabilitation nursing home, Carthage, North Carolina, 2009.

While many of these incidents can be labeled domestic terrorism, the rise of radical Muslim jihad deserves special attention. That is dealt with in Chapters 13 and 14.

The conclusion notes both changes that have been made and that need to be made to current approaches.

In the instances of Rapid Mass Murder recounted in this book, I have tried to answer the questions: Who, What, When, Where, and How. I am not concerned whether the perpetrator was bullied or picked on, was evil or just plain crazy. It is enough that he or she is killing innocent people and needs to be stopped. I leave to others the question of why.

Notes on Terminology

In law-enforcement circles, the perpetrators of mass killings have become known as "Active Shooters." A couple of experts that I have quoted frequently in this book decline to use that term.

John Benner owns and is chief instructor at Tactical Defense Institute, a shooting school about an hour east of Cincinnati in Ohio. He is a Vietnam veteran and for twenty years was the head of the Hamilton County, Ohio, multi-jurisdictional SWAT team. At TDI, he teaches school teachers and ordinary citizens how to cope with mass killers. As he puts it: "We are all active shooters, but we are not active killers."

Ron Borsch, also a Vietnam veteran, retired in 1997 after thirty years with the Bedford, Ohio, Police Department as a patrol officer, SWAT team operator, and trainer.

In 1998 he founded SEALE Regional Police Training Academy, where he was the manager and lead trainer until 2015. SEALE stands for South East Area Law Enforcement, a mutual-aid cooperative of seven suburbs of Cleveland that fields its own SWAT Team, Bomb Squad, Drug Unit, Negotiations Team, and Academy. From 2000 to 2015 Borsch specialized in teaching tactics and mass-killer counter measures to police first responders in his tactical-first-responder course attended by officers from ten states.

He says the terms "Active" and "Shooter" are neutral and can refer to anyone who shoots regularly. The term "Active Killer" refers to someone who is a criminal and is self-explanatory.

I have chosen to use the term "Active Killer" rather than "Active Shooter," except where the term is used in a direct quote.

Neither Benner nor Borsch uses the names of the killers in their presentations. Benner feels that by not using their names he is denying them the notoriety most of them are desperately seeking. Borsch says use of their names gives them "instant celebrity status."

"That is what these people, at least some of them, are interested in. So with that instant celebrity status, they go from being a nobody to all of a sudden being a somebody," Borsch says. "When the media learn to not publish his picture or his name, that we shun him forever, that he will not be recognized for whatever he did do, then we're going to start to taper off these things."

Again, I have decided to follow the examples of these two expert trainers, so you will not find the names of the perpetrators in this book.

Ron Borsch is manager and lead consultant with PACT Consultant Group, which he founded in the early 1990s. He has a newsletter that goes out to more than seven hundred law-enforcement professionals and keeps a database of mass murders going back to 1975. He has coined several terms that I have used with his permission: "Rapid Mass Murder" (RMM); "Tactical Loitering;" and "SOLO," which stands for "Single Officer's Lifesaving Others." The SOLO term is used when a lone officer braces an active killer, and it refers to the principle that in large facilities single officers can and should be going in different directions in search of the murderer. Borsch also coined the term "Stopwatch of Death©."

ABOUT THE AUTHOR

Chris Bird has been a journalist for more than forty years and a handgun shooter for more than fifty. He was born in England, and his interest in shooting has steered him through the bureaucratic red tape of owning handguns in England, Canada, and Australia. As a commissioned officer in the Royal Military Police of the British Army in the 1960s, Bird was stationed in Berlin, West Germany, and Belgium, serving as company weapon-training officer and winning awards for shooting in competition.

After leaving the military, Bird migrated to Canada, where he worked as a cowboy in British Columbia, while shooting and hunting extensively.

He became a journalist and worked as a crime and investigative reporter for the *Vancouver Province* newspaper and the Canadian Broadcasting Corporation. He has also worked as a salesman, a private investigator, and a shotgun guard for an armored car company in Australia.

The call of the sea lured him away from his Canadian career to embark with his wife Anita on a two-year voyage from Vancouver, Canada, to Sydney, Australia, aboard *British Privateer*, a twenty-seven-foot sailboat that he built himself. They sailed back across the Pacific and took up residence in Anita's home state of Texas.

Bird has adopted the state as his spiritual home, and they live in San Antonio. Arriving in Texas in 1989, Bird worked as a police reporter for the San Antonio Express-News, mostly covering crime and law enforcement at all levels from municipal to federal. He is author and publisher of *The Concealed Handgun Manual*, which is now in its sixth edition. He is also author and publisher of *Thank God I Had a Gun: True Accounts of Self-Defense*, now in its second edition. He has written articles for *SWAT* magazine, *Concealed Carry Magazine*, and *The Gun Mag*.

Bird is certified in Texas as a concealed-handgun instructor. He is a former president and a former director of the Texas Concealed Handgun Association. He is a member of the Texas State Rifle Association, the National Rifle Association, the Second Amendment Foundation, and Gun Owners of America.

In 2013 he and Anita returned to the sea to sail their thirty-six-foot sailboat from Corpus Christi, Texas, to Bermuda and back to North Carolina.

ACKNOWLEDGMENTS

Most books owe their existence to people whose names do not appear on the cover. *Surviving a Mass Murder Rampage* is no exception. Many people have made this book possible. I will try to thank as many as possible here, but if I have omitted anyone, please accept my apologies.

As mentioned in the introduction, I could not have written this book without the help and cooperation of John Benner and his instructors at Tactical Defense Institute. These include Chris Wallace, Forrest Sonewald, Deborah Fletcher, John Motil, Cameron McElroy, Gary Hoff, Wyatt Roush, David Bowie, Dick Wheeler, and Jeff Lehman. Ed Lovette, a former CIA officer, taught us about situational awareness and terrorism, while Greg Ellifritz, a police officer from Columbus, Ohio, taught us about bombs.

While at TDI, I met Dick Caster, former Executive Director of the National Association of School Resource Officers, and Jim Irvine, President of the Buckeye Firearms Association, both of whom read most of the manuscript and provided invaluable help. Benner and Irvine got together after Sandy Hook and created the FASTER program that teaches armed teachers how to protect themselves and their students.

Greg Crane, who invented the ALICE (Alert, Lockdown, Inform, Counter, and Evacuate) program kindly allowed me to take one of his instructor courses, taught by Kenny Mayberry, a university police officer from Missouri, with assistance from David Dickinson.

I am also indebted to the following people, who shared memories of incidents in which they were involved: Joe Zamudio, retired Texas Ranger Ramiro Martinez, Assistant Principal Joel Myrick, Jake Ryker, Deputy Sheriff Tracy Bridges,

Suzanna Hupp, Jeanne Assam, Pastor Terry Howell, Vic Stacy, and Chief Operating Officer Mark Vaughan of Vaughan Foods.

Ron Borsch, retired police officer and trainer, has made a study of active-killer incidents and shared statistics from his database of incidents. Retired police psychologist Dr. Alexis Artwohl, psychiatrist Dr. Robert Young, pediatric orthopedic surgeon Dr. John Edeen, and members of Doctors for Responsible Gun Ownership shared their thoughts and expertise.

Several sheriffs provided insight: Sheriff Bobby Grubbs of Brown County, Texas; Sheriff Wayne Rausch of Latah County, Idaho; Sheriff Paul Van Blarcum, of Ulster County, New York; and Sheriff John Whetsel, of Oklahoma County, Oklahoma. In addition, Capt. Bill Mackey of the Moore County, North Carolina, Sheriff's Office ploughed valiantly through thousands of pages of documents concerning the Pinelake Rehabilitation Center shooting.

David Thweatt, Superintendent of Harrold Independent School District, and Ralph Price, Argyle Independent School District police chief, provided information about armed teachers in Texas. Clark Aposhian, president of the Utah Shooting Sports Council, provided similar information about teachers in Utah.

Dr. John Lott, President of the Crime Prevention Research Center, shared some of his material with me.

John Giduck, author and terrorism expert, allowed me to quote from his books and shared his insight into current terrorism trends.

Thanks to my friend Jerry Lane, who with his son Chase went up the University of Texas Tower.

Many thanks for all her help to my friend Ginny Simone, host and producer of *NRA News*.

Thanks also to Tom Hudgins, who designed the cover and suffered through several changes. My thanks to Mary Rowles, Mark Noble, Richard T. Williams, and all the folks at Independent Publishers Group, who provide so much more than book distribution.

PROLOGUE

"When you see an individual who shoots
a nine-year-old girl, something has to be done."
— Bill Badger, a seventy-four-year-old retired colonel
from the South Dakota National Guard

The most frequent use of a gun in self-defense is when an ordinary citizen feels threatened by a human predator and produces a gun — usually a handgun. The potential robber, rapist, or murderer sees the gun, realizes his victim-selection process needs revision, and takes off faster than a shotgun slug goes through a sheet-rock wall. No one gets hurt. Usually, the incident is not reported to the police, and there is seldom a report of the incident in the local paper or on the local television news — no blood, no story.

At the other end of the media-attention scale is when a disturbed individual turns up at a place where many people congregate — a school, a mall, a church, a workplace — and starts shooting, killing and wounding as many as possible. It is these incidents that get national attention across the air-waves, cable television, and newspapers. Screams for more gun control by the country's professional whiners, who think more laws will solve everything, typically follow. They hate the idea of ordinary citizens carrying concealed handguns for protection, and they hate the people who take responsibility for their own safety.

January 8, 2011, started as a normal, cool, winter day in Tucson. But it was destined to be anything but normal. It was to be a day that the citizens of Tucson and all of Arizona would remember for a long time.

The sky was clear, and the sun was shining. To the north of the city, preparations were being made for a political event in a shopping center on the east side of North Oracle Road and the south side of West Ina Road. There was a Safeway grocery store at the east of the center and a Walgreens pharmacy just north of it. This area was outside the City of Tucson, where Pima County Sheriff's Department enforced the law.

In front of the Safeway, several people prepared for a "Congress on Your Corner" event, where members of the public could meet and talk to their member of Congress, Gabrielle Giffords. A Democrat, Giffords, then forty, was elected to Arizona's Eighth Congressional District in 2007 and had been reelected three times.

The event was supposed to start at 10 a.m., so shortly after 9 o'clock several staff members and interns started putting up a couple of tables displaying literature about Giffords. They made a line of folding chairs stretching north along the grocery store wall towards the Walgreens so visitors could sit while waiting to talk to the congresswoman. The event was just north of the main entrance to the Safeway under the store's overhang.

Front of the Safeway where the shooting took place.
Gabriel Giffords banner is far right; Walgreens is at left.
(Pima County Sheriff's Department photo.)

Giffords's outreach director, Gabe Zimmerman, was organizing the event, while Daniel Hernandez, an intern who had been with her Tucson office only a few days, was responsible for getting people signed up on one of three clipboards before they met the congresswoman. Hernandez also had another job.

"It was my job to sit in the back and make sure if I saw anything suspicious to let Gabe and some other staff members know," he later told law-enforcement officers.

These events can get a little hectic, so they needed some control of the crowd, he said. They used stanchions and ropes as well as the tables to funnel people towards Giffords.

A large banner in front of the Safeway read "Gabrielle Giffords, United States Congress" proclaiming the event, along with a U.S. flag and an Arizona state flag.

At 9:45 they got a call saying Giffords was on her way, and Zimmerman told Hernandez and the other staff members to man their posts.

Roger Salzgeber and his wife Faith arrived in front of the grocery store about 9:40 a.m. Salzgeber retired after thirty-five years of running a wholesale cactus and succulent nursery business in Tucson and had been a volunteer in Giffords's campaign.

"I had put in about thirty hours a week during her run for Congress this last time and wanted to just drop by and say 'hello' and wish her well," Salzgeber told investigators.

He and his wife were third in line. "There was one gentleman, and then a couple, and then us. So we were just sitting on the chairs, talking to each other, my wife and I, and some of the people around us," he said.

Susan Hileman, 59, had gone to the Giffords event and had taken with her a neighbor's nine-year-old child, Christina Taylor Green, Hileman's husband Bill told a detective.

"My wife is kind of a mentor to her. And they were just trying to get a young person interested in politics," he added.

Susan Hileman said she picked up Christina from her home and drove to the Safeway. "She prepared her question, which was going to be about pollution and what the government could do about making our environment better," Hileman said.

She wanted to show Christina that she could grow up to be a Gabbie Giffords. The girl was enjoying the attention of the constituents in the line.

"Then we noticed the congresswoman was there. Pretty woman, blonde hair. She was tall and straight and slender. The sun was shining. I said to Christina, 'This could be you someday.'"

Kenneth Veeder told a detective he was there because he had a problem with the Veterans Administration in Phoenix, and he wanted to see if Giffords could help him. He was well back in the line, somewhere between fifteenth and twentieth, he said. Veeder was talking to Mary Reed and her son. "I was talking to this lady because her daughter and son were there. Her daughter was an aide to Giffords. She wanted to go up and thank Giffords for letting her be an aide up in Washington. Then, all of a sudden, her son said — I had my shirt on, and it says Infantry Airborne, 'cause I was a combat officer in Vietnam — he says: 'You're a paratrooper?' And I go: 'Yeah.' And so I was talking to her younger son 'cause he wanted to be a paratrooper."

Reed said, "We were talking about Vietnam, and I told him I wanted to rub him, because anybody that made it in and out of Vietnam three full times was a good luck charm."

Bill Badger, a seventy-four-year-old retired colonel from the South Dakota National Guard, was in the line of people hoping to talk to Giffords. He used to fly helicopters and fixed-wing aircraft for the U.S. Army before retiring and moving to Tucson. He said he was in frequent contact with Giffords and her staff and had been invited to attend the event.

Badger said there were two tables with literature on them and two staffers behind them. The staff told him he would have to get in line if he wanted to talk to the congresswoman.

"So I went down and got in line, and there were probably twenty people in line ahead of me," he later told two detectives from the Pima County Sheriff's Department.

Ronald Barber was Giffords's district director. Typically he would drive her to these events, but she had another appointment after the "Congress on Your Corner" meeting, so she drove there in her Toyota 4Runner. Barber arrived moments after the congresswoman, while she was greeting her staff. He said the first visitor was a reservist who had just come back from Iraq and wanted to show her a certificate he received. Sara Rajca, Giffords's staff photographer who also does outreach for her, took photographs of the congresswoman and the reservist.

Barber told investigators, "The second constituent was a couple who came up and started talking to the congresswoman. The way this is set up, I always stand right beside her. The purpose of that is so that if there are issues that we need to address for that couple or that person, I can bring our staff over or listen or give them information."

He was listening as the two constituents were talking to Giffords when Chief Judge John Roll stepped up. Barber knew the sixty-three-year-old judge because they were at college together. Roll was the Chief Federal District Judge for the State of Arizona. He told Barber he just wanted to greet Giffords because she had been working on some issues for him. Barber invited the judge to come back behind the tables to where he and the congresswoman were standing.

"I didn't want to have him wait in line. It was just a brief interaction. So he came around and through this opening between the two tables and stood beside me. And he and I were talking about issues," Barber said.

Twenty-four-year-old Joe Zamudio was not supposed to be anywhere near the Safeway grocery store in Tucson on January 8, 2011. He usually worked Monday to Friday at his mother's art gallery, selling paintings and delivering them to customers. Saturday was supposed to be his day off, but his mother asked him to come in to help with a special event. He and his mother finished breakfast at a nearby bakery about 10 a.m.

He got into his truck and drove across the shopping center parking lot to the Walgreens drug store next to the Safeway. As usual, he was accompanied by his dog Buddy, a black Labrador mix, and he had his gun, a Ruger P-95 semi-automatic, in an inside jacket pocket. The fifteen-round magazine had only about eight rounds in it.

"I don't keep my clips [magazines] fully loaded," Zamudio said.

What was not usual was that he had a round in the chamber. Usually, when he put the gun in his pocket in the morning, he would put the magazine in but would not rack the slide to put a round in the chamber.

"That morning — who knows why? — I chambered a round," he said.

Zamudio is left-handed, so carried the gun in his right-hand inside coat pocket for a cross draw.

He parked and, leaving Buddy in the truck, he walked towards the entrance of the drug store. He intended to buy a pack of cigarettes, and that too was odd. He said he bought a pack the evening before and had smoked only one. Ordinarily his cigarettes go everywhere with him, but on this day he had left the smokes at home so he needed to buy more.

As he walked towards Walgreens, he noticed a crowd of people around a table in front of the Safeway. Although he didn't know it at the time, it was the outreach event where Giffords was meeting with her constituents.

"I thought, I wonder what's going on?" Zamudio said.

He decided to get his cigarettes first then see what had attracted the crowd.

The Shooting

Alex Villec had been an intern for Giffords. He was in Tucson on vacation before returning to school in the East. He stopped by the congresswoman's office the previous day and had been persuaded to help out at the event. He had helped out at "Congress on Your Corner" events previously and knew the system. He was standing behind one of the tables, while Giffords was behind him talking to constituents.

A young man, wearing a beanie, a black hoodie-type sweatshirt, and khaki pants, came up to the table and asked Villec if he could talk to the congresswoman. It was the sort of routine question that Villec was there to answer. He told the young man he could get into the line, and Giffords would see him in fifteen or twenty minutes.

"He was a little standoffish, kind of defensive, didn't seem to care what I had to say. He walked to the back, seemingly complying," Villec said.

A minute or so later, the young man returned, which struck Villec as unusual. He thought he was waiting in the line.

"But he came back, was stone-cold faced, barged through the table that was separating him from me and the congresswoman. I didn't see the gun itself but heard the gunshots. Took a second to register what was actually happening. Saw the congresswoman go into a natural self-defense posture to shield herself from all this being inflicted upon her," he said.

Barber did see the gun. "I saw this guy with a gun coming through the opening in the tables. And I heard him shooting.

It was a pistol, I believe. He was a thin guy as I recall. And he just started pulling the trigger."

Barber saw the gunman shoot Giffords in the head at point-blank range, and then he was shot in the leg near his groin. "I could see blood coming out of me, and I went down."

Daniel Hernandez, one of the interns, heard someone yell: "Gun." Then he heard someone shooting. He was trying to figure out what was going on when he saw Barber fall.

"Then I knew it was actual gunshots," he said.

He saw outreach director Zimmerman on the floor, then he ran over to where Giffords was lying up against the glass of the Safeway store. He checked Zimmerman for a pulse but couldn't feel one. He checked Giffords and found a faint pulse. She was breathing shallowly. Barber was conscious and alert. He told Hernandez to stay with the congresswoman, which he did. She was suffering from a head wound, and he staunched the bleeding with a smock from the Safeway meat department.

Meanwhile the shooter had shot Giffords and most of those around her before heading along the line towards the Walgreens pharmacy, shooting as he went.

Roger Salzgeber, who had volunteered in Giffords's campaign, told investigators that he and his wife were near the head of the line when the killer seemed "to come out of nowhere" and started shooting.

"My wife kind of tumbled backwards and pulled a chair over her, and I went after him [the suspect]."

Badger, the retired Army colonel, heard the shooting and saw the killer shooting at people. "Everybody started to duck, and just as I ducked, I felt a bullet hit the back of my head. It just burned the back of my head."

The killer had almost reached him when Badger said someone picked up one of the folding metal chairs and hit the suspect on the back of the head with it. There was a pause in the shooting giving Badger a chance to grab the killer's left arm while Salzgeber grabbed his right.

"The two of us brought him down and got the gun out of his hand," Salzgeber said.

The Glock Model 19 in 9mm caliber with an extended magazine clattered to the ground where Ken Veeder grabbed it.

Patricia Maisch, 61, who was also in the line, said she was lying on the ground, "waiting to be shot," when she heard someone yell to grab the gun. She tried kneeling and leaning over the killer but couldn't reach the gun. However, she was able to grab a fresh magazine that he had pulled out of his pocket, presumably to reload his gun.

Badger told *ABC News*: "I had this guy by the throat and the other guy [Salzgeber] on the other side had his knee right on the back of his neck, and so anytime he would move I would apply the choke hold and meantime the other individual would put pressure on the back of his neck. All he said was, 'Ow, ow, ow,' when we would push down on him. And I told the other gentleman, 'hold him down until the police get here,' and that's what we did."

The suspect's legs were flailing, so Maisch sat on them.

Meanwhile Joe Zamudio had decided to get his cigarettes from Walgreens before he checked out the group of people in front of the Safeway.

"That decision is the hardest one for me, because I feel like if I hadn't gone into the store first, and I had gone down there, then I would have been in a better position maybe to stop him sooner," Zamudio reflected.

He went into the store and got his cigarettes. He had swiped his debit card to pay for them but hadn't finished the transaction when he heard the shots.

Zamudio realized immediately that what he was hearing was gunfire. He ran out through the door of Walgreens, heading for the sound of the shooting.

Joe Zamudio.

"I know when I came through the doorway, I had my hand on my gun, and the safety was off," he said. He did not draw his gun.

A man outside the door was shouting: "Shooter, shooter, get down." Zamudio ran past him towards the group of people.

When shooting starts the flight response will kick in for most people. In various mental states, from thinking self-preservation to outright panic, they will run as fast as a deer from a cougar away from the gunfire. However, there are a few people, who from instinct or training, will head for the sound of the guns. Joe Zamudio is one of these few.

There was a burst of gunfire: very fast, too fast for accurate shooting, Zamudio said. "He was shooting at a pile of people. They had nowhere to move: there was a wall behind them, columns in front; they were penned in there. It was literally like shooting fish in a barrel. He didn't have to aim; that's why he was able to hurt so many people so fast."

"This is where it really got scary," he said.

He saw an older man [Veeder] getting up off the ground with a gun in his hand. He could see an extended magazine protruding from the bottom of the gun.

"Luckily, I saw that the slide was locked open."

He realized that the gun would not fire in that state, so he did not draw his own gun.

"I'm still moving, and it's still pretty intense. I've got my hand on my gun; I'm like scared. All these people are hurting, screaming already, crying. The man [Badger] who's holding the guy on the ground is all bloody. That was the first person I saw all bloody.

"It becomes crystal clear: somebody just shot a bunch of people, and I see this guy holding a gun, so I think that he's the shooter," Zamudio said.

He heard the man holding the gun say: "I'll kill you, you mother------, I'll kill you."

Veeder told a detective the gunman knocked him down. As he was getting up he saw the killer trying to reload, but one of the other men, Badger or Salzgeber, grabbed him, and the gun fell to the ground.

"I grabbed the gun, and the clip [magazine] he was reloading fell out. The lady grabbed it, and I said: 'Give me the clip; I'm going to shoot the son of a bitch.'

"She goes: 'You can't do that.'"

"And I: 'The hell I can't.' Because I would have shot him. That's how angry I was." Veeder discovered later he had been shot in the leg.

Zamudio told me: "The problem for me is, as an outside responder, who didn't see the shooter shoot people, I see a guy holding a gun and a bunch of people shot so I thought, I need to shoot him. But I saw he couldn't shoot me, and in that split second I decided I didn't have to, so I didn't."

Zamudio charged the man and grabbed the gun, twisting it away from himself and towards the man holding it. Zamudio pushed the older man up against the wall and told him to drop the gun. At that point, Badger, who was holding the shooter on the ground, and Patricia Maisch, who was helping him, yelled at Zamudio that the man he was holding was not the shooter.

The young man being held down by Badger, Salzgeber, and Maisch was the gunman.

Initially Zamudio was suspicious of what he was being told, but then realized Badger and Maisch were telling him the truth. However, he was not going to allow the older man to keep holding the gun.

Zamudio told the man: "Just drop it; put it on the ground. Make us feel safe; nobody feels safe right now."

Veeder let go of the Glock, and it fell to the ground. Zamudio told him to put his foot on it. Zamudio then helped Badger hold the suspect down until the police arrived. Relieved by Zamudio of holding the suspect down, Maisch ran into the grocery store and grabbed a handful of paper towels to tend to Badger, who was bleeding from the head wound.

Law Enforcement Arrives

Pima County Deputy Sheriff Thomas Audetat was on patrol in the Foothills area when he was dispatched to the scene of the shooting. He pulled into the parking lot in front

Glock Model 19 with magazines used by the killer and a Smith & Wesson Extreme Ops folding knife found on him. (Pima County Sheriff's Department photo.)

of the Safeway at 10:15 a.m., according to his report. He got out of his vehicle and was directed by bystanders to the sidewalk between the Safeway and the Walgreens, where he saw a man being held down by two or three other people.

"I immediately went to the suspect and placed my knee in his back and grabbed one of his hands. I then put him in handcuffs," the deputy reported.

Another deputy recovered the Glock semi-automatic. Audetat called over another deputy to help him.

"I told the two citizens who were still helping me hold down the suspect to back away and let the deputy come in. The citizens did so," the report stated.

Audetat searched the suspect, finding two fully loaded magazines for a Glock in his front left pocket. The gunman bought the Glock Model 19 legally from Sportsman's Warehouse on November 30, 2010.

In the right front pocket the deputy found a folding knife with about a four-inch blade. Audetat reported that the shooter was wearing peach-colored foam earplugs. The two deputies took the suspect to Audetat's vehicle and later took him to the Foothills District Office and then to the Pima Sheriff's headquarters. Other than saying he pleaded "the Fifth," the only thing the suspect said was: "I just want you to know that I'm the only person who knew about this."

He was later charged with murdering six people — nine-year-old Christina Taylor Green, Chief Federal District Judge John M. Roll, Gabe Zimmerman, and three others. He was also charged in the wounding of thirteen — including Representative Gabrielle Giffords, who apparently was the target of the shooter. Among the wounded were Bill Badger, Ron Barber, Susan Hileman, Mary Reed, and Ken Veeder. Although shot through the brain, Giffords survived and in 2014 was continuing a long recovery period.

In November 2012 the gunman pleaded guilty to nine-teen charges and was sentenced to seven consecutive life sentences plus 140 years in prison.

Running to the Sound of Gunfire

As the only person other than the shooter who had a gun at the scene, Zamudio showed admirable restraint and judgment. He is aware that if the slide on the Glock had not been locked back, he might have drawn his own gun and shot the wrong man.

I asked him why he ran to the sound of gunfire. This was his response: "I didn't think about it — it was a reaction. I believe now, when I think about it, that having the gun and being comfortable and familiar with it gave me a giant con-fidence boost…to be able in that situation to do something appropriate. I know that I am very comfortable carrying a gun all the time, and I feel responsible to help people in my daily life, with or without a gun. I always hold doors for ladies, and I always stop and help somebody with a flat tire. I'm like a nice guy; I always help people. I think that it's my natural nature to want to help and to protect, plus the confidence of knowing if there is a shooter out there shooting people, I can stop him."

Joe Zamudio learned to shoot from his father, a Vietnam veteran who worked for the prison service. Although his father and mother split up when he was two, he maintained a good relationship with his father while living with his mother, he said. His father was seriously injured in a motorcycle accident and could not get around much after that. One thing he and his father could share was shooting, Zamudio said.

Since the shooting, Zamudio said he always carries his gun with a round in the chamber.

"There would never be time to chamber one," he said. "You don't have that extra second."

Bill Badger said his military training kicked in, but he got involved because, "When you see an individual who shoots a nine-year-old girl, something has to be done."

Alex Villec, the intern who directed the gunman to the end of the line, is an example of someone whose flight response kicked in. Villec first took cover behind one of the stone pillars supporting the Safeway overhang. He knew he had to get out of there, so he sprinted across the shopping center parking lot to the Wells Fargo bank.

There is absolutely nothing wrong with this course of action, particularly as Villec was unarmed. But even if armed, flight may be the best and safest solution. If you stay and exchange fire with a gunman, you are likely to be wounded or killed. You also run the risk of missing your target and hitting innocent bystanders. In Villec's case flight worked — he was unscathed.

Stopped by Ordinary People

There is one factor about the Tucson shooting that makes it different from most other mass shootings. Professor John Lott of the Crime Prevention Research Center has said many times that mass killers almost always pick on "gun-free zones" to conduct their multiple murders. Unlike the locations of most rapid mass murders, the shopping center north of Tucson was not a "gun-free zone." Any law-abiding citizen could carry a concealed handgun there. In 2010 Arizona passed a law allowing ordinary people to carry handguns concealed or in the open without permit or license.

One thing that was not unusual about the Tucson incident is that it was stopped by ordinary people — either armed or unarmed — who attacked the killer. It is difficult to quantify because experts have different definitions of mass killings, but it appears that civilians or law enforcement abort about half the incidents. Of those, two-thirds are stopped by civilians, mostly unarmed because they occur in so-called gun-free zones, and one-third by law enforcement.

In Tucson nineteen people were hit by gunfire, including the six who were killed. However, the casualties would perhaps have been twice that had the killer been able to change magazines and continue shooting. It was several unarmed citizens who fought back and brought the carnage to a close before law-enforcement officers arrived.

This book shows how the response to rapid mass murders has changed in the last fifty years and what ordinary people can do when facing the unthinkable: a stranger trying to rack up a kill record of innocent victims. It also shows that in many mass killings the real first responders are usually not the law-enforcement officers or the paramedics that follow them, but the ordinary citizens who happen to be on the scene at the time — people like Bill Badger, Roger Salzgeber, Ken Veeder, Patricia Maisch, and Joe Zamudio.

In August 2015 U.S. Airman 1st Class Spencer Stone led an unarmed response, assisted by Oregon Army National Guard Specialist Alek Skarlatos, university student Anthony Sadler, and British businessman Chris Norman. They brought down a radical Muslim terrorist armed with an AK-47, who was shooting up a high-speed train from Amsterdam to Paris. Their effective actions were acknowledged and commended internationally.

Chapter 1

THE TEXAS TOWER: THE RISE OF SWAT

Allen Crum: *"Are we playing for keeps?"*
Officer Ray Martinez: *"You God damn right we are."*
Crum: *"Well, I guess you'd better deputize me."*
Martinez: *"Consider yourself deputized."*

Ramiro "Ray" Martinez and his wife VerNell woke about 6 a.m., in time for VerNell to get to work at her job as an executive secretary for Steck Vaughn, an Austin publishing company. She had to be at work at 8 a.m., while Martinez did not go on duty until 3 p.m. He would look after their two-year-old twin daughters until he took them to nursery school later in the morning. Martinez had been a patrol officer with the Austin Police Department for more than five years.

It was August first, 1966. He was twenty-nine, and he and his wife had just returned from San Antonio where they had celebrated their fifth wedding anniversary. After his wife left for work, Martinez played with his daughters until it was time for them to leave. He took them to the nursery about 10:30.

When he returned, he laid out his uniform on the bed. His wife had pressed his heavily starched shirt. He checked his wool pants to make sure they were properly pressed and clean.

"Then I polished all the brass on my belt," he said.

The heavy leather belt had a holster on the right side for his Smith & Wesson revolver.

"It was a .38 Special caliber on a .44 frame. They call them the heavies."

The revolver was loaded with Remington-Peters rounds with round-nosed lead bullets, he recalled. He had two small pouches on the left side of his belt buckle. Each one opened at the bottom to drop six rounds into the hand. He also had handcuffs.

"I was proud of my department; I was proud of my uniform," Martinez said.

Shortly before noon, he started preparing his lunch.

The Shooting Starts

Meanwhile, about 11:50 a.m., Allen Crum was at work in the University of Texas Co-op across Guadalupe Street from the University of Texas Tower. The Tower was built between 1932 and 1937 and is 307-feet tall. Crum, then forty, was the first-floor supervisor at the Co-op. He had retired after twenty-two years in the U.S. Air Force where he had been a tail gunner in a B52.

According to his statement, Crum had walked to the front of the store and was standing beside one of the cash registers. He noticed a group of students milling around a boy on the ground. They were dragging the boy on the grass, and as they dragged him more students gathered around.

"I told my cashier that it looked like a fight, and I thought I would go check to see if I could stop it."

When he left the store, a boy was beginning to run across the street toward the Co-op. At the same time, Crum heard the sound of a shot, though at the time he did not recognize it as a rifle shot.

The boy ran past Crum and yelled that the boy on the grass had been shot. Crum heard several more gunshots, this time recognizing what they were, though he didn't know where they were coming from. When he reached the east side of Guadalupe Street, he found the boy had been shot in the right buttock. Crum tried to stop the flow of blood.

He heard more shots and thought perhaps the shooter was on the roof of the Student Union building, which was next to where the boy had been shot.

"Several of us yelled for everyone to take cover," Crum stated. He stayed with the boy but realized the people in the store didn't know what was happening. So he called on one of the students to get the wounded boy under some nearby bushes and showed him how to stop the blood flow. He ran back across Guadalupe to the Co-op. Traffic was flowing normally along the street, but he noticed some students redirecting traffic from the south. Inside the store he instructed an employee to get customers away from the windows and back into the store.

Looking out of the window, Crum realized no one was stopping traffic coming from the north, so he ran up Guadalupe in that direction. He redirected traffic onto Twenty-third Street away from the campus.

"I realized that I made a fine solitary target, and I went to the east side of the street where I tried to find a telephone to call the store and my wife. My wife knew it was my lunch hour, and I knew she would worry," his statement reads.

He reached the building immediately west of the Tower without finding a phone. He thought he would find one in the Tower where he could call the store and his wife.

"I stood behind a pillar on the east side of this building. I waited until the individual started firing on the east side of the Tower, then I ran across the street into the Tower building."

Back at their house, Martinez turned on the television to watch the 12 o'clock news. It started as usual, then shortly into the broadcast somebody handed a message to Joe Roddy, the anchor. He looked at the message and, as he remembers, said: "We want to advise you that there is a shooter on top of the University of Texas Tower. We have reports of a number of injuries so far, and we'll keep you posted. Stay away from the university area."

Martinez continued preparing his lunch as he waited to hear more about the shooting.

Ramiro Martinez when he was a Texas Ranger. (Photo courtesy Ray Martinez.)

Roddy made another announcement: "I have been handed a note, and there are reports of one or two deaths and quite a number of people wounded. The shooting is continuing, and the police are converging on the scene. Please stay away from the university area. We'll keep you posted."

Martinez decided it sounded serious, so he called the police station and asked if the department needed any help. He was put through to Lieutenant Kendall Thomas. Martinez asked the lieutenant if he needed any assistance. Thomas said they did and suggested he come in. Martinez asked if he should report to the police station or go to the scene. Thomas told him to go to the university area, find a main intersection, and direct traffic away from the campus.

Martinez then called his wife and told her: "There's a man on top of the University of Texas Tower shooting people, and I'm going to go to work early. I'm going to find an intersection around the campus to keep people from coming into the campus."

VerNell Martinez told her husband to be very careful, and he promised he would. He dressed in his uniform, cinched on his gun belt, and got into his 1954 Chevrolet. As he backed out of his driveway, a neighbor who had obviously been listening to the news shouted, "Go get him, Tiger!"

At the intersection of Barton Springs Road and South Lamar Boulevard, he saw two detectives, a lieutenant, and a sergeant, but they were heading south on Lamar away from the university campus. Martinez thought this was odd. "I later found out they were going to the lieutenant's house to get deer rifles."

He listened to KTBC radio station on his car radio as he drove north on South Lamar. Neal Spelce, the reporter, was giving a shot-by-shot account of what was going on. However, the officer was not getting everything Spelce was saying. The radio in his '54 Chevrolet would fade in and out. In those days the radios were not transistorized. "They were tube type, and I had a weak tube."

Martinez continued north on Lamar. At an intersection he pulled alongside an unmarked car driven by a detective sergeant from forgery. He rolled down the window and asked the sergeant what was happening.

"There's a guy up there at the university shooting," the sergeant replied. He added that he thought another police officer, Bobby Sides, had been killed. Sides had been shot and wounded in 1964 by a burglar who had killed another police officer. The sergeant didn't seem too concerned, Martinez said. He discovered later that the officer who was killed was not Bobby Sides but Bill Speed.

At another traffic light further north, a woman in a car with a little boy honked at Martinez and indicated that he should roll down his window. She said: "Junior here says you need Batman and Robin to go over there and take care of that bad man."

Martinez drove on. It took him a while to reach the university campus due to the traffic lights and traffic that was bad even in those days. He reached Nineteenth Street, now called Martin Luther King Boulevard, turned east and went up the hill. When it leveled off, he could see motorcycle officers had the main intersections under control. He decided they didn't need any help, so he turned north up San Antonio Street and found a parking spot behind the Saint Austin's Catholic Church at Guadalupe and Twenty-second Street.

Martinez got out of the car, not realizing he was in a two-hour parking zone. "Once I got out of the car, I could hear all this shooting going on — rifle fire — and I could hear sirens."

He knew whatever was going on was serious.

"It sounded like a war zone. Once I got onto Guadalupe Street, I could see the Tower, and right away I determined that, if I can see the top of the Tower, that son-of-a-gun can see me. So I started using concealment. I ran behind buildings, behind trees. Of course the campus had fewer buildings than it has now, so there was a lot of trees out there."

Martinez ran until he reached the South Mall on the south side of the Tower. Behind him was the Littlefield Fountain, where sculpted horses were being sprayed with water. On a sidewalk beside a rock wall, he saw some blood and later learned that was where Officer Bill Speed was shot.

Houston McCoy, then in his mid-twenties, was the officer assigned to the murder of Officer Billy Speed. In a supplementary offense report, he outlined what he did that hot August day.

He went to the university area and obtained two rifles. He also obtained two boxes of .30-06 shells and one box of .30-30 rounds from Everett Hardware Company on Guadalupe Street. He indicated in the report that the company had not been reimbursed for the ammunition.

"After attempting to shoot the subject from several locations, I ascertained that I was too shaky to do any good and gave the weapons back to their owners."

After hearing on the radio that officers were needed to go up the Tower, he went to the University Police Security

Office. A university employee led McCoy and several other officers through service tunnels to the Tower.

Martinez had been trained as a combat medic in the U.S. Army, but he decided it was more important for him to get to the Tower and help stop the shooting before attending to the wounded.

"I could see people wounded and dead all on the South Mall. The thing I can recall I saw was a pregnant woman lying on that concrete. It was very hot, and she was like frying on the damn thing. She was wounded."

"I ran as fast as I could by the dead and the wounded, zigzagging. If he saw me, I don't know. If he shot at me, I don't know. But I ran as the shooting was going on. I made it to

The Tower at The University of Texas at Austin from the South Mall. The observation deck is below the clock. Three drain spouts (center) direct rainwater from the deck. Friend Jerry Lane and his son Chase are pictured in the foreground.

the building. It's an administration building, and the Tower sits in the middle of it."

Martinez walked around to the west side of the building and entered the hallway leading to the elevators that go up the Tower. He didn't go up the Tower because he wanted to get some help for the wounded outside. He thought a commercial armored truck could reach the wounded and get them out of the line of fire.

At the time, the Austin Police Department had about eight hand-held radios, but they were in the captain's office. "They were not issued to the rank and file," Martinez said.

The radios were provided by the Secret Service for use when President Lyndon Johnson came to town. The radios would then be issued to supervisors responsible for Johnson's security. Patrol officers did not have hand-held radios, however, their patrol cars did have two-way radios.

"Once you got out of your patrol car, you were on your own, because you didn't have communication with the police station."

Arrival at the Tower

Having arrived in the Tower building, Allen Crum said in his statement he talked to several of the university security officers and asked them if they had called the police. They said they had. They directed him to where the telephones were, and he tried to call the Co-op and his wife. The lines were busy. As he turned away from the telephone, he saw Officer Jerry Day.

"I went up to him and offered my help," Crum said.

They got a radio from one of the security officers, intending to keep in contact with other officers, but they could not get the radio to work, he said.

Someone came up to Day and told him there were people lying on the Mall to the south of the Tower.

"We went directly there, and we saw one man on the grass and two women, a man, and a boy student on the concrete Mall," Crum said.

He and Day realized there was not much they could do for the wounded. The sniper was still firing rapidly, and they could not figure out where he was located.

"At this time, we both thought there was a possibility of two people in the Tower."

Jerry Day felt he might be able to get a shot at the sniper, if he could find a window from which to shoot. They went up to the north side of the library floor of the building, which is part of the Tower. There, Day took a shot at someone on the observation deck, but according to Crum missed.

He and Day returned to the street floor, where they found W.A. "Dub" Cowan, an officer from the Texas Department of Public Safety, Intelligence Division, who was carrying a rifle in addition to his revolver.

"I asked this man if he would give me the rifle, and I would volunteer to go with them. They agreed," Crum stated.

As Martinez was looking for a telephone, he came across Day and Crum, who he said was wearing a white shirt. He knew Day, but didn't know who Allen Crum was and didn't realize he was not a law-enforcement officer.

"I didn't know him from Adam," Martinez said.

He found a phone and tried to reach the police department. It was a phone with a dial, and as soon as he dialed the first digit he got a busy signal, because the system was overloaded and jammed.

While Martinez was on the phone trying to line up an armored truck to move the wounded, Day and Crum left. He didn't see where they went.

At the time Austin had no emergency medical services, and what they called ambulances were actually hearses from the local funeral homes.

"It was pretty backwards because normally they just hired students, and they didn't know the first thing about first aid; they were just drivers," Martinez said. They would put patients on a gurney in the hearse and drive as fast as they could for the hospital.

Then he saw a campus security officer. In those days, campus security officers had uniforms and looked like policemen, but they were unarmed. All they had was a nightstick and a flashlight. However, they did have hand-held radios, so Martinez asked if he could use the officer's radio.

"I tried to use the hand-held radio to communicate with the police department; couldn't find the channel."

Up the Tower

Having failed to reach his department, Martinez decided he needed to go up the Tower to where he assumed a group of officers was preparing to assault the sniper on the observation deck. When he got to the elevator, he found a young man with a clipboard who asked Martinez his name and wrote it down. Martinez thought at least somebody knows what he's doing.

"To this day, I never found out who he was or anything."

Martinez got into the elevator and punched the button for the top floor, which was the twenty-seventh.

"You could hear the firing that was going on outside. It was muffled, but you could still hear it in the elevator," he said.

As the elevator was going up, Martinez watched as the little numbers indicating the floors were flickering.

"It felt pretty serious. I'm a Catholic, and I was taught in the event of imminent death, if you say an Act of Contrition, God will forgive you your sins. So I said an Act of Contrition as I was going up. I didn't know what to expect at the top. Of course I was hoping there was a whole squad of police — an assault squad."

Martinez had pulled his gun out and pointed at the doors as the elevator arrived at the twenty-seventh floor. When the doors opened, he found himself looking down the barrels of two guns, a revolver held by Jerry Day and the rifle pointed by Allen Crum.

After all three lowered their guns, Martinez walked out onto the floor. He saw a little table with a telephone on it. Cowan was on the phone trying to establish communications. There was another man who appeared to be drawing a diagram on a piece of paper.

"I was disappointed. I said: this is it? This is the whole enchilada? There's no squad here — no assault squad or anything."

Martinez had learned in the Army that you always secure the ground you are on before you move forward, because you don't want anybody to come in behind you. So he and Day started checking all the offices on the floor.

Martinez came to one door that was locked. He shoved against it and heard a voice say: "Who is it?"

"Police."

"Just a second."

The people inside had barricaded themselves, so they started unstacking furniture. "Once they opened the door, I guess a dozen to fifteen people came out of there."

Martinez remembers that two of them were nuns in their black-and-white habits. They got on the elevator and went down. One man who came out was wearing glasses and was clearly upset. Martinez later identified him as M.J. Gabour from Texarkana.

"He was carrying a pair of white women's shoes, and they were bloody, and he said: 'That s.o.b. killed my family, all my family; give me your gun, and I'll go get that s.o.b.' He was trying to get my gun, and I said: 'Nope, you're not.' And I wrestled with him. I restrained him and walked him to the other elevator. Jerry Day was helping. So we opened the elevator door, and I shoved him and Jerry Day in there, pushed the button for the first floor and sent them down," Martinez said.

He could see the metal stairway leading up to the observation deck. There were bloody footprints on the steps. He turned to go up the steps when, as Martinez remembers it, this interchange took place.

Crum: "Where are you going?"

Martinez: "I'm going to look for the guy."

Crum: "Not by yourself, you're not. I'm going to go with you. We'll do it service style: I cover you, you cover me."

Martinez: "That's fine, come on."

"I was so happy, because it was lonely up there," Martinez recalled.

Playing for Keeps

They went warily up the stairs, hearts thumping, not knowing what to expect. They came to a landing where Martinez could see down a short hallway that linked the two staircases.

"I could see a face, looking at me. It was one of the Gabour boys — dead. He was looking at me. His eyes were bugged, and his tongue was protruding out."

It was sixteen-year-old Martin, known as Mark, Gabour.

"So I eased upstairs to where he was. I peeked around the corner, and I could see a woman. She was dead."

It was Mark's aunt, M.J. Gabour's sister, Marguerite Lamport. Beyond her was Mark's mother, Mary Gabour, who was wounded, and at the end of the hallway was Mark's brother, Mike Gabour.

"He was conscious, but he was severely wounded. And he pointed up because there's where he was, the stairs went up again and then they took a right. And he said: 'He's up there.'" Martinez remembers.

Allen Crum stated he asked Mike Gabour how many people were shooting. The young man said, "one." Crum asked if he could see the shooter. Mike replied: "No, he's outside."

Martinez confirmed that Marguerite Lamport was dead. Mary Gabour was still alive but was lying face down. The officer was afraid she might drown in her own blood, so he and Allen Crum turned her over. Mike Gabour had shoulder and head wounds. They pulled him back, out of the line of fire, in case the sniper appeared and shot down the stairway.

Martinez and Crum continued on up the stairs, finding a large, metal trashcan on the steps. Martinez pushed the trashcan aside, and that's when an interesting exchange took place between the officer and his unofficial partner.

Crum: "Are we playing for keeps?"

Martinez: "You God damn right we are."

Crum: "Well, I guess you'd better deputize me."

Martinez: "Consider yourself deputized."

This was the first indication Martinez had that Crum was not a law-enforcement officer.

"I didn't have a second thought, because we had already passed all those dead and wounded, and he was with me, and he had a rifle. What more could you ask of a man?" he said.

At the end of the stairway, a desk barricaded the steps. They continued up the stairs and pushed the desk out of the way so they could reach the twenty-eighth floor. They pushed the desk around, using it as cover. All the time they could hear the shooting outside. They followed a blood smear across the floor, and behind a couch they found Edna Townsley, the receptionist.

"She was still alive, but she was dying. There was nothing we could do for her," Martinez said.

The only exit on to the observation deck was a glass-paneled door on the south side near the southeast corner. The sniper barricaded the door from the outside with a metal dolly he had used to bring his supplies up to the deck.

Much of the twenty-eighth floor inside the Tower was used for storage, but there were a couple of windows near the southwest corner. Martinez looked out of the windows, hoping to see the sniper so they could shoot him from inside, where the stone wall of the Tower would provide them with good cover.

"We couldn't see anything except a lot of debris, empty shells. It looked like a war zone out there," Martinez said.

So he went back to the glass door and started pushing it until the dolly toppled over with a crash. He expected the sniper would have heard the crash and come to investigate, but with the noise of the shooting and a radio he had cranked up as loud as it would go, he apparently didn't hear the crash as the dolly went over.

On the Observation Deck

Martinez pushed open the door and looked to his right to the southwest corner of the observation deck. He couldn't see the sniper there.

The observation deck is about sixty-feet long on each side and five-feet wide. On each face of the Tower above the deck is a large clock, and on each side of each clock is a buttress stretching up from the deck. These create protrusions that provide some cover but narrow the deck to three feet. They also make it more difficult to see if the deck is clear. A four-foot-high stone wall surrounds the observation deck. On each side, three large drains pierce the wall to direct rainwater off the deck. The drains are four-inches wide and two-feet tall and slope downwards.

Martinez stationed Crum just outside the door facing towards the southwest corner.

"If he comes 'round this corner," Martinez instructed, "shoot him."

Martinez, armed only with his revolver, headed opposite to circle the Tower in an anticlockwise direction.

Crum would later be joined by Jerry Day.

Initially the sniper leaned on the four-foot-high parapet and made accurate shots out to five-hundred yards with a Remington Model 700 in 6mm caliber equipped with a four-power Leupold scope.

In those days almost every Texas pickup had a gun rack in the rear window that often held the owner's deer rifle. When students, other civilians, and a few police officers realized what was happening, they grabbed their rifles and started shooting at the sniper. This made shooting over the parapet untenable, so the sniper was reduced to shooting through the drain spouts, which severely limited his field of fire. This is why most of the killing and wounding happened in the first twenty minutes. Then the shooters around the Tower realized what the sniper was doing and started shooting up the drains.

One of the drain spouts through which shots were fired by the killer and fire was returned from the ground. Campus buildings can be seen through the spout.

Even though the sniper wasn't hit by any of the ground fire, it was hitting all around him and making his accurate shots more difficult or even impossible. Of course the steady drumbeat of rifle fire from the ground was hazardous to Martinez's health as he was moving along the east side of the Tower. The rifle bullets were chipping away

Jerry Lane standing where the killer was sitting. He is pointing in the direction the killer's carbine was pointed.

at the stonework above him showering him with chips of limestone and dust. To avoid getting hit, he adopted what he called a "duck walk" or squatting walk to keep below the parapet. He would leap over the drains to avoid getting hit by the bullets coming up them.

Before reaching the northeast corner of the deck, Martinez looked back and saw Officer Houston McCoy following him. He was encouraged to see McCoy carrying a shotgun in addition to his revolver. But the younger officer was standing straight up.

"I motioned to him to get down, and then a couple of shots hit above his head, and he got the message," Martinez said.

Shootout on the Deck

As the two officers approached the northeast corner, they heard a shot from close by. Allen Crum had fired the shot in the direction of the southwest corner of the deck. In his statement, he said he fired the shot on purpose. However, he told Martinez afterwards he had been checking the 35 Remington rifle to make sure he knew how to operate it, and it went off accidentally.

"The problem was that he was not familiar with the rifle. It wasn't his rifle," Martinez said.

The accidental shot worked to the advantage of the two officers. Martinez reached the northeast corner of the deck and looked along the north side, but couldn't see anyone. He continued duck walking to the first buttress coming down from the clock.

Then he spotted the sniper. He was wearing overalls, and had a white sweatband around his head.

"He was in a sitting position. He had an M1 carbine and he was bracing his left elbow on the left knee, aiming like he's got a target, like he was going to shoot, and I was afraid Allen Crum had left his position."

Officer Martinez as he emerged from the Tower after engaging the killer. (Photo courtesy Ray Martinez.)

The sniper was pointing the carbine down the west side of the deck towards where Crum's accidental shot had hit the southwest corner.

"Thinking he was going to shoot Alan, I opened fire," Martinez said. "I could tell that I hit him in the left side because of the way he reacted: he jumped up, and he was trying to turn around, and I kept advancing and shooting, because I saw his muzzle flash at least one time from the M1 carbine."

McCoy, aiming at the sniper's white headband, fired two rounds from his shotgun, then Martinez grabbed it from him and fired one more shot into the sniper.

It was over.

In an hour and a half, the sniper had killed fourteen people in and from the Tower and wounded thirty-one. He had murdered his wife and his mother before ascending the Tower.

Martinez started waving the shotgun yelling, "Stop! Stop! We got him! We got him!"

But nobody on the ground could hear over the noise of the continuous gunfire, so he put the shotgun down and said, "I'm getting the hell out of here."

Martinez said that while he was stalking the sniper he was operating like a robot. But the effect of seeing the gunman dead changed that. "At the time I saw the body, I became a human being again," he said.

As the adrenalin drained from his limbs, he had trouble walking: "My knees were weak, and my legs were like rubber."

Martinez got into the elevator and went down to the ground floor. The lieutenant in charge of homicide and another lieutenant met him. They thought he had been wounded, because he had blood all over his shirt from where he had been moving the wounded members of the Gabour family. The lieutenants tried to get him into one of funeral-home vehicles that acted as ambulances, but Martinez protested that he was uninjured, so he was taken to the police station to write his report.

At the police station, he told Chief Robert Miles and a city council member who was there what had happened. Then he asked if he could phone his wife. He was given access to a telephone and called her at work.

He said he just wanted to let her know he was all right. She said: "Why shouldn't you be; you've been working traffic."

He said that he would tell her about it later. A few minutes later she called up and said she had heard that he was wounded.

Martinez said he replied: "Dear, if I was wounded, I wouldn't be here at the police station; I'd be at the hospital. I'll tell you about it later."

The Aftermath

When the sniper was identified, he was found to be a twenty-five-year-old former U.S. Marine, who had qualified as a sharpshooter.

There was some dispute afterwards about who killed the sniper and whether Martinez missed with some or all the shots he fired from his revolver. This was at least partly the result of the report of the autopsy conducted by Dr. C de Chenar. He found death was caused by injuries to the head and heart. Chenar listed eight "holes of pellets" in the head. In the neck and chest, he listed twelve "penetrations." He stated that "one, under the arm, is of larger diameter, close to 1 cm." The doctor also stated: "Around the shoulder, about a dozen of grazing or penetrating injuries. The left arm bone [humerus] is severely destroyed by several large caliber penetrations."

It appears that Chenar did not remove the missiles that caused the wounds and weigh them, as is normally done in an autopsy, and there was no diagram of the body. However, he seems to account for more than thirty-two wounds. Three 12-gauge shotgun rounds, each comprising nine pellets of .33 caliber were fired, as well as six .38-caliber rounds from Martinez's revolver. This totals thirty-three missiles, which indicates that Martinez hit the sniper with most or all of his shots.

Martinez says the sniper tried to bring his carbine to bear on him but couldn't.

"If I had been missing, he would have been able to bring the M1 carbine down on me," he said.

Ramiro Martinez left the Austin Police Department in 1968 and later became a Texas Ranger. He published his memoirs in 2004: *They Call Me Ranger Ray,* published by Rio Bravo Publishing. (See Bibliography.) The book has an excellent chapter on the Tower incident. The shooting has never particularly bothered him.

"I wake up thinking about it sometimes. It's nothing that's disturbing, but I relive it."

If he reads something about the Tower shooting or on the anniversary of it, he relives what happened.

Houston McCoy died at his hometown of Menard in central Texas in 2012. Allen Crum died of a heart attack on March 9, 2001.

Reflections

Martinez felt that a better job could have been done in learning from what had happened. A thorough examination of the incident was not done. Martinez feels Chief Robert Miles was afraid of losing his job, as there was a lot of criticism over what had happened, in particular why it had taken so long — an hour and a half — to resolve.

As far as Martinez knows only three things came out of the incident. A lieutenant and a detective were tasked with finding suitable rifles for use by police in case of a similar incident. Detectives were instructed to get plans of all high-rise buildings in the city. Officers were issued cards with home telephone numbers of senior officers, so they could be called at any time.

Martinez was also amazed that it took so long before anyone thought of assaulting the Tower itself. He was told that the chief and the chief of patrol were both at the hospital where Billy Speed had been taken, rather than directing the response.

In the mid-1960s, police departments were unprepared for the phenomenon of mass killings that became more frequent from the 1990s onwards. Officers in those days were usually armed with .38-caliber revolvers and perhaps had access to a shotgun. But they had little tactical training, and there were no SWAT teams.

SWAT Teams

In the subsequent four decades, changes in response to rampages by active killers were all about law enforcement: this, despite the reality that the police usually arrive at the scene too late. While mass shootings occur in churches, malls, work areas, and other venues where large groups of people gather, it was the shootings at schools and colleges that drove most of the changes.

Martinez felt the civilian shooters at the Texas Tower did not get enough recognition for what they did. "They pinned him down," he said.

Martinez said the sniper would have doubled the number of dead and wounded if the shooters on the ground had not intervened.

Two patrolmen and a civilian spearheaded the assault on the Tower. On their own initiative, they put themselves in harm's way. No senior officer was present at the Tower until after the shooting stopped. In retrospect, it appears that the Austin Police Department was ill-equipped to deal with a mass killer. But in 1966 it is doubtful that any police department in the country was prepared for what happened at the University of Texas. That was about to change.

The shooting at the Tower was partly responsible for the creation of Special Weapons and Tactics (SWAT) teams and ultimately the militarization of police departments and federal-government agencies.

"It was the thing that took law enforcement into the sniper, SWAT mode," said John Benner, owner and chief instructor at Tactical Defense Institute near Cincinnati in Ohio. He commanded a forty-five-man multi-jurisdictional SWAT team in Hamilton County, Ohio, for twenty years.

Police realized they had to have more than a revolver and a shotgun to respond to such incidents.

"Now we've got tactical teams because of the Texas Tower shooting, and we've got all this gear, and now we're SWAT qualified, and we've got SWAT teams all over the place, and I'm a big proponent of that. I think SWAT is a misunderstood thing. We save a whole lot more lives than we take," Benner said.

Referring to his own twenty-year record with the Hamilton County SWAT team, he added, "The bottom line is we never killed anybody, but we saved a lot of people's lives."

A 2003 study by the Illinois State Police Academy entitled "Rapid Deployment as a Response to an Active Shooter Incident" stated of the Texas Tower incident: "Many regard this incident as the impetus of dramatic change in police training and response. Some agencies issued long-range rifles and trained their officers in the role of counter-sniper, while other agencies formed more comprehensive para-military teams with even greater capabilities. The genesis of what would become Special Weapons and Tactics teams (SWAT) undoubtedly began at 11:48 a.m. on August 1, 1966."

The first major-city police department to organize a SWAT team was Los Angles. According to its web site, the Los Angeles Police Department (LAPD) SWAT team was created in 1967 and consisted of fifteen four-man teams that were drawn mostly from patrol-division officers with military experience. The unit became full-time in 1971.

It was created to cope with barricade and hostage situations. However, once a SWAT team has been formed, it has to be used to justify its existence. That is just the way of bureaucracies. Therefore, SWAT Teams also serve high-risk warrants and conduct drug raids where subjects are dangerous and probably armed...reasonable uses of these highly trained officers.

"LAPD SWAT Team members have effected the safe rescue of numerous hostages, arrested scores of violent suspects, and earned hundreds of commendations and citations," states the LAPD web site.

As SWAT teams evolved they adopted light military weapons such as sub-machine guns, carbines, military-style semi-automatic rifles, and sniper rifles, as well as pump and semi-automatic shotguns. They use battering rams and explosives to break down doors and have access to armored vehicles.

The Austin Police Department didn't get a SWAT team until 1979, thirteen years after the Tower shooting.

By the 1990s most mid-size and large cities in the United States had SWAT teams. Smaller cities often grouped together to form a SWAT team. The federal government also got into the act, with almost every federal agency developing its own tactical team.

This proliferation of SWAT teams has led to the militarization of law-enforcement agencies. SWAT-team members tend to be dressed and equipped like military

Members of the Dallas, Texas, SWAT Team in the 1980s.

commandos and have armored military vehicles provided by the federal government. This has widened the gap between law-enforcement officers and citizens.

There is another effect. There is a tendency, particularly by large urban police departments, to have policies requiring patrol officers to call in the SWAT team rather than deal with a situation themselves, as they used to do. This tends to discourage officers from using their initiative. This is acceptable if time is not a controlling factor — it takes time to assemble a SWAT team. This weakness was demonstrated tragically at Columbine. (See Chapter 3.)

John Benner defended the use of local law-enforcement SWAT teams.

"I certainly have no proof of this, but if you had regular officers doing what SWAT teams are doing — doing the raids, dealing with barricaded people, all that kind of stuff — you would have a lot more deaths on both sides than you do with SWAT teams."

He said that in the twenty years he was in command of the Hamilton County SWAT team, they never fired a shot at a perpetrator. He thinks that is fairly universal. Even now the team he was in charge of, comprising fifty or sixty officers, still hasn't killed anybody.

"There have been some shots fired, but it's been very rare. One of them was at a vehicle, to stop a vehicle, but that's been about it."

He says the Hamilton County SWAT team has a military vehicle that they drive up into the suspect's yard. This encourages the suspect to come out without the use of force.

In the 1990s SWAT teams would also be called out for what became known as "active shooter" incidents. As mentioned in the Introduction, I have referred to these perpetrators as "active killers."

Many in law enforcement discourage ordinary citizens from becoming involved in ongoing situations in any way except as victims or witnesses. For decades, police managers have told the public to call 9-1-1, give criminals what they want, and don't fight back. This of course doesn't work with active killers. This has resulted in more victims instead of citizens taking action to protect themselves and others.

As we will see in this book, many untrained citizens have chosen to take effective life-saving actions. In dire circumstances they have the right to assess the risk to themselves and others and make their own decisions about enhancing everyone's survival. Law enforcement could better serve the community by not discouraging them from protecting themselves. Instead of scolding them when they do get involved, they should thank them and provide all interested citizens with information, including referral to training resources, that can help them be more effective.

Chapter 2

THREE SHOOTINGS: VICTIMS FIGHT BACK

"I was beating on him as much as I could.
They had to pull me off him." — Jake Ryker

Early in 1996 in central Washington State, a tragic event occurred. It would start a trend that continued throughout the twenty-first century and today shows few signs of stopping. Students would arm themselves, enter their schools or colleges, and start shooting their fellow students and teachers. Often these killers had mental problems and/or grudges against particular individuals, but they also shot people at random.

Although school and college shootings had occurred before, the shooting at Frontier Middle School in Moses Lake, Washington, on Friday, February 2, 1996, was the first of a rash of mass killings in the late 1990s that was covered extensively by the national media and brought the problem into the country's living rooms.

On that winter day, a fourteen-year-old student walked from his home to Frontier Middle School. The youth was wearing a black western rig, later described as a Clint Eastwood-like outfit, and carrying a .30-30-caliber hunting rifle. He was also armed with a .357 Magnum-caliber revolver and a .25-caliber semi-automatic pistol.

He entered his algebra classroom and started shooting with the rifle. He shot and killed Manuel Vela, 14, Arnold Fritz, 14, and teacher Leona Caires, 49. He seriously wounded Natalie Hintz, 13, shooting her in the back and arm.

While holding fourteen other students at gun-point, he reportedly said: "This sure beats the hell out of algebra, doesn't it?"

Hearing the shooting, math teacher and gym coach Jon Lane rushed into the classroom where the killer was about to choose a hostage to assist him in escaping from the school. Lane volunteered to be the hostage, grabbed the rifle, and wrestled the killer to the ground, controlling him until the police arrived.

With this incident as a warm up, there followed five mass shootings at schools around the country in which six youths killed twelve students, a principal, and a teacher. They also wounded forty-seven others.

February 19, 1997, in Bethel, Alaska, a sixteen-year-old student, armed with a Mossberg 500 12-gauge shotgun, shot and killed one student, wounded two more, then shot and killed the principal. He fired one shot at police then surrendered.

October 1, 1997, in Pearl, Mississippi, a sixteen-year-old student murdered his mother at home then went to school, where he killed two students and wounded seven with a Marlin .30-30-caliber rifle. He was chased down and held at gunpoint by an assistant principal armed with a .45-caliber semi-automatic pistol.

December 1, 1997, at Heath High School in West Paducah, Kentucky, a fourteen-year-old boy fired a Ruger .22-caliber pistol at a prayer group, killing three students and wounding five. He then dropped the handgun and surrendered to the school principal.

March 24, 1998, at Westfield Middle School near Jonesboro, Arkansas, two boys, aged eleven and thirteen, opened fire from ambush with rifles. They killed four girls and a teacher. Nine other students and a teacher were wounded. A deputy sheriff arrested the boys while they attempted to escape from the area.

May 21, 1998, at Thurston High School in Springfield, Oregon, a fifteen-year-old student opened fire with a sawed-down rifle. He killed two students and wounded twenty-three before other students stopped him. The gunman killed his parents before starting his rampage at school.

Of the six school shootings mentioned above, three ended when unarmed potential victims fought back, police caught two after the shooting had ended, and two of the killers surrendered. Law enforcement ended only one of the incidents, but that did not change law-enforcement's responses.

Despite enormous amounts of publicity, school shootings are quite rare. A study on school-associated violent deaths, put out by the Centers for Disease Control and Prevention covering the years 1992 to 2010, states that school-associated violent deaths varied between fourteen and thirty-four per year for students aged five to eighteen. In 1998 a Justice Policy Institute report stated the chance of a student becoming the victim of a school-associated violent death is slightly less than one in a million.

Pearl High School, Mississippi

The incident that occurred in Pearl, Mississippi, on October 1, 1997, is instructive because a civilian with a handgun brought it to an end.

Shortly after 8 a.m., Joel Myrick, an assistant principal at Pearl High School, was walking back to his office with a cup of coffee in his hand. He was dressed as usual in a pinstripe suit, white shirt, and tie.

He crossed a large area known as the Commons that was about the size of a basketball court with a high ceiling. About six hundred students were milling about in this vast area. They had just arrived and were waiting around for the school day to begin. It would be unlike any other school day they had ever experienced.

Assistant Principal Joel Myrick.

As Myrick reached his outer office, he heard a loud explosion. Immediately, he set down his coffee and stepped back out into the Commons.

There was another loud boom. Most of the children in the Commons ran for the exits, many of them screaming. As some ran towards Myrick, he held open the door and they flooded into his outer office. After fifteen or twenty children had run past him into his office, Myrick heard the third boom.

He realized someone was shooting. He started moving carefully out into the Commons looking for the source of the gunfire. A stairwell blocked his view of part of the Commons. By this time the area was almost empty of students. After moving a few steps, Myrick saw the barrel of a rifle, then as he moved further, a large youth wearing a long coat. He was walking with the rifle pointed forward and down, towards the center of the Commons, where there were four columns, each about three-feet thick.

As Myrick watched, he saw the gunman lift the barrel of the rifle slightly and fire another shot. Myrick saw chips of concrete fly from one of the columns as two girls fell to the ground. The shooter, later identified as a sixteen-year-old student, kept walking towards one of the columns where several children were trying to hide. But one boy was left exposed.

"He pulled his book bag up to his chest, and he said: 'No, man, no.' And [the gunman] shot him within about four or five feet," Myrick said.

The two other children behind the column turned and ran. The gunman worked the lever of the rifle, chambered another round, and fired at them. The bullet hit the floor behind them and broke up. They were hit by fragments of the bullet and went down. The student with the rifle was walking away from Myrick thumbing rounds into the magazine through the slot in the receiver of the .30-30-caliber Marlin rifle.

"I was contemplating running [at the gunman], but I was scared. Because there was about forty or fifty feet between me and him, and I thought, if I start running and he turns around, I'm dead, because he's killing folks," Myrick said.

The assistant principal said he has been hunting all his life and knows what the .30-30 round will do to a deer.

The gunman turned and started to walk towards one of the halls that lead off the Commons. Myrick sprinted along the side of the Commons towards an exit that led to where his truck was parked. In the truck he kept his .45-caliber handgun.

"I knew I had to get to my gun, because I was defenseless, and I couldn't do anything with him at that point. I knew there was no one else around that could do anything with him," Myrick said. "He was king. He was god of that school, and he could take life whenever he got ready, and he was doing it."

About halfway to the exit, Myrick turned and looked back. "This is the image I'll remember for the rest of my life. I looked, and I saw seven bodies laying around in various positions. I could smell gunpowder," he said.

The gunman was walking away from him down the hall with the rifle held diagonally across his chest. Myrick had his truck key in his hand even before he reached the back door. He sprinted across the parking lot to his pickup, opened it up, and reached under the seat for his gun. The .45-caliber Colt compact semi-automatic was in a soft case. Myrick undid the zipper and took it out. It had a full magazine but no round in the chamber. He paused a moment realizing that he was holding a loaded gun on school property, then he racked the slide, chambering a round, and put on the safety. Myrick said that once he had the gun in his hand he felt "unbelievably safe" during the rest of the incident.

Myrick took off running, with the gun pointed up in the air and his finger alongside the trigger guard. He didn't want to enter the building through the door from which he had exited, so he started running clockwise around the building.

Myrick fondly remembers an elderly black custodian named Irene who summed up the whole situation in two words. She was standing in the next entrance with one foot each side of the door so she could run in or out depending on the threat. She looked at Myrick running past with a gun in his hand, and she said: "Oh, my."

Myrick turned the corner of the building and ran towards the front door. He figured that was the closest entrance to where he had last seen the gunman. He thought the shooter was probably searching classrooms, closets, and bathrooms looking for more unarmed victims.

When he was about forty yards from the front door, the gunman emerged from it still carrying the rifle. Myrick stopped and settled into a classic Weaver stance, pointing the gun at the threat, and yelled, "Stop!"

The gunman turned his head and looked at Myrick, but kept walking to his car, which was parked at the curb. Behind the gunman, cars were leaving the parking lot, and kids were running. Myrick didn't have a clear shot at him, and the gunman didn't point his gun at Myrick.

"I made the decision not to shoot at him at that point. I safed my weapon again and took off running towards his car."

Before Myrick could reach the car, the gunman had taken off, burning rubber as he accelerated away.

"I remember looking at the white smoke coming off his tires."

Myrick ran as fast as he could to cut the gunman off before he could escape from the parking lot onto the street.

The gunman was slowed by traffic at an intersection on school property. Some cars were still bringing students to school, and others were trying to leave the area as fast as they could. A car was stopped in front of the gunman at a stop sign. The gunman backed up and went around the car, but the delay allowed time for Myrick to reach the exit ahead of him.

Myrick Stops the Killer

Myrick was standing with one foot on the road when the gunman turned the corner about thirty yards away. There was nothing on the other side of the road but trees, so this time the assistant principal would have a clear shot.

"I was going to shoot him as he came across my field of fire, because the junior high was right down the road, and that's where my son goes to school," said Myrick. "I don't know where he was heading, but I knew he had just shot up a bunch of folks with a high-powered rifle, and he was getting away. I just figured I needed to stop him."

When the active killer turned the corner and headed straight for him, Myrick took up his position, covering the shooter with the .45 in a two-hand hold. He clicked off the safety. When the gunman saw him, he swerved off the road onto the grass away from Myrick. The grass was wet, and the car spun out, coming to a stop across the road about fifteen feet away from him, Myrick said.

The assistant principal kept the gunman covered and told him not to move. The killer's knuckles were white from where he was gripping the steering wheel, and his glasses were askew on his face, but he didn't move. Still keeping him covered, Myrick walked quickly to the car.

"I knew I had him at that point. I moved right up to the car and held the pistol a couple of feet from the side of his head. I told him: 'If you do anything, I'm going to kill you.'

And he never moved. He never said a word. In the seat next to him was the rifle lying muzzle down."

Myrick noticed that the student had black electrical tape around both of his hands. He found out later that the killer had stabbed his mother to death before coming to school and had cut himself.

Myrick got the gunman out of the car and made him lie face down on the grass. The assistant principal pulled the student's jacket up over his head, partly to immobilize him and partly to see if he had any other weapons on him. Myrick put his foot on the back of the student's head to make sure he didn't move, then asked why he had done this.

"Mr. Myrick, the world has wronged me, and I couldn't take it anymore," the gunman replied.

"I didn't think twice; I said: 'My God, wait till you get to Parchman,' which is the state penitentiary," Myrick recalled.

A few minutes later a police car pulled up, and the police officer took over, handcuffing the gunman. Myrick cleared his gun then ran back into the school. He found the killer had murdered two girls and wounded seven other students.

Although no one but the killer knows for sure, Myrick believes he would have continued his murderous rampage if he had not been stopped. He still had two rounds in his rifle and thirty-six rounds on him at the time of his capture. Myrick said, "I truly believe that he would have continued to do what he was doing."

In June 1998 the killer was sentenced to life in prison for his rampage, which he tried to blame on the leader of a satanic group that he belonged to.

Joel Myrick has received hate mail. He has received more than twenty letters from around the country from people blaming him for what happened. Some were bizarre enough that he was concerned for his safety.

"The gist of what they were saying was that I was the problem. [The killer] was not the problem; that I created [the killer] because I'm a big bully that carries a gun."

Myrick has been a hunter and shooter all his life and is a member of the National Rifle Association. He is also an officer in the National Guard. He believes children are being desensitized to killing because of the graphic violence they see in movies and the violence they participate in when playing video games. This is the same sort of indoctrination that soldiers receive to enable them to kill an enemy.

Myrick says kids need to feel a sense of belonging. If there is a common thread to the school shootings, it is that the shooters felt alienated from the student body. "They were really not a part of the mainstream culture," he said. "They were a little bit outside."

In 1999 Myrick moved from Pearl to a job as the principal of a high school in northern Mississippi. He has been working to develop a sense of community in his school, so all students feel that they belong. If he sees a kid sitting alone, he will go and talk to him or her, he said. He also speaks to adult community groups to get them to become involved in the school and its students.

"I've really made a big effort to try to draw kids into the mainstream of the school, so everybody feels like they're part of the school, and nobody is just left out."

Myrick is in favor of taking the initiative and trying to head off such incidents before they start. However, in a school situation, once someone has decided to go on an armed rampage, it is not easy to prevent it. "You are not going to stop them by making the school into a prison, although I do believe an armed security guard is a great deterrent, because some of these shooters are cowards," he said.

If these youths knew there was a good chance they would be shot or killed it would deter some, Myrick said. Under the current system, schools proclaim loudly with signs that they are drug- and gun-free zones.

"It's a shooting gallery. What better place to go and shoot than a gun-free zone," he said.

Myrick did not have a concealed-handgun license, though he could easily have got one in Mississippi. He said it is legal for him to have a gun in his home and in his vehicle. He is usually not far from one or the other, but does not want to carry one on his person.

He believes having teachers carry guns would create a problem. Students jostle teachers in crowded hallways. Female teachers with guns in their purses would be vulnerable because they have to put down the purses to teach.

"You're not maintaining a posture of keeping your weapon secured in a crowded hallway. That's why I think that an armed guard would be better."

Myrick did feel that with sufficient training it would be an advantage to have a teacher or administrator have a gun locked inside the school building.

"I would love to have a gun loaded in my desk, drawer locked. It would be safe there; it would be inaccessible," he said. "It would really be safer than the one in my truck that's there now, because I'm not watching my truck, and if you wanted to take a pipe and knock my window out and snatch my gun, you could."

He acknowledges that, if he had had a gun in his desk at Pearl High School, he could have reached it a lot quicker and perhaps saved some of the students from being shot. He stressed that whoever was allowed to keep a gun on school premises should receive training and have strict instructions about when it could be used.

Thurston High School, Oregon

A school shooting that was stopped by unarmed students happened in Springfield, Oregon, in 1998.

Jake Ryker didn't know he had already been shot in the chest when he charged the shooter in the school cafeteria that Thursday morning, but it probably wouldn't have made any difference if he had.

It was Ryker's seventeenth birthday — May 21, 1998. He was just getting up from a table with his friends at Thurston High School. It was just before 8 a.m., and the students were getting ready for their first class. Ryker had a history assignment to turn in.

That's when a fifteen-year-old student walked through the cafeteria door and opened fire on his fellow students with a .22-caliber Ruger semi-automatic rifle with a fifty-round magazine. The gunman had sawed off the butt of the rifle to make a pistol grip and to make it easier to conceal under his trench coat.

This killer had already murdered his parents — both teachers — before coming to school. And in the breezeway a few feet from the cafeteria door, he had executed Ben Walker with a shot through the head.

At first Ryker didn't see the gun as the killer came in, but he did hear the shots. When the gunman started shooting at the students around his table from about twenty feet away, Ryker pushed his girlfriend, Jennifer Alldredge, to the ground. That was when he got shot. But he thought as he landed on the ground that the blow was from someone's arm or fist. He was unaware that a bullet had gone through his right lung and broken a rib. He looked up to see the gunman approaching the end of the table where he and the others had been sitting.

"He grabbed my friend Mike, held him down, and shot him in the head," Ryker said, referring to Mikael Nickolauson. "That's when I got up and started running. I tripped over this girl Christina and hit the ground. I hit my

chin or my forehead or something. I remember my face
bouncing off the floor."

Jake Ryker, Student at Thurston High School.

Ryker looked up to see
the killer pointing the rifle to
fire again and heard the click
as the firing pin snapped on
an empty chamber.

"I knew when I heard
that click that if anybody was
going to hit him, now's the
time," Ryker said.

The gunman had fired all
fifty rounds in the magazine
and struggled to reload the
rifle as Ryker came up off the
floor and ran at him.

"When he saw me, he
started back-peddling."

Ryker, a high-school wrestler six-feet four-inches tall,
swept the gunman's feet from under him in a wrestling tackle,
and the rifle went flying.

"I hit him hard enough that it knocked him over. His feet
went up in the air, and I came down on top of him."

Another teenager picked up the rifle, and several others
joined in the attack on the killer, including Ryker's brother
Josh. But the gunman was not ready to give up. Ryker could
see he was armed with a knife, but he also had a Glock 9mm
semi-automatic pistol in his waistband under his trench coat.

"When he hit the ground, that's when he started going
for that Glock," Ryker said. "I thought he was going for the
knife. I put my hand on the knife and grabbed his face, but
then he took the gun out. That's when I grabbed the barrel
of the gun. By that time, he had it up in my face, so I was
looking down the barrel."

The previous weekend, Jake Ryker, his fourteen-year-old brother Josh, and their father Robert had been shooting at a local range. They had been shooting a .45-caliber Colt Gold Cup semi-automatic. The pistol is a target version of the .45 semi-automatic that had been the standard issue for the U.S. military. Robert Ryker, at that time a chief petty officer in the U.S. Navy, knew all about the big pistol. He was explaining the safeties on the .45 to his sons. He told them that if you push on the muzzle or the slide of most semi-automatics they will not fire.

"If you push the slide back an eighth of an inch, it throws it out of battery. I said that if somebody stuck one in your face or pointed one at you, you could push back on the slide, and it won't go off," Robert Ryker recalled. "But then I said, if he's still got his finger on the trigger, and you release the slide, it'll shoot, because it'll slam back in battery, and the hammer will fall."

Jokingly, Robert warned his sons not to try this move except as a last resort. He said he never expected that less than a week later his oldest son would be fighting for his life with someone who had stuck a pistol in his face.

"I was taught that very same thing when I was in the Navy as a gunner's mate, and when I went to gunnery school they showed us that. Our chief told our class don't ever try this unless you know you're going to be dead anyway," Robert Ryker added.

Ryker Grabs the Gun

When the student gunman stuck the muzzle of the Glock 9mm in Jake Ryker's face, Ryker grabbed the muzzle with his left hand. Remembering his father's advice, he tried to push the slide back out of battery.

"I figured that would be the best thing for me to do with that thing pointed in my face," Jake Ryker said. "If not, I was going to get a bullet between my eyes. So I grabbed the end of it. When I grabbed it, I guess I didn't grip it strongly enough, but I got it away from my face, and it discharged."

The 9mm bullet went through the knuckle of Ryker's left index finger, burned the top of his thumb, ricocheted off the floor, then ripped through another boy's buttocks. But Ryker's grip on the slide prevented the gun from cycling, and it jammed.

By this time several boys, including Adam Walburger and Josh Ryker, had piled on the shooter and managed to get the Glock away from him.

"Adam was helping Jake, and I grabbed the legs, because he was kicking and fighting," Josh Ryker said. "We kept fighting him until we got pulled off by the adults."

"I was beating on him as much as I could. They had to pull me off him," Jake Ryker said.

It wasn't until another boy, Chris, pulled him off the killer that Jake Ryker realized he had been wounded. Chris grabbed him where his rib had been broken, and Ryker felt a stab of pain. The boy rolled Ryker over and pressed down on his chest where blood was welling from his chest wound. Ryker noticed blood all over Chris's hands. He noticed his own left index finger hanging by a piece of skin from his hand. Chris told him he had also been shot in the chest.

When the killer was arrested, police found that, in addition to the .22-caliber rifle and 9mm pistol, he was armed with another handgun and had more than a thousand rounds of ammunition on him.

Jake Ryker has been called a hero for his actions in the school cafeteria, but he plays this down, pointing out that he was not the only teen to charge the gunman, just the one in front. He said he did not have time to be afraid.

"By the time I got to stop and think about what the hell I just did, I was actually in the hospital," he said.

Ryker spent about a week in the hospital. Doctors were able to save his finger, and he was fit enough a year later to survive Marine boot camp. In November 1999 the killer was sentenced to 111 years in prison for murdering his parents and two Thurston students and for wounding twenty-five other students.

Robert Ryker is a concealed-handgun-license holder and life member of the National Rifle Association. He is proud of his sons' knowledge and ability with firearms. He believes this knowledge enabled Jake to take down the shooter and almost certainly save the lives of more students.

"He knew enough about guns, had been around them enough, so he respects them like anybody should," Robert Ryker said. "But he knew when he could make his move, because he was familiar with them."

Jake said he remembers shooting at beer cans with his grandfather with a .22-caliber revolver when he was six- or seven-years old.

"I got my first BB gun for Christmas when I think I was eight," he added.

Ron Borsch was the manager and lead trainer at the post-graduate SEALE Regional Police Training Academy in Bedford, Ohio. He was a consultant and trainer with the Bedford Police Department. A Vietnam veteran, he retired after thirty years as a patrol officer and SWAT team operator and trainer. Borsch has also served as a consultant to police departments on their responses inside schools. In addition, he has amassed a database of almost two hundred mass-shooting incidents in the U.S. and abroad. He does not include terrorist incidents.

Borsch says that about half the mass shootings end when the killers either quit and surrender or commit suicide. Of the other half, two-thirds are ended by civilians and one-third — one-sixth of the total — are ended by police. Law enforcement and government largely ignored the successful responses by ordinary citizens who happened to be on the scene and took action.

The late Bill Barchers of Hard Tactics Corporation did some research into active-killer incidents. His company taught military-style tactics and skills to law enforcement. Barchers, who died in 2013, had retired from the U.S. Army after a twenty-year career in special operations.

On his blog, now discontinued, he summarized his active-killer research. He stated that the best possible outcome is where the intended victims resolve the incident by confronting the shooter. Examining forty-nine incidents, Barchers stated that police resolved only nine incidents, while the victims resolved fourteen.

"We find that the most likely way to survive an active-shooting incident is not to run. It is to turn and attack the shooter. The problem is, attacking the shooter runs contrary to most current politically correct and police thoughts."

Fortunately, this attitude is changing, albeit slowly.

"Our research indicates that when victims defend themselves, they not only without doubt save their own lives, but they save others' lives," Barchers stated.

He went on to relate that victim-resolved incidents result in far fewer fatalities than shooter-resolved incidents. Additionally, police-resolved shootings produce more casualties than victim-resolved shootings.

"Interestingly, however, in the fourteen incidents in which the victims themselves stepped up to resolve the incident, they did so with a minimum loss of life," Barchers stated.

Chapter 3

COLUMBINE:
SWAT IS NOT THE ANSWER

*"We didn't have a clue who they were. But they were
hurting kids. I couldn't imagine something
like this happening."* — Deputy Paul Smoker

At Columbine High School in Jefferson County, near
Littleton, Colorado, two youths, aged seventeen and eighteen, planned to use propane bombs on timers to kill as
many students as possible as they had lunch in the school
cafeteria. They planned to shoot students fleeing the explosions, according to the Jefferson County Sheriff's Office.

The sheriff's report states there were indications that
the two killers planned to conduct their massacre on April
19, the anniversaries of the 1993 FBI attack on the Branch
Davidian compound near Waco, Texas, and the 1995 bombing of the federal building in Oklahoma City.

However, it was April 20, 1999, when the two youths
drove to the school in their cars and parked them near the
entrances to the cafeteria. Some time about 11:14 a.m., they
got out of their cars and toted two twenty-pound propane
bombs in duffel bags into the cafeteria and placed them near
two lunch tables. They returned to their cars to wait for the
explosion. The bombs were set to explode at 11:17. The two
youths had calculated that was when the maximum number
of students, about five hundred, would have been in the cafeteria. They waited for the explosions, but the bombs failed
to go off. Had they detonated, the sheriff's report estimated
that most of the 488 people in the cafeteria would have been
killed or seriously injured.

The sheriff's report stated: "Because of faulty wiring and poorly constructed devices, the twenty-pound propane bombs did not detonate."

However, reliable and credible sources say the reason the propane bombs did not go off had to do with the clocks that were used as timers. The two killers bought one of the clocks to test, and it worked to set off a test device. They later bought more of the same make and model of clock, which they attached to the bombs they left in the cafeteria. But between the time they bought the first clock and the second batch, the manufacturer changed the material of the clock hands from metal to plastic, which did not complete the electrical circuit necessary to set off the bombs.

Both of the youths' cars contained bombs set to explode after the cafeteria bombs. These did not explode either.

Initially the two killers wore black trench coats to hide the guns they carried. At some point they apparently discarded the coats, as they were seen on security cameras without them. The eighteen-year-old carried a sawed-off pump-action 12-guage shotgun and a Hi-Point 9mm carbine. The seventeen-year-old carried a TEC-DC-9, a 9mm semi-automatic pistol that looked like a small sub-machine gun. He also carried a cut-down Stevens 12-gauge double-barreled shotgun.

At 11:19 Jefferson County Dispatch received a 9-1-1 call from a citizen who reported an explosion and grass fire in a field three miles south of the school. The two gunmen had set several explosive devices in two backpacks as a diversion. The killers apparently wanted to lure first responders to the field while they carried out their attack on the school. Some but not all the devices exploded, starting the fire. The Littleton Fire Department extinguished the fire.

Also at 11:19 the killers were seen on a vantage point at the top of a flight of steps near the west entrance to the school. One of them was heard yelling, "Go, go!" Both pulled their shotguns from duffel bags they were carrying, and the killing began.

Rachel Scott and another student were eating lunch on the grass outside the west entrance to the school when the two gunmen opened fire. Scott was the first student killed by the duo. Her companion was wounded.

Five more students on the grass came under fire; two were hit. Three other students were shot at and two hit. The seventeen-year-old killer advanced on the wounded students and shot them again at close range. One died; one survived.

Throughout their rampage, the two killers set off pipe bombs and other explosives that they carried in backpacks and duffel bags. Thirty bombs of the seventy-six that were found at the school did explode.

The 9-1-1 Call

Meanwhile, Jefferson County Deputy Sheriff Neil Gardner, the school's resource officer, was finishing his lunch in his patrol car. At 11:22 Gardner received a radio call that a female was down in the school's south parking lot. He responded with emergency lights and siren.

At 11:24 a teacher and two custodians entered the cafeteria and urged the students to take cover. The students started hiding under the tables.

About the same time, teacher Patti Neilson, acting as a hall monitor, saw the two gunmen outside and thought they were students making a school video production using toy guns. She headed through the west entrance intending to tell them to stop, when one of them fired at her, shattering the glass in the entrance windows. The glass shards hit her in the shoulder, arm, and knee. Glass shards also hit student Brian Anderson, who was trying to escape through the west doors. Teacher and student escaped into the library, where at 11:25 Neilson called 9-1-1 while hiding under the counter at the front of the room.

She told the operator: "The school is in a panic, and I'm on the floor in the library. I've got students down! 'Under the tables kids; heads under the tables.' Kids are screaming, and teachers are trying to take control of things. We need police here."

The 9-1-1 operator urged her to stay on the line and assured her police were on the way. She asked if Neilson could lock the door or block it to keep anyone from coming in.

Neilson said the shooter was outside the library in the hallway, and she was afraid to go there. "I don't know what's happening in the rest of the building."

The operator tells her to try to keep the kids calm.

"I told the kids to get on the floor. I told them…all of the children on the floor under the tables. Yes, they're all under the tables."

The 9-1-1 operator: "Keep everyone low to the floor."

"Yes, yea, everyone is. Everyone stay on the floor. Stay under the tables."

She described the shooter as a large male student, but she didn't know his name. Initially she thought the gun he had was a "play gun," until he shot at her.

The operator asks her name.

Neilson replies: "Patti."

"He's in the library. He's shooting at everybody."

Operator: "Okay, try to keep as many people down as you can."

The Response

Deputy Gardner, the resource officer, arrived in the parking lot at 11:24 and parked near the west door, one floor above the cafeteria and on the same level as the library.

The sheriff's report stated there was so much traffic on the police radio that Gardner could not tell the dispatcher he was on the scene. The bright yellow shirt that was part of Gardner's school-resource-officer's uniform made him a highly visible target, and as he got out of his patrol car, he came under fire. The eighteen-year-old gunman, who was standing at the west doors, fired about ten rounds from his 9mm carbine, then the gun jammed.

Gardner leaned over the roof of his patrol car and fired four shots at the gunman at a range of sixty yards while the gunman was clearing his carbine. After clearing the jam, the gunman fired several more shots at the deputy. None of the shots from the two combatants scored a hit.

After the gunman ran back into the school building at 11:26, Gardner was able to get through on the police radio, telling dispatch: "Shots in the building. I need someone in the south lot with me."

By 11:30, about four minutes later, five more Jefferson County deputies arrived on the scene. They found "chaos and hysteria." Terrified students and teachers were running in all directions from the school. The deputies could hear explosions coming from inside the building. Escaping students talked of gunmen with semi-automatic rifles, bombs, and hand-grenades. Other students reported four and six gunmen and some students taken as hostages. According to their training, the deputies set up a perimeter to ensure the suspects did not escape. They covered school exits on the east, south, and west sides of the building.

More officers were arriving, including several from the Denver Police Department. They organized a shuttle to get students to safety, after initially providing cover behind the patrol cars.

Deputy Paul Smoker, a motorcycle officer, was not far away when Gardner yelled, "There he is!" Gardner fired several shots at a young man armed with a rifle standing inside the double doors at the west entrance. Smoker moved to where he could see the gunman and fired three shots before the youth disappeared. Gardner had engaged one of the gunmen twice. Meanwhile other officers were evacuating students and teachers with priority given to the wounded.

According to the sheriff's report, Smoker later said: "This was not the dope deal gone bad. There was an unknown inside a school. We didn't know who the bad guy was, but we soon realized the sophistication of their weapons. These were big bombs, big guns. We didn't have a clue who they were, but they were hurting kids. I couldn't imagine something like this happening."

Despite the explosions and sound of gunshots inside the building, the officers remained outside the school and were ordered to hold their perimeter while the killing continued inside. As Patti Neilson reported to the 9-1-1 operator, the gunmen entered the library where there were fifty-six people. In seven and a half minutes — between 11:29 and 11:36 — the gunmen murdered ten and wounded twelve. The last victim was killed at 11:35. The killers left the library and wandered randomly around the second floor, shooting into empty rooms. They went down into the cafeteria and finally returned to the library, where they killed themselves.

Five members of the Denver Police Department SWAT team arrived at Columbine at 11:49. Jefferson County SWAT team commander Lieutenant Terry Manwaring assembled an *ad hoc* SWAT team comprising a dozen officers from Jefferson County, Denver, and Littleton. Many of the officers did not have their SWAT gear with them, including bullet-resistant vests and weapons. Manwaring split them into two groups, with the first group entering the school at 12:06 p.m., forty-seven minutes after the active killers fired their first shots.

According to the sheriff's report, the killers committed suicide between 12:05 and 12:08. In the sixteen minutes of their killing spree, the two gunmen murdered twelve students and one teacher. They wounded twenty-one others, with three more injured while escaping. The active killers fired 37 12-gauge rounds and 151 9mm rounds for a total of 188 shots fired.

Twelve law-enforcement officers fired 141 times, with sixteen rounds fired by four deputies, four by a Lakewood police officer, and the rest by seven Denver police officers. The sheriff's report stated: "The majority of the [law-enforcement] shots were fired toward the west entrance and the library windows. This was done when shots were exchanged with the gunmen and when law-enforcement and medical personnel were evacuating students. There were no injuries as a result of shots fired by law-enforcement officers."

"Tactical Error"

It was the shooting at Columbine that demonstrated the inadequacy of SWAT teams to deal with active killers.

The first officers to arrive set up a perimeter and waited until the SWAT team arrived. The first tactical officers entered the building forty-seven minutes after the incident began, by which time the shooting was over and the perpetrators had shot themselves.

"Columbine was a true tactical error, because we didn't understand the problem. Law enforcement did not understand the problem," said John Benner of Tactical Defense Institute. "But Columbine was the thing that really changed law enforcement, because we realized we can't sit out here. We've got to go in."

So how could law-enforcement officers go into a building to find and stop an active killer, who is trying to murder as many unarmed victims as possible, while the officers remain as safe as possible?

Benner said they went to the tactical experts and asked their advice. The result was to train small teams of regular officers to go in. The first officer on the scene would wait until he was joined by three or four officers, and they would enter the building together.

"We still didn't fully understand the problem. I am including myself in this," Benner acknowledged.

The small-team approach was better than waiting for the SWAT team, but it still didn't work. It took too long.

"You can't wait. It takes time, is the problem, and that's the thing we didn't understand. Unfortunately, we've got enough numbers now that we understand the problem better. So Columbine changed from a tactical-team response to a multi-officer response, which was still a mistake," Benner said.

Another retired law-enforcement officer who saw the light was Ron Borsch, lead trainer for the SEALE Regional Police Training Academy in Bedford, Ohio. In 2000 shortly after the 1999 Columbine High School rapid mass murder, Borsch began to specialize in tactically training patrol officers.

"For a few years, I followed the lead of national tactical alleged 'gurus' using multiple-officer formations. Eventually it became apparent to me that these gurus were not paying attention and adjusting to past and current events, so I parted company with their methods," he said.

The formation of choice was the diamond. The front officer looked ahead, the next two watched the sides, while the last member watched for threats from behind. This formation was designed by the military and worked well outside, but in a school hallway it exposed the lead officer to a threat from a classroom on one side. The assailant would see the lead officer before the officers on each side could see him, Borsch said.

In the training he taught, he had the lead officer drop back a few steps behind the officers watching the sides.

However, after extensive research, Borsch concluded that a multiple-officer formation of four or more had never arrived in time to stop the killing.

"Around 2006 I dedicated myself to only the Single Officer's Lifesaving Others (SOLO) concept in Tactical First Responder courses."

In his years at the SEALE Regional Police Training Academy, Borsch trained officers from more than a hundred law-enforcement agencies from ten states.

Each time he held a Tactical First Responder course or did a presentation, he always asked his audience if anyone knew of a rapid-mass-murder incident that was stopped by four or more officers.

"I could not find a single incident until 2008," he said. "Experience would indicate that delaying engagement in the initial action in order that more officers may deployed results in fewer lives being saved, not more."

Columbine prompted a lot of discussion about what could be done among law-enforcement and security professionals. The Illinois State Police Academy report, mentioned earlier, examined a technique called "Rapid Deployment," in which patrol officers do not wait for SWAT teams, but enter the kill zone and run to the sound of the gunfire. They bypass the wounded and head straight for the active killer or killers. The aim is to engage the gunman or gunmen as soon as possible to stop the killing. The minimum size of the entry unit is usually four patrol officers, preferably armed with shotguns or carbines. This system is also known as "Immediate Action, Active Shooter Response, Violent Intruder — Police and Educators Response" (VIPER), or "Quick Action Deployment" (QUAD).

Researchers who assembled the report studied forty-four mass-shooting incidents. In case after case they found that the shooter had escaped before police arrived or that he had committed suicide. But in five cases ordinary citizens had confronted the gunman and held him until the police arrived.

From the forty-four cases they studied, the researchers came up with an "average" active-killer incident: "A single, white-male shooter, aged thirty, will enter a well-populated location and open fire without warning. This shooting spree will probably be over in two to three minutes, usually long before even a single police officer can arrive. The suspect will almost certainly be familiar with the locale and will initially target specific people, but is very likely to fire randomly before he stops. This shooter will probably be armed with more than one firearm and will fire about twenty-five rounds, killing three to four victims and wounding an additional five people. After the shooting spree, the suspect is likely to end up dead, probably by committing suicide. The incident is almost guaranteed to take place during daylight hours and will probably occur inside a building."

In its conclusions, the report states: "Immediate action taken by personnel who are on-site when the shooting starts is the most effective way to stop the killing."

Richard E. Fairburn of the Illinois State Police Academy and primary author of the report acknowledges: "this research illustrates that almost all of them (active-killer incidents) will be over long before even the quickest teams can hope to make contact with the shooter."

He also recommends that all officers should be trained to respond immediately when they are close to an active killing in progress.

Of course the report does not recommend arming school teachers or other citizens — at the time Illinois had no provision for concealed carry by ordinary citizens. The closest it comes is to refer to some terrorist incidents in Israel. "Reports suggest many of these terrorists are being shot by armed Israeli citizens, who happened to be on the scene or arrived before military or police units."

Arming Teachers

Utah is a trail blazer in allowing ordinary citizens with concealed-carry licenses, including teachers, to carry their guns in schools and colleges. The Utah concealed-carry law went into effect in 1995. There was no prohibition in the law, as there is in most states, for carrying concealed handguns in schools and universities. School districts and the University of Utah tried to contest this in the courts and lost. In September 2006 the Utah Supreme Court ruled in favor of concealed carry in schools and universities, not just for students and employees, but also parents and other visitors.

"Where we're at now is that schools and universities cannot have their own rules regarding the carrying of firearms," said Clark Aposhian, president of the Utah Shooting Sports Council. With the exception of one accidental discharge, Utah has not had any incidents involving firearms in schools or colleges and certainly no school shootings, Aposhian said.

On September 11, 2014, a sixth-grade school teacher at Westbrook Elementary School in Taylorsville, a suburb of Salt Lake City, negligently fired an accidental shot in a faculty bathroom, killing the porcelain toilet. The teacher was injured in the lower leg by fragments from the toilet. The shooting happened before school started, and no one else witnessed the incident. She was subsequently charged with a misdemeanor and resigned from her job. "It was an accident, and that's all it was. It was negligent, absolutely," Aposhian said.

On October 2, 2006, another school shooting grabbed headlines across the country. An active killer murdered five young girls and wounded five others at a one-room Amish school-house in Bart Township in Pennsylvania. The killer then committed suicide. This prompted a reaction from a school district in Texas.

Harrold ISD Superintendent David Thweatt in his office.

Harrold Independent School District nudges up against the Oklahoma border about thirty-five miles west of Wichita Falls. The district covers two hundred square miles but has only one school that teaches kindergarten through grade twelve to 125 students. It is on the eastern edge of Wilbarger County, a typical west-Texas county with a population of thirteen thousand, spread over an area that is just smaller than the state of Rhode Island.

David Thweatt is the school-district superintendent and has been in the district since 2004. When he arrived he found the school was in need of both repair and some upgrade in security philosophy. It is on a major highway, and people could just walk in, he said. He improved passive security by locking all the doors except the front one and installing surveillance cameras. Thweatt can see the front entrance from a screen in the corner of his office.

The nearest law enforcement in Wilbarger County is the sheriff's office at Vernon, the county seat. Harrold is about seventeen miles from the county court house.

"We're about thirty minutes from any type of first responders. And that's given the fact that they're right there and not on the other side of the county, because we're on the very edge here. So that's problematic within itself," Thweatt says.

His office is as crowded as an antique store, with old-fashioned high ceilings, tall windows, and walls that appear to be a foot thick. He has several clocks, plaques from the National Rifle Association, the Texas State Rifle Association, and other gun organizations fighting for space on his walls.

Living out in the country, most residents have guns and are familiar with them. They have rifles, shotguns, and handguns for self-defense, but also to shoot rabbits, snakes, skunks, wild hogs, bobcats, and cougars, Thweatt said.

"That concerned us because we had our magnetic locked doors, we had everything, but this was the milk-delivery man. We would have let him in because we knew him; he was a friend," Thweatt said, referring to the killer at the Amish school.

He was skeptical of the standard emergency plan for U.S. schools, which he referred to as: "Lock the doors, and hope for the best."

So Thweatt came up with a plan to arm teachers and school staff. He took it to his attorney and asked him to research the legality of it. About November or December of 2006, the attorney said it was legal on the state and federal levels. Thweatt took it to his school board of seven and told them if they passed the policy they would attract national media attention.

He said: "I'm not worried about that; I'll be the spokesman. I'm not worried about that, in any way, shape, or form, but you will be in the spotlight."

A couple of the board members said they really didn't want the district to be the poster child for armed teachers, so perhaps they should consider other options.

"So we sat on it," Thweatt said.

They would revisit the plan after the next major mass shooting.

Chapter 4

VIRGINIA TECH: FORTY-SEVEN CASUALTIES IN ELEVEN MINUTES

"Nobody tried to get up and be a hero."
– a student in Room 211

The Virginia Polytechnic Institute, better known as Virginia Tech, has a sprawling campus of some twenty-six hundred acres in the southwest part of the state not far from the Blue Mountains. In 2007 about seven thousand employees catered to more than twenty-six thousand students, nine thousand of whom lived in dormitories on campus.

No walls or fences enclose the university. Anyone can walk or drive onto the grounds, although access to dormitories is controlled by key-cards. West Ambler Johnston is one of those dormitories.

According to the Virginia Tech Incident Review Panel's report, about 7 a.m. on April 16, 2007, a twenty-three-year-old Korean-born student entered the West Ambler Johnston dormitory building. He had a history of mental and behavioral problems, including stalking female students. He had a mailbox in that building and had access to the lobby, but only after 7:30 a.m. He lived in another dormitory building nearby. Somehow he got into West Ambler Johnston, probably by following someone in, and went up to the fourth floor.

Emily Hilscher, a nineteen-year-old freshman student, had just been dropped off by her boyfriend, Karl Thornhill, a student at nearby Radford University. She was in her room when the Korean-born student entered her room. Ryan Clark, who lived in the next room, apparently heard some sort of commotion, maybe shots fired or screams, and went to investigate. Another student whose room was on the other side of Hilscher was woken up by the noise and thought Hilscher had fallen out of bed. She found the resident assistant who called for Emergency Medical Services (EMS) on a non-emergency line. When EMS and a police officer arrived, they found Hilscher and Clark in Hilscher's room shot at close range and mortally wounded.

The killer escaped from the building without being seen and returned to his room in nearby Harper Hall. No connection was ever found to link the gunman with Hilscher or Clark, and his motive in that shooting remains a mystery.

Initially, police thought the shooting was a domestic dispute between Emily Hilscher and her boyfriend Karl Thornhill, who they were told owned a gun. They informed the university administration but did not urge any action such as canceling classes or even warning the students.

Thornhill became the prime suspect and officers from the Virginia Tech and Blacksburg police departments searched for him. Both departments put their emergency response teams (ERTs) on alert in case they had to conduct a high-risk arrest of Thornhill. Officers from Virginia Tech and Blacksburg ERTs had trained together and knew each other.

Shortly before 9:30 — two hours after the first killings — the university's emergency policy group decided to put out a statement, reporting the double shooting and warning students and staff to be cautious. This statement was put on the university web site and also sent by email.

After changing out of his bloody clothes, the killer went to the post office in Blacksburg to mail a package to *NBC News* in New York. It would be opened two days later. The package included a diatribe of rage and resentment against the university and its students, as well as the infamous video clips of him holding guns, which were shown on national television.

About 9:30 a Montgomery County deputy sheriff stopped Karl Thornhill in his pickup on a road outside the campus but inside the Blacksburg city limits. Detectives who questioned him found him co-operative and unlikely to be the perpetrator of the two murders.

Norris Hall

Also about 9:30, the killer entered Norris Hall. He was armed with two semi-automatic handguns — a 9mm Glock and a .22-caliber Walther. He chained and padlocked the three main entrance doors to the building from the inside. This prevented anyone from entering or leaving. It also delayed the police response. A faculty member later found a bomb threat note the killer put on the inside of one set of doors.

Norris Hall is a three-story older building containing faculty offices and classrooms. The gunman was familiar with the building because he had a class there that semester — the class was on Abnormal Behavior. He went up to the second floor and poked his head into several rooms where classes were in progress.

The Virginia Tech Incident Review Panel's report describes what happened next. The report estimated that the killer started shooting about 9:40. He walked into Classroom 206, where Professor G.V. Loganathan was teaching Advanced Hydrology Engineering. Without warning the gunman shot and killed the professor then turned his guns on the students. He killed nine and wounded two. Only two students in that class were unscathed. The killer made several visits to four classrooms, shooting some students six times or more.

Students and faculty in nearby classrooms heard the shots but did not immediately realize what they were hearing. Some thought the sounds were from a nail gun being used in nearby construction, others thought they were noises from experiments in the chemistry lab on the first floor.

General plan of Norris Hall.

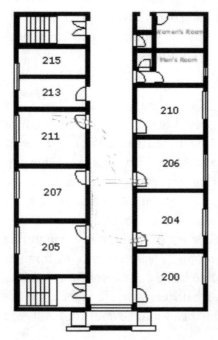

John Benner of Tactical Defense Institute says that in most of these mass murders, when someone starts shooting, people often don't recognize the sound as gunfire and depending on the building layout sometimes they don't hear the shooting at all.

"What we are seeing is that it takes a long time for somebody to recognize what is going on and to call 9-1-1," Benner says.

We don't know the time period between the first shot and when the first 9-1-1 call is made, he adds.

The report continued stating that the gunman crossed the hallway and entered Room 207, where Professor Christopher Bishop was teaching a German class. He shot Bishop and several students near the door, then walked among the desks shooting others. Bishop and four students died, and six more were wounded. One student tried without success to wrench free the podium that was bolted to the floor to barricade the door.

The killer headed for Room 211 where a French class was in progress. The professor, Jocelyne Couture-Nowak, realized that she and her students were hearing gunfire and asked student Colin Goddard to call 9-1-1. The call was routed to Blacksburg Police Department then transferred to Virginia Tech police who received it at 9:42. The police response started.

Other students in the room tried to use the instructor's table and the flimsy desks to block the door, but the gunman pushed his way in and started shooting. He killed Couture-Nowak first and wounded Goddard then murdered several other students. Goddard dropped his cell phone when he was hit. It was picked up by Emily Haas who kept the line open and fed information to the dispatcher throughout the ordeal. She kept her eyes closed and played dead, only talking when she knew by the sound of the shots that the gunman was out of the room.

In his definitive book about the law-enforcement response to Virginia Tech called *Shooter Down*, author John Giduck recounts the actions of the only student who tried to fight back. Twenty-year-old Air Force Cadet Matthew La Porte was sitting in in his uniform in the back of Room 211 when the killer forced his way in and started shooting. Cadet La Porte ran along the window side of the room leaping over desks and students until he reached the front of the room. He turned towards the active

Air Force Cadet Matthew La Porte. (Photo courtesy Stevens Photography.)

killer and charged him. He soaked up eight rounds before he collapsed and died a few feet from his murderer.

As Giduck puts it, "Cadet La Porte did what he had been trained to do, what his character and personal desire to serve the nation in uniform compelled him to do: fight to protect those who could not fight for themselves."

Strangely there is no mention of La Porte's actions in the Virginia Tech Incident Review Panel's report. In 2015, La Porte was posthumously awarded the Airman's Medal, the Air Force's highest medal for valor in a non-combat situation.

The active killer would return to Room 211. In addition to the instructor, he killed eleven students and wounded six. Only one student escaped unscathed in Room 211.

The killer returned to Room 206 where he shot more students then tried to get back into Room 207. However, students pushed a desk up against the door, then two wounded students and two who had not been hit held the legs of the desk with their hands while digging their feet into the carpet to prevent the killer pushing his way in. The gunman beat on the door and pushed it open an inch, then fired several shots around the door handle. He eventually gave up and tried to get into Room 205.

The students in Room 205 came off best. They were attending a scientific computing class when they heard the shots. They held the door closed with their feet while keeping low to the ground. The killer tried to force his way in, but the students kept him out. He fired through the door but did not hit anyone.

The gunman went to Room 204 where Professor Liviu Librescu was teaching solid mechanics. The seventy-six-year-old Romanian Jew was a survivor of the Holocaust and came to the U.S. from Israel in the mid 1980s. When the killer tried to enter the room, Librescu braced himself against the door and yelled for his students to jump out of the window. They responded by pushing out the screens and jumping from the second-floor windows, a drop of nineteen feet to grass and bushes. The smart ones lowered themselves from the windows then dropped about thirteen feet.

While the students were escaping, the gunman shot and killed Librescu through the door then got into the classroom and started shooting the students waiting at the windows to escape. Ten students got out of the windows and reached the ground, some breaking bones when they hit the ground. The gunman shot three students in Librescu's class, killing one.

Police Arrive

According to the report, police officers started to arrive at Norris Hall three minutes after the university police department received the first call. The officers were slowed by the chained entrances but eventually found a locked door to a maintenance shop. They shot the lock with breaching rounds from a shotgun and entered the building. Two police teams entered and ran up the stairs to the second floor where the shots were coming from.

Meanwhile, the killer had returned to Room 211 where he fired one shot into La Porte's head then the police heard the last shot as the killer pumped a round into his own head, ending the worst massacre by a gunman on a U.S. university campus. Although the police did not shoot or overcome the killer, their arrival is probably what prompted him to end his killing spree. He still had more than two hundred rounds left so he could have continued his rampage or shot it out with police.

The review panel's report estimates that between 9:40 and 9:51 — eleven minutes — the active killer shot and killed twenty-five students and five faculty members in the hallway and in four of the classrooms.

According to John Giduck, he wounded twenty-three other students. Another four students were injured when they jumped from the windows in Room 204. In those eleven or so minutes, the killer fired at least 174 rounds from his two semi-automatic pistols — a rate of about one shot every four seconds.

In addition to Matthew La Porte, another hero of the Virginia Tech shooting was undoubtedly seventy-six-year-old Professor Liviu Librescu, but he was from a different generation. He sacrificed himself by holding the door while ordering his students to escape through the windows. He understood the responsibilities of leadership — the leader, like the captain of a ship, saves himself last. Another professor who successfully saved students and also died was Kevin Granata. He was in his office on the third floor. Another professor was holding an exam on the same floor. One girl who had completed her exam was going down the stairs but came back to report someone shooting on the second floor. Granata told the other professor to lock his students in his, Granata's, office because classrooms did not have locks. Granata then went down to the second floor to investigate. The gunman shot and killed him in the hallway.

We talk of flight or fight as a response to danger. Flight is a respectable and preferable course of action. Students who jumped from the windows in Room 204 followed Librescu's order and saved their lives. Those who tried, some successfully, some unsuccessfully, to block the doors have nothing to be ashamed of. They saw that action was needed and took it.

But if you are trapped, what about the other option: fight? *Time* magazine quoted one student in Room 211, who cowered under a desk while other students were being executed around him. He was waiting for it to be his turn. He heard the gunman reload three times, but no one apparently thought to attack him while his gun was out of action.

Another student in the same class who feigned death told *Newsweek*: "Nobody tried to get up and be a hero."

Ironically, that was in Room 211 where La Porte did fight back, but the student obviously had his head down and did not see the cadet's valiant charge.

The review panel's report states: "Several students, some of whom were injured and others not, successfully played dead amid the carnage around them, and survived. ...This worked for at least some students."

The report made no mention of Matthew La Porte or anyone trying to rush the shooter. Apparently this was fine with the panel. Its recommendations concerned action by police, to make sure that exterior doors cannot be chained shut, and that bomb threats be taken seriously. The focus of the report seems to be to absolve the police and administration of any responsibility, while failing to address how students could save their own lives. There was no recommendation that students should be taught to fight back.

The Aftermath

"Virginia Tech was also a game changer. Law enforcement was in the absolute best position that they could possibly be in," said John Benner. "On campus at the time of the second shooting, they had two in-service tactical teams that were geared up and ready to go, and they still lost [almost] fifty people, either killed or wounded."

He said it only took the SWAT teams about eight minutes to get into Norris Hall from the time the Virginia Tech Police Department received the call. In almost all cases the unknown factor is the time it takes from when the shooting starts to when the first 9-1-1 call reaches the police.

"The time that we don't know is: how long did it take to call 9-1-1, and how long did it take for them to process the call? Those are things that in most instances we don't know: when it starts to the time somebody calls 9-1-1," Benner said.

The review panel's report estimated the time from when the shooting started to when the first 9-1-1 call reached the Virginia Tech police was about three minutes. Add the eight minutes it took the SWAT teams to reach Norris Hall and the shooting lasted about eleven minutes. With forty-seven faculty members and students killed or wounded, the active killer was hitting between four and five victims a minute, some of them as many as eight times.

"Time is a real problem," John Benner said. "The only answer is armed people inside."

Immediately after the Virginia Tech shooting, the local and national media were all over the incident like blowflies on a dead cow in August. They concentrated on the victims, on the university, on the police response, and on the active killer's obvious mental problems and that the country obviously needed more gun-control laws. There were the *pro forma* comparisons to Columbine. The media were aided and abetted in calling for more gun-control laws by the usual suspects: the Brady Campaign to Prevent Handgun Violence, the Violence Policy Center, and other anti-self-defense groups.

While the media and anti-second-amendment organizations' responses were predictable, the political response was muted. It was encouraging that after the shooting many politicians kept their mouths shut about gun control, saying it was too early or inappropriate to raise the issue.

Many Democrat politicians had been stung by the party's enthusiasm for disarming law-abiding citizens. It is an issue they didn't want to deal with. After prompting by former President Bill Clinton, they have come to realize that gun control likely cost the Democrats control of Congress and the Presidency in 2000.

Newsweek noticed the hush from Democrats in the wake of Virginia Tech. Even such rabid anti-gun politicians as then Congressman Rahm Emanuel didn't want to talk about gun control. The Democrats recruited some pro-gun politicians to run for Congress in 2006 and tried to court gun owners, albeit with their fingers crossed.

When Attorney General Eric Holder suggested reinstating the so-called assault-weapons ban in February 2009, sixty-five Democrat congressional representatives wrote him a letter telling him to back off.

The response to Virginia Tech from the pro-gun, pro-self-defense citizens and organizations was also predictable. The feedback I heard again and again from people interested in taking responsibility for their own safety was: "If only one student there had had a gun...."

But Virginia Tech was a "gun-free zone." Even students and faculty members with concealed-handgun licenses were forbidden to take their guns on campus. In 2005 a student with a concealed-handgun permit was disciplined for bringing a gun on campus.

For more than two years, the Virginia Citizens Defense League had been trying to get a law passed in the legislature that would prevent public colleges and universities from banning guns from their campuses. The bills were stalled in committee after much lobbying by Virginia Tech and other institutes of supposed higher learning in the state.

Apparently Virginia Tech spokesman Larry Hincker was pleased the bill in 2006 was defeated. He was quoted in *The Roanoke Times* as saying: "I'm sure the university community is appreciative of the General Assembly's actions because this will help parents, students, faculty, and visitors feel safe on our campus."

Right.

Students for Concealed Carry on Campus

In the days and weeks after the Virginia Tech shooting, some people spoke in favor of allowing students and faculty members who have concealed-handgun licenses to carry handguns on campus just as they can off campus.

The shooting at Virginia Tech made some students realize how vulnerable they were, and it spawned an organization called "Students for Concealed Carry on Campus" (SCCC).

According to its web site, Students for Concealed Carry on Campus is a national, non-partisan, grassroots organization comprising more than forty-three thousand college students, professors, college employees, parents of college students, and concerned citizens, who believe that holders of state-issued concealed-handgun licenses should be allowed the same measure of personal protection on college campuses that current laws afford them virtually everywhere else.

The organization has members in all fifty states. It states that its leadership includes people of diverse political backgrounds: conservatives, moderates, and liberals.

The web site states that SCCC has two main functions. "The first function is to dispel the common myths and misconceptions about concealed carry on college campuses, by making the public aware of the facts. The second function is to push state legislators and school administrators to grant concealed-handgun license holders the same rights on college campuses that those licensees currently enjoy in most other unsecured locations."

The organization pushes for change at the state level to remove prohibitions against concealed carry on college campuses. It seeks to get states to follow Utah's example in prohibiting publicly funded "colleges from refusing to honor state-issued licenses."

SCCC believes in honoring private-property rights, therefore, it pushes concealed carry on private colleges through negotiation rather than legislation.

It does seem ridiculous that young soldiers who have served their country in Iraq or Afghanistan should come home and be denied the right to carry concealed handguns for protection while students at a college or university.

Various people weighed in to support students and faculty members being able to protect themselves on campus. Texas Governor Rick Perry was quoted as saying that Texans with concealed-handgun licenses should be able to carry anywhere. He included college campuses, bars, courthouses, and churches.

Suzanna Hupp, whose parents were killed in the Luby's Cafeteria massacre in Killeen, Texas, in 1991, told a reporter from *Time* magazine that she put some of the blame for Virginia Tech on politicians. She was angry because the shooting was preventable, she said.

"The politicians haven't figured it out. They have created gun-free zones, and all of the dreadful things that have happened were in these gun-free zones," Hupp told the reporter. The story of the Luby's Cafeteria massacre is told in Chapter 9.

Alan Gottlieb, chairman of the Citizens Committee for the Right to Keep and Bear Arms, agreed. He said every tragic school shooting and some other mass shootings had one thing in common. "They all happened in so-called 'gun-free zones.' You can pass all the laws you want, but the only proven way to stop shootings in 'gun-free zones' is an armed response."

After Virginia Tech, I spoke to Sheriff Wayne Rausch of Latah County, Idaho. The University of Idaho, with a student body of ten thousand, is located in Latah County and the city of Moscow. At the time the university had a policy of no guns on campus, but that changed in 2014. The governor of Idaho, C.L. "Butch" Otter, signed a bill allowing permit holders to carry concealed handguns on university campuses.

Rausch favored more law-abiding citizens, including adult students, getting permits to carry concealed handguns. However, he has experienced occasions when permit holders have hindered police, while intending to help. In most cases permit holders should use their guns only to defend themselves or their families, he says.

"An active-shooter situation is certainly an example of an exception, where I would like to see the armed citizen get involved," Rausch said, "because one of the questions that was posed to me by many of the people that called was: 'What could law enforcement have done differently at Virginia Tech?'

"Quite frankly I've spoken to a lot of my fellow sheriffs and chiefs, and we all agree: basically nothing. It's absolutely ludicrous to think that on a huge campus like that, when there is an isolated incident going on that is not only dynamic but changing fast, that somehow or another police are miraculously going to be able to pinpoint the exact location and have immediate response to shut it down before it gets worse. That's just not feasible; that's just not going to happen."

Rausch felt the most reasonable expectation is that law enforcement is probably going to get the information about a shooting from someone calling on a cell phone. When police are alerted, they go there and take care of it as quickly as possible. "On the other hand, the quickest answer to this obviously is that if you've got a classroom full of students, and you are lining them up to shoot them, and some of them are armed themselves, there is a possibility this may be shut down much quicker."

He said the deterrent factor of some students being armed should not be discounted.

"It seems to me that there must be some intimidation factor for the bad guy that, if I know I am among an armed populace, I could be picking a fight with someone who is going to kill me."

Lack of Fighting Spirit

While after Virginia Tech many people railed against the ostrich-like attitude of most educators towards guns on campuses, another more disturbing question was being raised: Why did none of the students in Norris Hall fight back? At the time, the attempt of Air Force Cadet Matthew La Porte to rush the gunman was not known to the media.

The answers varied, but the theme seemed to be that we have produced an emasculated generation of young adults, who have been socialized by educators to obey orders and avoid conflict at all costs.

Nationally syndicated radio-talk-show host Neal Boortz opined: "It seems that standing in terror waiting for your turn to be executed was the right thing to do, and any questions as to why twenty-five students didn't try to rush and overpower [the gunman] are just examples of right-wing maniacal bias. Surrender—comply—adjust."

National Review Online columnist John Derbyshire asked: "Where was the spirit of self-defense here? …Why didn't anyone rush the guy?"

Syndicated columnist Michelle Malkin stated: "Instead of teaching students to defend their beliefs, American educators shield them from vigorous intellectual debate. Instead of encouraging autonomy, our higher institutions of learning stoke passivity and conflict-avoidance. And as the erosion of intellectual self-defense goes, so goes the erosion of physical self-defense."

National Review columnist Mark Steyn refers to a "culture of corrosive passivity."

"It's deeply damaging to portray fit, fully-formed adults as children who need to be protected. We should be raising them to understand that there will be moments in life when you need to protect yourself — and, in a 'horrible' world, there may come moments when you have to choose between protecting yourself or others," Steyn wrote.

The late Bill Barchers of Hard Tactics Corporation thought the attitude applied not just to students. In his blog, he wrote: "After thirty years of cultural change in which our society has done much to emasculate men and generally make society less self-dependent and more dependent on government services, one of the outcomes is that the average citizen appears to be much more physically timid than the average citizen of forty years ago."

The Virginia Tech Incident Review Panel's report stated that data on the effect of carrying guns on campus are "incomplete and inconclusive."

"The panel knows of no case in which a shooter in campus homicides has been shot or scared off by a student or faculty member with a weapon."

However, in the report's own Appendix L on school mass shootings, it lists two cases where this happened. One of these was the shooting at Pearl, Mississippi, on October 1, 1997, when the active killer was stopped by the assistant principal at gun-point.

Appalachian School of Law

Compare the Virginia Tech incident with the other incident the Review Panel chose to ignore. It happened five years before and only a hundred miles west of the Virginia Tech campus. Another foreign-born student went on a shooting rampage on January 16, 2002, this time at the Appalachian School of Law, near Grundy, Virginia.

When Tracy Bridges and his friends got back to the law school after lunch they were late, so Bridges parked his Chevrolet Tahoe in a faculty spot near one of the exits from the classroom building. He and the friends with him climbed the stairs to the second floor and entered the class-room. About fifteen students were waiting in the room for the professor to arrive.

Bridges, 25, was in his third and final year at the law school. He was also certified as a peace officer in North Carolina and was a deputy with the Buncombe County Sheriff's Office in the far western part of that state.

The students were talking among themselves when they heard what could have been a shot, Bridges said. One of the students in the class was Ted Besen, another third-year student, who had been a law-enforcement officer also in North Carolina.

"We both kinda' looked at each other and kinda' jokingly said that sounded like a gunshot. And then when we heard the second and third; that's when we knew it was a gunshot," Bridges said.

He and Besen ran into the hallway, where they saw Professor Wesley Shinn who, according to Bridges, told them one of the students was in the building and that he had a gun. Shinn was referring to a forty-three-year-old naturalized U.S. citizen from Nigeria, who had been told he was to be dismissed for failing grades.

Tracy K. Bridges.

"We didn't know what he had done at that point. We didn't know if anybody was hurt or injured," Bridges said. He and Besen ran back into the classroom and herded all the students out of the room, along the hallway to a back entrance, and down a metal staircase.

"At that point we didn't know where [the gunman] was or anything, so my thinking was: get them outside. At least we have some escape routes if we get them outside."

Many of the students who escaped from the classroom went to a grocery store right next to the school, but Bridges had other things on his mind.

"My immediate thought was I needed to get to my vehicle, because I knew that I had a weapon in my vehicle."

It was fortunate that he had parked in a faculty spot, because the vehicle was much closer than it would have been had he parked in the student area. He ran to his Tahoe, unlocked it, and got his gun from its hiding place under the seat. The gun was a Ruger Speed-Six revolver with a 2¾-inch barrel in .357 Magnum caliber that he had received as a gift some years before.

Leaving his vehicle door open in his hurry, Bridges ran towards one of the front entrances, where he could see some students milling around where the gunman had come out of the building. The gunman was about twenty yards away when Bridges first saw him, and he was holding a small pistol, later identified as a Davis .380, a cheap semi-automatic. He advanced on the student, yelling at him to put the gun down and get down on the ground.

"They say you get tunnel vision, but I think I got tunnel sound [auditory exclusion], because I don't think I heard anything except for me screaming and yelling."

He did glance to his left at one point during his advance, where he saw Mikael Gross, a first-year student who also was certified as a peace officer in North Carolina. Bridges saw that Gross had a Beretta semi-automatic in his hand.

In training Tracy had been taught that at some point you have to make up your mind that you're ready to pull the trigger. "I had already made that decision; it was a question of when — how I could get the shot off and be safe about it."

As he approached the gunman, he saw that Besen and another student, Todd Ross, were in the way of a clear shot. Besen was in front of the student with the gun, while Ross was behind him. Bridges said he could hit the gunman without hitting Besen, but he was afraid the hot loads from his .357 Magnum would go clean through the gunman and hit Ross.

Bridges did not shoot, but as he got close, the gunman put his gun down on the ground and moved away from it. The moment for shooting passed.

"It seemed like once [the gunman] turned around and recognized that other people were armed — myself and Mikael....I'm not sure if he'd seen Mikael's gun, I'm not sure if he'd seen mine. There's no way to tell. I think once he noticed that we were armed, he laid his weapon down."

But the gunman wasn't finished. Besen was in front of the gunman, and he hit Besen on the jaw with his fist. Ross grabbed him from behind, and then the others joined in. They wrestled him to the ground, where Bridges got his arm in a lock. He asked Gross if he had any handcuffs. Gross said he did and ran back to his car to get them. When Gross returned, they handcuffed the gunman and held him until the first police officer arrived.

The police officer asked if anybody had been inside the building, so Bridges went in to check on who had been hurt in the shooting. Several students urged him to check on Dean L. Anthony Sutin. There was a lot of blood in the front lobby, but Bridges went straight up the stairs to Sutin's office.

"When I went into his office, he was lying there on the floor. I checked for vitals, and there were none."

It appeared to Bridges that Sutin had been shot several times in the body. Bridges left Sutin's office and entered the office of Professor Thomas Blackwell. He found Blackwell still sitting in his chair facing his computer with his head down.

"It looked like he had been shot at pretty close range in the back of the neck."

Again he checked for signs of life but found none.

Bridges went back downstairs to find Angela Dales, a thirty-three-year-old student, had been shot in the neck. The blood he saw when he first entered the building after capturing the gunman was hers.

Dales was shot beside some couches in a lounge area, but she apparently jumped up and ran towards the door. Although she was somewhat responsive when Bridges got to her, she had lost a lot of blood and died shortly afterwards.

In addition to Dales and the two faculty members, three other students were wounded but recovered.

Dean Sutin was a personal friend of Bridges. He had been a senior official in the U.S. Justice Department under Attorney General Janet Reno during the Clinton administration. He and Bridges were at opposite ends of the political spectrum, but they had an agreement: Bridges would read one of Sutin's left-wing books if the dean would read one of his right-wing books. They traded books frequently, Bridges said.

"He was very open to listening to what I had to say."

Rather than face the death penalty, the student killer accepted a plea bargain of multiple life sentences, which he is now serving.

Afterwards it seemed to Bridges that the pro- and anti-gun people were using the incident to further their own agendas. The anti-gun people were deploring the use of a gun to murder three people and wound another three. The pro-gun faction said that, in this case, having guns on campus saved lives.

In his book, *The Bias Against Guns*, Professor John Lott of the Crime Prevention Research Center uses this incident to show the media's unwillingness to portray the use of guns by citizens in a positive light. He wrote that he ran a Nexis-Lexis computer search and found 208 stories about the law-school shooting in the week following the incident.

However, only four reports mentioned that Gross and Bridges were armed with handguns when they confronted the active killer. Most of the stories stated that the shooter was tackled by the students, but failed to mention that any had their own handguns.

The day after the shooting, Katie Couric, then co-host of NBC's *Today Show*, interviewed Bridges. He got the impression that she didn't want to talk about the fact that he and Gross were armed.

"As soon as I mentioned the weapon, she very quickly said, but we need to mention that you are a law-enforcement officer," he said. This is borne out by the transcript of the show.

Bridges thinks that if students with concealed-handgun permits had been allowed to carry on campus at Virginia Tech, the incident might have ended differently. "I think it would have. That's my personal feeling," he said.

The difference between the two shootings was that at the Appalachian School of Law two armed students were able to stop the killing without firing a shot, after six people had been killed or wounded. At Virginia Tech nearly fifty people were killed or wounded before the gunman killed himself.

Harrold, Texas, School District Arms Teachers

The Virginia Tech shooting prompted the Harrold School District board to revisit Superintendent David Thweatt's plan to arm teachers and school staff.

"That was our wakeup call," Thweatt said.

He had already checked with lawyers and was advised that his plan did not violate any state or federal laws. Next he had to get insurance and work out the liability issues. Texas Association of School Boards refused to cover the school district.

"They basically said, 'We really don't want TASB's name associated with your policy.'"

The association had no problem with the school district hiring a security guard, but arming teachers, whatever next? Thweatt remembered the subsequent conversation this way.

Thweatt: "Let me get this straight. So you're okay with me hiring a high-school-educated security guard that's standing around, but you're not okay with me training people with master's degrees."

The woman from TASB: "It's different."

Thweatt: "You're damn right it's different. Mine is better, and you know it."

The school district got insurance elsewhere and saved money. In October 2007 the board passed the policy as part of its emergency operations plan. The board recognized that first responders, including law enforcement, were likely to take thirty minutes to arrive at Harrold School in response to an emergency. The sheriff's department is about seventeen miles away.

Under the Texas Penal Code the board has the authority to allow specific school employees to carry firearms on school property and at school events. The employees must

have Texas concealed-handgun licenses and "shall be provided additional training in crisis intervention, management of hostage situations, and other training as the Board or designee may determine necessary or appropriate."

The board also stipulated that only frangible ammunition, which reduces the chance of ricochets, could be used in guns on school property. Thweatt organized training for those teachers and staff members who wanted to be armed, including a one-thousand-round range course.

"We flew under the radar for a while."

Although everybody in the town knew what the board was doing, ordinarily no reporters showed up at the school district's board meetings, Thweatt said.

So it wasn't until August 2008 that the media in Wichita Falls got hold of the story, and shortly thereafter it became national news. Thweatt said they were accused by the news media of being paranoid and overreacting.

"That's how they defined it. 'Reading, Writing & Revolvers,' were the headlines," he said. In an effort to control the message, Thweatt agreed only to live interviews that he did from a studio in Fort Worth. After a month to six weeks the furor died down.

"That was a pretty crazy time. So finally after a couple of years when we were almost off the Google search list, then Sandy Hook comes along. That was the first major school shooting since we had passed our policy. So we got a lot of notoriety on that, simply because we had a policy in place that basically could have stopped that."

Chapter 5

SANDY HOOK:
THE RISE OF THE ARMED TEACHER

*"If we do not have willing, trained, and competent
armed people in the school or any other 'gun-free' zone,
we cannot win this or even stop it."*
– John Benner, Tactical Defense Institute

Newtown is a small community of about twenty-seven thousand people located in the timbered hills of southwestern Connecticut. Its population is overwhelmingly white, and a high proportion of its families have school-age children. With a median income of more than $100,000 and a median house price of $350,000, it is largely middle class.

Newtown was relatively unknown to the national media until December 14, 2012. Since that day Newtown and its Sandy Hook Elementary School have become household words. Most of the information about that day comes from the "Report of the State's Attorney for the Judicial District of Danbury on the Shootings at Sandy Hook Elementary School and 36 Yogananda Street, Newtown," and from contemporary news reports.

On that morning a mentally disturbed young man of twenty shot and killed his mother with a Savage Mark II bolt-action .22-caliber rifle. He shot her four times in the head, while she was in bed at the house they shared at 36 Yogananda Street.

He then drove his mother's Honda Civic to the school and parked it near the main entrance. When he got out of the car, he was armed with a Bushmaster XM15-E2S semi-automatic rifle in .223 caliber, a 10mm-caliber

Glock 20, and a 9mm-caliber SIG Sauer P226, both semi-automatic pistols. He also had more than five hundred rounds of ammunition in magazines, most of them for the Bushmaster.

Sandy Hook Shooting

The previous day student attendance at Sandy Hook Elementary was 489 plus 82 employees, including teachers and administrators. The front door of the school was locked as usual at 9:30 a.m. After the door was locked, visitors had to be buzzed in by someone in the main office. According to the time line in the report, a parent was buzzed in at 9:30, after the door was locked, to attend "the gingerbread house event."

Some time after the parent was buzzed in, the gunman reached the front doors and found them locked. He fired eight rounds from his rifle, shattering a plate-glass window to the right of the doors. He walked through the hole and entered the building.

About 9:34 the parent who was buzzed in heard gunfire, about fifteen shots, according to a statement given to police.

Barbara Halstead, the school secretary, was in the main office when she heard the glass shattering and saw the gunman, dressed in black and wearing a hat and sunglasses. He was carrying the Bushmaster rifle. According to the State's Attorney's report, he walked normally, did not say anything, and appeared to be breathing normally. To his left a corridor led eastward between two rows of offices and classrooms. Halstead in the main office saw the gunman shooting down the corridor.

In room nine, a Planning and Placement Team meeting was in progress, attended by the principal, forty-seven-year-old Dawn Hochsprung; the school psychologist Mary Sherlach, 56; several other staff members; and a parent. The people at the meeting heard unusual noises, but did not recognize them as gunshots. Hochsprung and Sherlach went out into the corridor to see what was causing the noise.

According to the report, Hochsprung yelled, "Stay put," to the others in room nine. However, teacher Natalie Hammond followed them into the corridor.

Hochsprung and Sherlach came face-to-face with the gunman. He shot and killed both of them, then wounded Hammond in the leg. She took one more round and lay still, playing dead. Another staff member at the end of the hallway was hit in the foot by a bullet and made it into a nearby classroom. When the gunman had disappeared, Hammond crawled back into room nine and blocked the door with her body.

The killer entered the main office but did not see Halstead or Sally Cox, the school nurse, in the adjoining office where both were hiding. Cox was under her desk and saw the gunman's legs as he came into the office, waited a few seconds, then turned and left.

At 9:35:39 Halstead made the first 9-1-1 call to Newtown Police. She reported that she saw the gunman. She was calling from the nurse's office after the killer had left that room.

At 9:35:56 officers in the police station were told about the shooting and left in their cars heading for the school.

At 9:36:06 Newtown Police Dispatch broadcast news of the shooting: "Sixty-seven [Officer McGowan], Sandy Hook School, caller is indicating she thinks there is someone shooting in building."

Officer Seabrook and Sergeant Kullgren heard the broadcast and headed for the school. Kullgren responded to the dispatcher: "S-six, I am en route."

A woman arrived at the school to see several children running away from the building. She parked her car and walked to the front of the building, where she saw the shattered window. Another woman arrived in the school parking lot and met the first woman at the front doors. Hearing gunfire, the two women ran to the dumpsters on the west side of the school to take cover. One of them called 9-1-1 to report the shooting.

At 9:36:48 the Newtown dispatcher broadcast the information: "Units responding, units responding to Sandy Hook school, the front glass has been broken out of the school. They are unsure why."

At 9:36:49 a staff member called 9-1-1 to report the school is in Lockdown and that he could hear gunshots. In the report the names of all live victims and witnesses are redacted, though the staff member was probably custodian Rick Thorne, who ran around the classrooms alerting staff and students about what was happening, while staying on the phone with the 9-1-1 operator.

At 9:37:27 the Newtown dispatcher broadcast an update: "All units, the individual that I have on the phone is continuing to hear what he believes to be gunfire."

At 9:37:38 the Connecticut State Patrol dispatched its officers to the school.

At 9:38:07 [Thorne] reported to 9-1-1 that he could still hear gunshots.

At 9:38:43 the parent in room nine, the conference room, called 9-1-1 and reported she believed the shooter to be right outside the door. She said five adults were in the room with her, and one had been shot twice. She told the Connecticut State Patrol dispatcher she believed the gunman had already fired one hundred times.

At 9:39:00 Officer McGowan arrived behind the school. Moments later, at 9:39:13, Sergeant Kullgren and Officer Chapman arrived at the school. All the officers reported hearing gunfire upon their arrival.

Meanwhile the killer entered rooms eight and ten. Both rooms were first-grade classrooms, but the report states it is unclear which room he entered first. In room eight he murdered substitute teacher Lauren Rousseau, 30, behavioral therapist Rachel D'Avino, 29, and fifteen children. One of the children was taken to Danbury Hospital and there pronounced dead. Only one child survived in room eight.

In room ten Victoria Soto, 27, was the teacher. She was assisted by Anne Marie Murphy, 52, a behavioral therapist. The gunman shot and killed both women and four children. In addition a wounded child was pronounced dead at the hospital. Nine children ran out of the room and escaped while the gunman was reloading or when his gun had jammed. Two more children were found alive in the classroom's restroom.

In classrooms twelve and six that flanked eight and ten, students and teachers hid in the bathrooms, where they could be locked from the inside. In the rest of the school, staff and students hid where they were, though some were able to escape from the building.

At 9:39:59 a single gunshot was heard on two 9-1-1 calls.

At 9:40:03 a second single gunshot was heard in the background of a 9-1-1 call. Police believe this was the shot with which the gunman committed suicide. He fired the shot from the 10mm-caliber Glock into his head. His body was found in classroom ten with the Glock beside him and the rifle several feet away.

He killed six women who worked at the school and twenty children aged six and seven, shooting most of his victims several times. He fired 154 rounds from the Bushmaster rifle, changing magazines frequently, even before they were empty, and two shots from the Glock. The police did not fire a shot.

Delayed Response

Despite several 9-1-1 calls reporting that the shooting was inside the school building, Newtown officers did not enter the building until 9:44:47. This was more than nine minutes after the first 9-1-1 call to Newtown police and nearly six minutes after the first Newtown officer arrived at the school.

Reasons for the delayed entry were reports that possible suspects were seen outside the school. Officer McGowan, who arrived first, was at the back of the school and apprehended and handcuffed a suspect who was later identified as a parent.

After considerable criticism of the police response to Sandy Hook in the media and elsewhere, the Newtown police chief asked the Connecticut Police Chiefs Association to analyze the police actions. In December 2013 the association released a report on the police response to the shooting.

The report states: "We concluded that the Newtown officers responded to the scene rapidly, positioned themselves appropriately, and followed their department policy. Since the shooter is believed to have committed suicide at 09:40:03 hours, Newtown Officers were on scene a total of 1 minute and 10 seconds before the shooter committed suicide. Unfortunately this was not enough time to assess the situation, confront the exterior threats, and tactically enter the locked building and engage the shooter."

The report also acknowledges that after the mass killing at Columbine, police realized the law-enforcement policy of "contain and wait" for a tactical team just gives the gunman more time to continue killing.

Newtown Police Department embraced the standard law-enforcement policy of quickly engaging the killer in April 2003. The officers responding to Sandy Hook followed the policy, but could not engage the killer before he shot himself.

"While we cannot prove the shooter killed himself due to the police arrival, the history of like incidents suggests this may be the case," the report concluded. Four Connecticut police chiefs signed the report.

The Catalyst

The Sandy Hook massacre shocked the nation and the world. Dozens of world leaders — from Australia to Azerbaijan, Malaysia to Mexico — expressed sympathy for the victims and their families. In a televised address, President Obama talked of coming together to take "meaningful action" to prevent such tragedies in the future "regardless of the politics."

Two things came out of the Sandy Hook shooting. One was to be expected: more calls for gun-control laws at the federal and state levels. Taking advantage of the tragedy to push his anti-gun agenda, Obama urged Congress to reinstate the so-called "assault weapons" ban, require background checks on all firearms purchasers, and ban all magazines holding more than ten rounds. His urgings fell on ears that were aware gun rights are a bipartisan issue supported by a majority of Americans. Congress passed no laws.

However, states like Connecticut, New York, Maryland, and Colorado passed new magazine restrictions, bans on military-style semi-automatic weapons, and additional restrictions on gun sales. But it is doubtful that any of the new laws would have stopped the Sandy Hook killer.

The other thing that happened was the realization in more open-minded states that, as Wayne LaPierre of the National Rifle Association put it, "The only thing that stops a bad guy with a gun is a good guy with a gun."

The massacre at Sandy Hook was a catalyst. Some school boards and school administrators started tossing around the idea of arming their teachers and other school staff. They were realizing that it is better to have armed staff in the schools than to wait for the police response.

The Sandy Hook school shooting was yet another example of the ineffectiveness of law enforcement to stop these murders. This is not an indictment of law-enforcement responders. They are not on the scene, and by the time they are alerted and arrive, the incident is most likely all over.

After the release of the State's Attorney's report on the shooting, John Benner, the retired SWAT team commander and owner of Tactical Defense Institute (TDI) in Ohio, put a statement on his web site that included this paragraph:

"This massacre was done essentially five minutes before the police even entered the building. You and I were not there. I throw no stones because I do not know how they were trained, what they ran into or the thought processes of all involved. It is easy being the quarterback when the game is over. My point is if we do not have willing, trained, and competent armed people in the school or any other 'GUN FREE' zone we cannot win this or even stop it."

For more than a decade, Benner and his instructors, mostly law-enforcement officers or retired officers, have been teaching civilians how to respond to mass killers. Since Sandy Hook they have also been instructing armed teachers and school staff.

"At TDI we believe without question (and have for a long time) in the arming of school staff (willing, trained, and competent). Quite honestly, I considered that a pipe dream until the Sandy Hook Massacre took place. Everything changed, and we had to start asking the hard questions. What is a real answer, because law enforcement is not effective," his web site statement said.

The FASTER Program

Shortly after the Sandy Hook shooting, Ken Hanson, an Ohio lawyer who does work for the Buckeye Firearms Association (BFA), complained to Jim Irvine, president of the association, that there was much talk but no action on what could be done to prevent other school shootings. He suggested training teachers to defend themselves and their students with firearms. Irvine called John Benner, and even before he had finished talking, Benner said he was already working on the idea.

Irvine asked Benner whether, if the Buckeye Firearms Foundation paid for it, he would put on a class at TDI. Benner agreed to put on a three-day class for twenty-four teachers and school administrators.

"It was simply an idea to hook up some of the school people with some of the training people and show this as a viable concept. That's all we were looking to do, but it just took on a life of its own," Irvine said.

More than one thousand people wanted to attend the class. When the foundation said it would pay for the class, people sent in donations, so they were able to schedule more classes. They named the program FASTER, standing for Faculty/ Administrator Safety Training and Emergency Response.

Buckeye people explained the FASTER program at school-board meetings, and they had a booth at a trade-show of the Ohio School Board Association, where the concept of arming teachers and administrators was explained. Irvine has been surprised at the reaction. No one called them crazy. School-board members and educators sounded interested and asked for more information.

"It really shocked us how well it was received," he said.

Irvine, an American Airlines pilot, lobbies school superintendents to arm those teachers and school staff who want to be armed. He starts by asking them about their qualifications for holding the post of superintendent of the particular school district. He encourages them to brag about their degrees and other qualifications, including certifications they have acquired after they left college.

Then he asks them how much time they've spent studying active killers.

"They have this blank look on their face, because it's none. They've never thought about it."

Irvine says he points out that if there is a mass shooting in any of their schools, it will be followed by law suits, and the superintendents will be on the witness stand trying to explain why they never studied the topic that killed the children for whose safety they are responsible.

"Everybody agrees the only way to protect them from violence is that you've got to have a gun there. All the experts know this, and here's the expert in education who hasn't spent a single day on it. They just never look at it that way."

Irvine said security cameras, single-point entries, and Lockdown drills may be helpful, "but none of that will stop the killer walking down the hallway about to slaughter the whole room full of kids — none of it — and everybody knows it."

He explains that he wants to help them understand the issue, and he wants them to learn about the potential problem, because he wants it to be a theoretical exercise.

"I don't want them ever to face it in real life, like the teachers in all these other districts where we've had shootings. Learn about it in an academic exercise, so that in real life they're never put in that spot," he said.

Irvine tells the superintendents that the Buckeye Firearms Foundation pays for the course and also picks up the hotel bills for the students. All they have to pay for is meals and ammunition. In a year Ohio went from one school district to thirty that had armed staff. Now there are even more.

Reaction to his pitch varies.

"It's funny: sometimes the reaction is hostile. It's bad of you, because you have burst their little denial bubble, and they don't like to think about really uncomfortable things," Irvine said.

He said that sometimes they get angry, but often he will get calls back in a week or a month from superintendents who want to know more about the program.

When Buckeye presents the program to a school board, most of them authorize employees with concealed-handgun licenses to carry at their schools, Irvine said.

"I think the ones that haven't, they just haven't done it yet. It's going to happen, because there is no other solution. I really believe every school that has a fire extinguisher in it is going to have a gun in it — every one — because it doesn't matter whether you love or hate fire extinguishers, they are safety devices in all our buildings to save our kids' lives. The gun is no different; it's a safety device, and we're going to put them in all of the schools to save all our kids' lives."

When trying to persuade a school board to endorse the program, three is the critical number, said Irvine. "If you get one person going in to the board, he is the one crazy person. He's easy to ignore. If you get two people going in, well, the crazy guy's got a buddy, so we can still ignore [them]. But if you get three, that's a committee. It's hard to ignore a committee. A committee makes recommendations; you've at least got to consider it."

He admitted that school violence is an extremely rare event.

"They've got to do something about it. It's negligence to say: 'We don't care; we're not going to do anything; we don't think it will happen here.' It's a negligent attitude, and it's going to cost them."

Harrold School District

In Texas Harrold school district's decision to arm its teachers suddenly didn't seem to be such an outrageous idea, in light of the Newtown shooting.

"After Sandy Hook, we were suddenly wise and prophetic," said Superintendent David Thweatt.

He speculated that most elementary schools in the country do not have school-resource officers — armed security guards or certified peace officers — on site. Thweatt said he was on a panel with the police chiefs of Austin and Dallas school districts, and they said they had school-resource officers at the junior highs and high schools, but not the elementary schools.

"That's a little known secret," he added.

The data show that active killers avoid locations where there are armed security guards or police officers, Thweatt said.

"But the mass shooters are only going where there are no guns. What they're wanting is the big body count."

Sandy Hook Elementary had physical security, but no one was armed.

"They had a buzzer; they had a locked door. You had to ring in, but he just shot it open. So what happens after Sandy Hook? Everybody puts in the same system Sandy Hook had. I haven't figured out to this day what's wrong with people. You know they spent thousands of dollars for a buzzer system, inconveniencing everybody."

As Harrold ISD is a pioneer in arming teachers, Thweatt has talked to congressmen and senators in about forty states who are interested in arming teachers. He has also answered questions from law enforcement and other school districts.

One law-enforcement agency asked Thweatt what was the minimum response time for first responders before they should consider a plan like his?

He replied: "I don't know. Within the first minute at Sandy Hook, everybody in the office was dead and he [the killer] was going down the hall. It just depends on how many casualties you want. No one's going to get there before three or four minutes — nobody. If you're okay with the casualties that you're talking about in three minutes, then don't have one. If you're not okay with it, arm the teachers."

School districts seem overly concerned about liability.

"I had one board member put it to me this way: the chances of this happening in our schools probably are not very good. If we pass this policy and something bad happens, it's our fault. If we don't pass the policy and somebody comes in, we can just wring our hands and say: 'Oh my, what a tragedy.'"

Thweatt said courts are going to have to get to the point where they consider that arming teachers leads to creation of a safe environment, and not arming teachers to an unsafe environment and being negligent. The problem is that we have been encouraged to be victims rather than to defend ourselves.

"We've moved towards an idea where the government does everything. It's a police-state mentality, that's all it is. It's very dangerous."

He said we are heading down a slippery slope. Most of his teachers share his philosophy or they leave.

If there is an active-killer incident at the school where the gunman is shot and killed, the media ask Thweatt: "What about those children who saw someone gunned down? You're going to traumatize them for life?"

He replies: "They're going to be less traumatized than being gunned down themselves."

Harrold ISD has twenty-four employees, including Thweatt. The way schools are designed it may take time before gunfire is heard or even recognized for what it is. He said you have to have armed people scattered strategically, so they can hear gunshots and recognize them. "You want ears everywhere."

Initially Harrold started out with all armed school staff carrying the same makes and models of pistols, but they found that the women had difficulty with large calibers, therefore, the women now use 9mms or .380s. Thweatt said their training involved shooting about a thousand rounds.

The school board approved an extra $50 a month for teachers and staff members who are authorized to carry in Harrold's schools. Thweatt has declined the extra money for himself.

"I'm just glad and happy you are giving me a weapon. I don't need to be rewarded monetarily," he told the school board.

While most of Harrold ISD employees approve of the gun-carrying policy, there are some people who don't have the right mindset to be armed. He said that, when looking for staff to be armed, "I want personalities who will run to the sound of gunfire."

There are twenty education regions in Texas, and Harrold is in Region 9, which has about forty schools. The superintendents get together from time-to-time and know one another. Some of his peer superintendents in Region 9 would make jokes about passing Harrold and not getting shot. After a while this got old, and Thweatt told them, "the problem I have with that is you guys are having a big laugh, but I have a problem. I really don't think dead kids are funny."

The ribbing stopped.

Argyle School District

The town of Argyle is in rural north Texas between Denton and Fort Worth in one of the fastest growing areas of Texas. With about two thousand students, the Argyle Independent School District operates four schools on three campuses. People approaching any of these campuses will be faced with an unusual sign.

According to school district superintendent Dr. Telena Wright, the issue of arming school employees came up as a result of Sandy Hook. Because of the age of the children killed, that shooting made schools across the U.S. review their security arrangements.

"We had a national security company that came and did an evaluation of our campuses," Wright said.

Argyle started the process with a community forum consisting of school-board members, school staff, parents, and anyone else in the community who was interested. They talked about Sandy Hook and that they would never know whether one of the staff members having a gun might have changed the outcome.

"But one thing we knew for sure was that, without a weapon, she had no chance, and those students had no chance, and those staff members had no chance. That's how it started: we didn't have an answer to the first couple of minutes, if you do have an armed intruder," Wright said.

Argyle had good security at the high school and middle school, which were both on the same campus, she said. They had a new building with check-in procedures, though they did not have a police officer. The school district also has an intermediate school and an elementary school.

In the spring of 2013, they were looking at three different options. One option was adding a sworn police officer as a school-resource officer. They discussed this with the Denton County sheriff and with the chief of the Argyle Police Department. They also talked about having their own police department. One school-board member suggested arming school staff.

"We need to see if we are doing everything we can to protect these children. That is kinda' how it started," Wright said. "More schools in Texas are getting their own ISD police departments."

Ralph Price, Argyle ISD police chief, and his patrol car.

They decided to hire a police chief and have him run a program to arm teachers and other school staff. Ralph Price was hired as the police chief in the fall of 2013. He retired after twenty-three years as an officer with Addison Police Department in North Dallas. His last assignment in Addison was as a school-resource officer at a private school.

The department consists of the chief and a couple of part-time officers who work after hours covering sporting events such as basketball and football games. During the day it is a one-man police department, Price said. "I can't be everywhere."

The chief has a fully equipped patrol car with a 12-gauge shotgun and an AR-15 semi-automatic rifle he prefers to call a patrol rifle. The car also has a radio tuned to the Denton County Sheriff's and Argyle Police Department's frequencies.

The staff members who carry concealed handguns have to go through a process to be qualified. They have to have a Texas concealed-handgun license. It is a voluntary position, but the superintendent, Wright, has the final say.

Wright said she was supportive of the program from the start.

"The community has been extremely supportive."

She said schools have got used to school-resource officers and having their own police departments, but they
have yet to get used to teachers and other staff members
carrying guns.

The volunteers have to go through a psychological screen-
ing process that lasts about four hours. They go through a
thorough training course in firearms and as first responders.

Greg Coker is a former U.S. Army special-operations
helicopter pilot and firearms instructor. He designed a three-
day school-staff-volunteer training course. During the thirty-hour
class, each student fires about nine hundred rounds.

The police department issues the handguns and holsters, and all are the same make and model of 9mm
semi-automatic pistol. This makes instruction easier,
because everyone is on the same page, and all the volunteers are familiar with the guns. They could lend each other
magazines in an emergency.

"I've got a standard that they have to achieve and pass,
and it's all timed," Coker said.

He covers safety, gun retention, first aid, deescalation,
and survival mindset. During the course, the students go to
one of the schools and run through various scenarios using
Simunitions. This is a system of using converted handguns
loaded with marking cartridges. Students wear protective
helmets and other gear, but the hits leave a mark. They also
sting if they hit an unprotected area.

Coker puts the students through several scenarios,
including one in a classroom, one in which an armed
person comes in the front door, and another with two
armed bad guys in the school.

As of June 2015 Coker had taught only Argyle ISD. He
has talked to other school districts and given them information, but Argyle is the only one he has taught.

The school staff members get two-day refresher courses twice a year, and Coker encourages them to shoot at least fifty rounds a month in practice.

Once the volunteer school employees are qualified, they carry their guns concealed on them all the time.

Price would not say whether they carry with a round in the chamber, but there is a policy so they all carry the same way. He said that all staff members — male and female — carry the same way. He acknowledged that the holsters have a security feature built into them.

"That gun does not come off during the school day."

Only the administrators, Price, and the teachers who carry guns know who is armed. The teachers who do not carry don't know who does.

The teachers know their guns must never come out unless there is what Price calls "an extraordinary event," he said. "Extraordinary event" appears to be a politically correct synonym for an active-killer incident.

"The only time that these teachers would ever take this gun out of that holster is if there is an active shooter on their campus. That is the only reason; there is no other reason: not to break up a fight, not if mom and dad came across to threaten them, not if somebody hurts them — that's not what this weapon is for. And they've all been trained on that, and they all know the stipulations that go with carrying a gun."

Price said he is comfortable trusting the armed teachers not to do anything irresponsible.

"There is no way that I believe, and this is just Chief Price's opinion here, that you could ever stop someone that's intending to do some harm in any given school in the U.S. If their intent is to come here and do harm, well they're going to do some harm before either I can get to them or the teachers can get to them."

The aim of the program is to minimize the amount of harm they can do before they are stopped, he added.

And those warning signs outside the campuses? Superintendent Wright said, "The signs are supposed to be a powerful deterrent."

Price declined to say how many staff members were armed. He would like the public to believe that every teacher is armed.

"The whole idea behind what we're doing is hoping that they will go somewhere else — not come to our schools."

As of June 2015 the Texas Association of School Boards reported 108 school districts in Texas (that they know about) had passed policies allowing school employees to carry concealed handguns on school property.

In an email the association stated: "There are some districts that have a local policy permitting identified staff (not marshals) to carry concealed handguns; and a number of those districts actively use the policy. Another (unknowable) number have adopted it as a deterrent. A few have told us that they adopted the policy only for very select staff with particular credentials (retired military, peace officers, etc., who are now working at a school as a second career)."

This sounds promising until you realize that there are 1,247 school districts in the state, which means that fewer than 10 percent are armed. However, compared to the Texas School Marshal program, 108 districts, potentially with armed teachers, is a great start.

Texas School Marshal Program

The School Marshal Program is another outcome of the Sandy Hook shooting. In 2013 the Texas Legislature passed a law creating the program, with the aim of improving school safety. It went into effect September 1, 2013, and the first course was held in the summer of 2014, according to the Texas Commission on Law Enforcement, which oversees the program. As of June 2015 eleven school districts were using the program, and thirteen individuals had taken the course and become qualified.

Students in the School Marshal Program must pass a psychological examination and have a Texas concealed-handgun license. They are school employees and not law-enforcement officers. The two-week, eighty-hour course includes more shooting, training scenarios, and use-of-force options.

According to the Texas Code of Criminal Procedure, school marshals "may make arrests and exercise all authority given peace officers." They are subject to regulations adopted by school boards and can act only "as necessary to prevent or abate the commission of an offence that threatens serious bodily injury or death to students, faculty, or visitors on school premises."

The law limits the number of school marshals to not more than one for every four-hundred students. A school marshal may carry a concealed handgun on school property, but the law stipulates that "if the primary duty of the school marshal involves regular, direct contact with students, the marshal may not carry a concealed handgun, but may possess a handgun on the physical premises of a school, in a locked and secured safe within the marshal's immediate reach when conducting the marshal's primary duty."

Why so few participants? Nikki Johnson, a School Marshal specialist with the commission, replied in an email that it was partly because the program is relatively new. She added, "the regulation on School Marshals is greater than that of merely allowing a CHL-holder to carry a firearm while at the district. A School Marshal has authority to act as a peace officer while performing his or her duties, while merely having a CHL does not. Some districts choose to have less regulation and no expanded authority."

Both Harrold's Thweatt and Argyle's Chief Price were critical of the School Marshal Program.

Thweatt took issue with the four-hundred-kids number and with the requirement that teachers have to lock up the gun. Four-hundred kids seems like an arbitrary number that doesn't take into account differences in schools or the layout of the buildings, he said.

"The problem I have with that particular policy is it's one for every four hundred, and then if you're in the presence of children, that gun has to be locked up. You can have that policy if you want, but that's just plain stupid, and it's going to be real obvious that you've got some kind of locked box or pouch hanging off you — again, idiocy."

At Argyle Chief Price said having the guns in locked containers in the classrooms would delay getting access to them, which could prove critical.

"Those teachers are in the classroom some of the day. Now, what happens when they are in the lunch-room? What happens when they are in the bathroom, auditorium? Think of all the times they are not in the classroom. When there's not a class, they're not in the classroom.

"So we don't know when that extraordinary event is going to happen, so what good is a gun at the teacher's desk? Even if it's at the teacher's desk, and the teacher is up at the bulletin board teaching, what good is that gun going to do her if somebody bursts into her classroom? You think that person is going to let her get to her desk, unlock the lock box, and pull the gun out?"

Price looked at the School Marshall Program and found it wanting. It was the requirement to keep the guns locked up that steered him away from the program.

"I would love for all my teachers to be school marshals and have that training and be certified, but until they revamp that and take that clause out of there, it's not going to happen here."

CHAPTER 6

TRAINING THE TEACHERS: THE OHIO EXPERIENCE

*"I'm tired of being a sitting duck. The best I can do
is say, 'hide.' I want to fight back."*
— L.P., an Ohio kindergarten teacher

For more than a decade, John Benner has been teaching law-enforcement officers that the first officer on the scene of an active-killer incident must go in and tackle the killer. He or she can't afford to wait for backup, because time is the big enemy.

Benner owns and runs Tactical Defense Institute (TDI), a shooting school set on 186 acres in the wooded hills of southern Ohio, about an hour's drive east of Cincinnati. Benner is an avuncular man in his sixties, who usually has a cigar clamped between his teeth. He is a Vietnam veteran and for twenty years commanded the Hamilton County, Ohio, multi-jurisdictional SWAT team.

As a result of Sandy Hook, many school boards and school administrators are learning that it is better to have armed staff in the schools than to wait for the police response. This is particularly true in rural areas, where school boards cannot afford to hire police officers or professional security guards and police response times may be twenty minutes or more. But it is also true in urban areas, where the police response is five minutes or less. Nothing beats having armed people at the scene before the shooting starts.

According to Benner, by March 2014 more than thirty Ohio school districts had armed teachers and school staff to protect their students. Much of this was due to collaboration between TDI and the Buckeye Firearms Foundation (BFF) that pays the tuition and lodging for school staff while they attend the three-day course.

I drove up to TDI at the end of March 2014 to monitor the FASTER — Faculty/Administrator Safety Training and Emergency Response — Saves Lives course. When I left San Antonio, Texas, the temperature was about seventy degrees. The morning after I arrived at Benner's facility, I believe my decade-old Dodge pickup was close to a nervous breakdown. It had never experienced snow before, and that morning it was covered in the white stuff.

First Day

The course started in the classroom, which was good, as it was still snowing intermittently. There were twenty-four teachers in the class — four of them women.

The students were all school staff, most from rural school districts — teachers, counselors, and administrators. For clarity and simplicity I have referred to the students in the course as "teachers" or in the scenarios as "responders." There were eight instructors, mostly active or retired law enforcement, but also including Jim Irvine of BFF and Deborah Fletcher, an economics professor at an Ohio university.

Fletcher said, "I'm helping out here for the weekend, which I do with some of the teachers' classes here at TDI. I think there are a couple of different reasons. It's nice to have a female instructor here, because sometimes women will have questions they don't want to ask a male instructor, and also because I teach for a living. I can bring a perspective from being in the classroom all day, thinking about the physical characteristics of the classroom, thinking about what it's like to have a roomful of kids there in front of you, and some tactical ideas from that experience."

Benner started the course by recounting the history of mass killings in the U.S. and describing the incidents that we have covered in the first few chapters of this book: the Texas Tower, Columbine, Virginia Tech, and Sandy Hook.

I explained in the Introduction that, as a way of denying them recognition, Benner refuses to use the killers' names. He also uses the term "active killers," rather than "active shooters." Benner says if you have your concealed-carry permit, you are an active shooter, but you are not an active killer.

"An active killer is going to be a person or persons who intentionally kill or attempt to kill multiple innocent persons, generally at a location thought to be safe for them — in other words, a gun-free zone," he said.

On average active killers shoot nearly five people a minute, which is why Benner has been teaching law-enforcement officers to enter as soon as they arrive at the scene, be it a school or a mall. Benner was quoting research done by Ron Borsch, the retired Ohio police officer mentioned in Chapter 3. He used to teach a Tactical First Responder course at the SEALE Regional Police Training Academy in Bedford, Ohio. As a result of his research, he has amassed a database of almost two hundred mass-shooting incidents dating back to 1975.

Borsch says that half of all active-killer events — he calls them Rapid Mass Murders — are stopped or aborted by someone confronting the killer. Half of the incidents that were aborted were stopped by the intervention of an unarmed civilian or civilians. An armed civilian terminated a quarter of those incidents, and a law-enforcement officer, usually acting alone, terminated the other quarter.

The other half of these incidents, those not stopped by others, are terminated by the killer himself — about 35 percent commit suicide — and the rest because the killer flees, surrenders, or runs out of ammunition.

Borsch says about 98 percent of the killers act alone. At Columbine and Jonesboro, Arkansas, there were multiple killers, but there may be other sites. About 80 percent will have a rifle or shotgun; 75 percent will have several firearms. They will kill or wound about 4.7 people a minute, and in two incidents they have killed or wounded more than one per second, he adds.

One problem with statistics on active-killer incidents is that different researchers have different definitions of such incidents. Borsch says his definition for Rapid Mass Murders is four or more people murdered within a twenty-minute time span in a public place. He also includes attempts, but does not include criminal actions by the military, police, street-gangs, or terrorists.

Most active killers will shoot until someone stops them or confronts them. They will have absolute control of life and death over whom they choose. They very rarely take hostages, and they do not negotiate. They try to avoid the police, and surrender or escape is unlikely.

Approximately 50 percent of shots fired by active killers are hits. That is not normal. It is a much higher ratio than the average police officer involved in a shooting incident, Benner said. In one school shooting, the killer shot eight people with eight rounds. How is this possible?

Active killers are likely to be shooting at very short range, almost contact distance in many cases, and at people who are no threat to them. People cowering under a desk or in a corner are not difficult to hit.

However, Benner added, an active killer will be no contest for a competent civilian or law-enforcement officer.

He showed the teachers a video, taken from a security camera, of the Columbine killers just wandering casually around, not using cover or tactics. They obviously felt safe.

Benner and Borsch have been teaching the single-officer response since before Virginia Tech.

"If you get there and hear shooting going on, it's your time to go and not sit there and wait for three or four other officers to get there to form a group and go in," Benner said.

W.H., a superintendent whose school board supports armed teachers:

"With all the different situations that have happened throughout the country, in different places, where people have gone into schools with guns and taken the lives of young people, I think one of the most important functions of the educational process is not only to educate, but to provide a safe and a secure environment for our staff and students. So based on some of the things that we've seen around the country, we choose to take an offensive position rather than a defensive position and approach it from that perspective. We were very selective in the process. We tried to pick people who had some gun training, who were very emotionally stable, and people we thought could make appropriate decisions in time of difficulty."

One factor that is usually unknown is the time lag between when the shooting starts and when someone actually calls 9-1-1. If people are not familiar with firearms, they may not realize the noise they are hearing is gunfire. At Virginia Tech some people thought the gunfire was construction workers using nail guns. Even if the police response is three minutes, it means the killer has time to shoot a dozen people. So it is better to have armed people among the school staff.

"I think arming you guys is the solution to the problem," Benner said.

The teachers must prepare themselves mentally for what they will encounter, Benner said. The first thought in their minds must be: this is a shooting situation. If it is unnecessary, that is fine, but they must make up their minds to do what they need to do — no half measures. When engaging the active killer, they must act with extreme violence.

They also have to realize they may have to shoot somebody who is perhaps thirteen or fourteen years old. Other people — adults and children — are depending on an armed teacher to save their lives.

"At that moment in time, you are the single most important person in the world," Benner said.

He told them to be prepared to encounter victims who may be begging for help. They must bypass them as they hunt the shooter down. At Columbine, when the police got inside, victims clung on to them and would not let go. They must resist clinging victims and concentrate on the mission.

"You are a hunter. You are going to hunt them down and kill them if necessary," he said. "Your job is not to stop and help anybody."

The people they are trying to protect are their co-workers, friends, and children they are responsible for.

"You have a dog in the hunt; police officers don't," Benner said.

Teachers may be afraid there is more than one killer or may be afraid of being ambushed. So far loners have perpetrated almost all the rapid mass murders at schools. At Columbine there were two killers and also at Jonesboro, Arkansas. But in both cases the gunmen stayed together. So far, active killers have not set up ambushes for responders. They are too concerned with racking up a large body count. The teachers may also have a fear of being out-gunned.

"If you are competent with your firearm and confident, you will win," Benner said.

The "Stopwatch of Death©" is a phrase coined by Ron Borsch in his training of first responders. It emphasizes the importance of time in responding to active killers. Borsch has identified two worst-case scenarios during which more than one murder attempt per second occurred for fifteen seconds: in 1996 in Tasmania, Australia, twelve were killed and ten wounded; and in 2011 in Tucson, Arizona, where six were killed and thirteen wounded.

At Virginia Tech the killer shot and killed or wounded forty-seven people in an estimated eleven minutes. According to the Stopwatch of Death, he killed or wounded 4.3 people a minute.

At Sandy Hook, it took three minutes to get three officers to the school, but it took six more minutes before they went in. From the time the active killer started shooting, it probably took a minute and a half before someone called 9-1-1. It probably took thirty seconds before the operator took the information and passed it on to patrol units. Six minutes after police arrived at the school, they went inside the building. According to the State's Attorney's report, the killer was shooting for about six minutes. In that time, he killed twenty-six people and wounded two, for a total of twenty-eight. Using the Stopwatch of Death calculation, the gunman killed or wounded 4.7 people a minute.

When engaging a gunman, stay calm and practice tactical breathing: breathe in through the nose, pause for three seconds, breathe out through the mouth, pause for three seconds, breathe in, etc. Use good tactics: head for the shooter as fast as you can go without missing what you need to see. Be aggressive: use speed, surprise, and violence in action. Shoot the killer down. When the fight is over, holster your gun and wait for police.

C.R., a Spanish teacher who hoped to persuade his school board to adopt the program:

"I am here because, in the wake of the Sandy Hook shooting, it became obvious gun-free zones don't work, and after doing a little bit of research, finding out that there were some districts considering arming teachers, I sought out this course, and this seems to be just the most common-sense solution out there to reduce the number of casualties, because these types of shootings, they're pretty much unavoidable. If people want to kill multiple people, they're going to, and this seems to be the best course of action in terms of reducing casualties and trying to make our children safer."

Benner gave teachers some advice on what to do when the police arrive after an active-killer incident. Stay calm and follow officers' directions. Keep your hands visible, and most important, do not have a gun in your hands when confronting law enforcement.

He discussed when the use of deadly force is justified. Four factors have to be present. First, the assailant's intent must be to cause you great bodily harm or death.

"Everybody can understand the death part of it; that's easy. What's great bodily harm? Can you define great bodily harm? And think about this: if we wait until great bodily harm occurs, we're too late," Benner said.

He mentioned the ultimate fighter competitions seen on television and suggested if one good punch or kick can knock down another fighter, imagine what it can do to an untrained citizen. The fighters on television have a relatively soft surface on which to fall, while we may fall on concrete. You hit your head on a concrete surface, and it may kill you.

"Think about that person's intent, and you have to be able to articulate that intent," he said. "You are supposed to be judged on what you honestly believe."

Sometimes the justice system gets it right, and sometimes it doesn't, he added.

Second, the attacker has to have the ability to cause you great bodily harm or death.

Third, he has to have a reasonable opportunity to cause you great bodily harm. When threatened by somebody armed with a knife, the person has to be close enough to cut or stab you. If he were too far away, he would not have the opportunity. If he moved towards you, then he would gain the opportunity when he got close enough.

Fourth, you have to be in jeopardy. "If I had a firearm, would that be a game changer? Absolutely. Then you would be in jeopardy," he said.

Benner talked about self-defense and the defense of others. "You're going to be defending others, which is perfectly legal to do."

Self-defense is the logical course of action under the circumstances. However, what people think is logical is likely to differ.

Benner urged the teachers to find out all they can about the local prosecutor; "his logic may have a profound impact on your life." What seems a reasonable course of action under the circumstances must be necessary to prevent great bodily harm or death to you or another person.

"We have a duty to retreat in most places. If you are an armed school-staff member, I don't think you have any duty to retreat. I think you have a duty to respond. That's what you're there for; that's what you're trained for; that's your job," he said.

Chris Wallace, a retired police chief from the Cincinnati area, urged school districts to have a firearms policy in writing. This should include what policies and procedures are in place that specifically say who can be armed, what type of training they need, what type of weapons they carry, how those weapons are to be carried, the type of ammunition to be used, the number of trainings per year with the firearm, and specifics on how to liaise with local law enforcement.

Teachers practice drawing and firing on the range.

Teachers shooting while moving forwards.

Most police departments will have their use-of-force policies available on the Internet, and these can be used as guides and can be adapted to the school district. Before he was police chief, Wallace was responsible for writing and updating his department's policies.

"Nobody sits down and writes a policy from scratch if they can help it," he said.

An advantage of using law-enforcement policies is that they have been tested in court. He said that a school district should have someone check on police-model policies, in case anything has changed as a result of new case law.

As a police chief, Wallace was conscious that a police department "lives and dies" on its written policies and procedures concerning the use of firearms.

He recommended checking the staff annually for indictments and protection orders. It is a good idea to liaise with local law enforcement so officers can get to know the armed school staff. The staff members will also have to have some range time, and the police range would be ideal.

Benner described some of the changes that occur in the body when faced with a life-threatening situation. Tunnel vision is when you become fixated on the threat to the exclusion of all else. This is dangerous, because you effectively lose all peripheral vision and may not see another threat approaching from the side or the rear.

Increased heart rate happens during any life-threatening situation. Fine motor skills will deteriorate, making your fingers as dexterous as your toes. Auditory exclusion, sometimes called "tunnel hearing," means you will not hear gunshots or even orders shouted at you.

Once you are involved in a shooting incident, you have the right to remain silent, Benner said.

"Anything you say can and will be used against you in a court of law — use your right. The police are going to come: they are going to question you. Your statement is that you want to speak to your attorney before you give a detailed statement. Do not give a statement right after being involved in a shooting, whether it is in a school or any place else."

Most police departments don't question an officer involved in a shooting for at least forty-eight hours after the incident.

Benner elaborated: "That should be a clue. Two sleep cycles and you will remember better what happened. You will be able to see small details and pick things up and understand better what occurred. So it's very important for you to remember that. You have the right to remain silent — use your right. Just tell them: 'Officer, I will cooperate with your investigation 100 percent. I'm going to do that through my attorney.'' Remember, anything you say before that is admissible. Once you invoke your rights, law enforcement cannot question you any further."

It is a natural human reaction to want to justify your actions to the officer. If you make a statement at the time and you later remember more details and you try to add them, you will likely be accused of lying.

"Keep your mouth shut. Get a good criminal attorney."

Between snow flurries, the teachers went outside and were lined up facing a steep wooded bank where they "roped" their guns. This consisted of unloading their semi-automatics; then, with the slide locked back, pushing about a foot-long piece of bright-yellow, flexible, plastic tubing down the barrel and out through the magazine well, so both ends were visible. The slide can then be dropped and manipulated, but anyone can see the gun is unloaded.

The teachers trooped back into the classroom and lined the walls of the room in the shape of a horseshoe. John Benner then asked if anyone's gun was not roped. I confessed. As an observer I didn't think the roping applied to me, but when guns were roped, everybody's gun was roped, including the instructors'. I was ushered outside, and I roped my gun under the probing eyes of two instructors.

As part of the mental preparation to get the teachers comfortable with pointing guns at other human beings, Benner had them do just that. "Pick someone, and shoot them."

Some of the teachers were hesitant. They looked around to see what everybody else was doing, then followed Benner's instruction.

Anyone constantly drilled in the basic safety rules of "never point your gun at anything you are not willing to destroy" or "treat all guns as though they are loaded," would be appalled. However, Benner justified it this way: "The reason we do that is because people are trained not to point a gun at anybody; and the bottom line is, they may fail in a force-on-force situation if they have never done that. So consequently, we don't want the first time they have to point a gun at anybody to be when they've got to use it, and they very well could have a failure.

"With a roped gun, it's not possible for the gun to be loaded, but it's still the same thing. You're still pointing that gun at somebody. If you've done something before, you're more likely to do it again. But if you've never done something, and now suddenly you've got to do it, it may not work."

John Motil, a gunsmith and one of the instructors, taught the teachers a proper two-handed grip, pointing the thumbs at the target. He taught a 60/40 percent grip with support hand *versus* gun-holding hand. He was not concerned with foot placement, but did have the teachers check for eye dominance.

Motil recommended lime green or blaze orange for a front sight. He didn't like the white three-dot sights because the front sight could get confused with one of the rear sight dots. He also dealt with trigger control.

Benner demonstrated a ready position, with the gun held in both hands just in front of the chest and with the gun barrel horizontal. He could shoot from there, and as he pushed the gun forward to eye level, he got the sights on the target.

He showed us a draw where the gun is pulled upwards to chest level, then rocked forward while the support hand is held high on the chest. This ensures that if you are in a car you are not drawing into the steering wheel.

Every time you bring the gun out, do it correctly, because everything you do is practice, he emphasized.

Chris Wallace said if you feel resistance when reholstering, stop. Reholster with the thumb on the back of the slide and the finger away from the trigger.

It had been snowing most of the morning, but about lunch time the snow stopped and a weak sun appeared, although the temperature was in the low- to mid-thirties.

B.D., a school monitor who was invited to the course by a teacher from her school:

"When I initially got my conceal-and-carry, it was because I wanted to exercise my right, but it has become more than that, and it's unfortunate that it's become more than that. But I have learned — and even today with what we have done in the morning session — just how evil the world is and how it could happen. Our school district is small, and people don't think it could ever happen to you — that it could happen to

us. Unfortunately I don't think there's rhyme or reason as to the time or where it happens. So you start looking at statistics and what could happen. I believe in exercising my right, and I feel empowered. I feel like it's good to protect yourself, and it's good to make yourself knowledgeable — to educate yourself and not be behind blinders."

After lunch the teachers started on the main range. The first target had eight three-inch dots that they shot from a range of ten feet. They started by shooting one shot at a time, followed by two shots, and then three shots. This was followed by shooting at two dots alternately.

Wallace demonstrated three methods of drawing from under a cover garment. He showed clearing the coat with the thumb, sweeping the coat aside, and lifting the shirt.

The teachers moved on to figure targets that contained vital areas outlined in the shape of a Coke bottle. They had circles in the high chest and the head. Teachers used the garment-clearing methods Wallace had showed them. They were told to draw and fire one shot using one hand from a range of five feet. For most of them, this involved clearing a bulky coat, then pulling up a sweater, drawing the gun, and holding it at chest height close to the body.

At ten feet they drew and fired two rounds. They stepped back two paces then drew and fired two rounds. They repeated this four times with two rounds, but the fifth time they fired five rounds. They repeated the whole stage, but initially shot at a small circle above the target's right shoulder, then head shots, and finally, at about thirty-five feet, shooting three at the body and two at the head.

Benner talked to them about concealed carry and types of holsters. Motil dealt with cleaning the gun.

Second Day

The next morning the weather started in the teens but warmed up during the day to about twenty-eight degrees.

Benner and Motil started a fire for the teachers to warm their hands. Early in the morning, I was recording Benner when he noticed that the hand holding my digital recorder was shaking. He drove back up to the house to get me a warmer coat and a thicker pair of gloves.

Benner talked about trigger control, taking the slack out of the trigger, and trigger reset. There is usually about an eighth-of-an-inch of slack in the trigger of most semi-automatics. Taking out the slack means pressing the trigger through that eighth-of-an-inch of slack. Trigger reset means holding the trigger back after the shot has fired and letting it go forward under control until it trips the sear, then pressing again to fire another shot. The finger stays in contact with the trigger throughout the cycle. The teachers started shooting on the range with emphasis on trigger reset.

The teachers kept coming back to the fire to warm up, but I noticed the groups on the targets were tightening up.

The class learned how to shoot while moving forwards and backwards, with Forrest Sonewald, a retired police officer, instructing. He emphasized a heel-and-toe movement when advancing and dragging the feet when backing up. The object in both directions is to provide a stable platform from which to shoot.

"The first thing I need to do is unlock my knees, lower my center of gravity, and treat my legs like shock absorbers. The other thing I want to do is, when I walk, rather than putting my foot down, I want to roll, heel to toe. As I move forwards, you can see how much more centered I am and stable," Sonewald said.

"Moving backwards, same thing. You can also see when I move backwards, I'm dragging my feet. Some places advocate stepping; others advocate doing a single drag step. The best thing that we've found is dragging the feet. It allows for normal movement, and if I encounter something moving backwards, I'll hit it, know it's there."

He told the teachers to look at his body posture. Even when moving backwards, Sonewald was leaning forward aggressively. He reminded the teachers they had been told continually on the range that their posture should be forward-aggressive. They would continue to hear it.

"If I stand upright and I encounter something moving backwards, next thing I know I'm going to go butt over tea kettle."

The teachers practiced moving forwards and backwards using their fingers as guns until they got the techniques. Then they practiced using live fire, while shooting at head-and-shoulders steel plates and moving forwards and backwards between ten and fifteen yards, reloading as necessary.

P.G., a school counselor and twenty-one-year veteran of the U.S. Air Force. He was wearing an NRA cap:

"One of the reasons that I am here is just to get more proficient with the pistol and the possibility of one day being able to conceal-and-carry or just openly carry a weapon in school, in order to defend students in case there is somebody coming in that means them harm."

John Benner demonstrated passing the gun from one hand to the other, using the trigger finger and maybe the second finger to "wipe" the gun into the other hand. This was a preliminary to shooting one-handed and to shooting two-handed around barricades with the gun in the support hand. In shooting one-handed, the shooter should face the target squarely and hold the support hand on the chest so it doesn't act like a pendulum.

The teachers practiced holding the gun in the right hand (if right-handed) then "wiping" it into the left hand and shooting one or two rounds. They also practiced at ten yards shooting with the left hand and with the right as support hand.

Benner says that in a raid he doesn't switch hands, but for a left-hand opening he twists his gun sideways. If going slowly, he does switch hands and closes his right eye. With an active killer you have to move fast before he kills more people.

Chris Wallace taught the teachers how to "dip" their gun muzzles down to avoid pointing their guns at people in front of them. With large traffic cones representing people, the teachers wove among them, shooting at the steel when they could and dipping their guns when the cones came between them and the targets.

The class split into three groups of eight to learn the use of space when rounding a corner. Each group had a different instructor. I watched the group led by Chris Wallace. He told the teachers not to hug the corner — stay back from the corner at least six feet if you have room, and you will see the assailant's sleeve or gun before he sees you. When you see him, stop.

Some instructors teach their students to get through a door as quickly as possible. They often refer to it as the fatal funnel. In a school or commercial building, the door-frames are often made of steel and the walls of concrete, which will give you cover from fire.

Wallace advised, "Never kill anybody from inside the room if you can kill them from outside the room."

As you see some one-or-more people when you are cornering, you can assess them one-by-one. You need to turn your upper body towards the threat. Use as much space from the corner as is available.

Back on the range, Sonewald demonstrated shooting around barricades using a technique called the "drop out." I know, you thought a drop-out was someone who didn't finish high school. However, the drop out is also a way of moving your head, hands, and gun in a controlled manner around cover with minimum exposure to incoming fire. If you are moving around cover to the right, your right foot is forward but inside the cover and your left foot is back as though it was in the opposite corner of a box. Your left leg remains locked straight, while you bend your right knee. This moves your upper body to the right while you look for the shooter. If you are rounding cover to the left, reverse the procedure. If you are right-handed and rounding cover to the left, tilt your gun ninety degrees to the left and use your left eye to align the sights.

The teachers practiced the drop out on both sides of the barricades. The barricades were made of old election campaign signs — a much better use for them than their original purpose.

Benner said, don't warn the active killer, or you will be reacting to him rather than having him react to you.

"Don't verbally challenge anyone unless you don't think he is the active killer."

He emphasized that the teachers have to practice what they have learned or they will lose the skills. They have to have good habits, because when they are involved in an incident isn't the time for thinking about technique. It has to come automatically.

Teacher shooting around a barricade using the "drop-out" method.

"You're going to have to have good habits, especially in the environment that you're in. Folks, you guys are pioneers at this. If we have a problem in any of the schools, if we have a problem with people making mistakes, in firing extra rounds, or hitting somebody that doesn't need to be hit, guess what? This program will go to hell, quite honestly. So you guys have to make it work. It's really up to you to do that."

K.B., assistant school-district superintendent:
"I think that at some point the things that are happening around the world are going to happen in our schools. And honestly, I would like to be the school district that posts a sign that says, 'Authorized personnel may be armed,' so that we're not a soft target anymore."

Benner said the Secret Service is responsible for the safety and security of the president's children. It has unlimited resources, so it can use the best possible way to keep them safe.

"They are professionals at what they do. They are excellent at protecting people," he said. "So if they are going to protect the president's children, how do they do that? They put armed people at the school. So that is obviously the best way to do it. The Secret Service believes it is. Why would that not be right for the rest of the children?"

The teachers finished the afternoon by taking turns going through two Live-Fire Houses, locating and shooting the active killer. The active-killer targets were the ones holding guns set amid others that were unarmed.

The Live-Fire Houses had only fronts — there were no outside walls — so bullets fired at targets hit the earth berms that surrounded each house on three sides. The first Live-Fire House had walls made of plywood and a catwalk above the rooms, so an observer could watch the action below. The second Live-Fire House had a roof. The interior walls were made of chipboard, pockmarked with bullet holes.

Checking targets in Live-Fire House 1.

Immediate Medical Treatment

After a break for dinner, the teachers returned to the classroom for a session on emergency medical treatment taught by Cameron McElroy, a professional firefighter and paramedic.

Civilian emergency medical services (EMS) will stage in a safe location until police determine the area safe. This results in what can be an extended period when the wounded are on their own.

McElroy several times emphasized that the teachers' first priority is to stop the killing. Only then can they treat the wounded. Most of the lecture concerned stopping the loss of blood, whether by tourniquet or pressure dressing.

He quoted a study that reviewed forty-five mass shootings with a total of 437 victims. Dead-to-wounded ratio was twelve-to-one. So we are more likely to be faced with dead bodies than wounded needing attention.

McElroy said there are three zones of care. The hot zone is under direct threat, where stopping the killer is the first priority. The warm zone is out of the direct line of fire. This allows for rapid and aggressive treatment. The cold zone is where EMS can enter and treat the wounded more expertly than we can.

In caring for the wounded, assess their conditions and prioritize whom you are going to treat first. Get onlookers to help.

The first task is to stop the bleeding. Whether the blood is pooling or spurting, it needs immediate attention. If the wound is in an arm or leg, use a commercial tourniquet, probably from a medical kit. If no proper tourniquet is available, one can be improvised from such things as triangular bandages, gauze, or clothing. The tourniquet should be at least two-inches wide. Use a steel pin or a stick and twist it until the bleeding stops. It is extremely painful.

Tourniquets are your friends, McElroy said. They have had a bad reputation in the past, but it is undeserved. If the tourniquet is placed before shock sets in, there is a 90 percent survival rate. Place the tourniquet and go on to the next victim.

A tourniquet cannot be used on a junction wound, which is a wound at the junction of the body and a limb. Pack the wound with gauze, a towel, T-shirt, or similar and apply direct pressure. Press down with your full weight for two or three minutes to allow the blood to clot. If there is a void like an exit wound, fill it with packing, combat gauze, and/or a blood-clotting agent like Quickclot.

For less severe wounds, apply a trauma dressing and compress the wound without pressure. Dressings can be made from T-shirts and duct tape. Use good-quality duct tape.

McElroy said the number one cause of combat deaths is bleeding from the extremities.

It is important to make sure the victim's airway is not blocked. If the victim is talking, the airway is clear. Roll him onto one side and pull up one leg. Turn his head to one side to prevent him choking on his own vomit.

If a victim has a penetrating chest wound and is sucking air through it, it needs to be sealed with plastic, duct tape, or pads and the edges sealed with tape. Seal entrance and exit wounds.

Remember, you may have to treat your own wounds, but still your first priority is to eliminate the threat to prevent further casualties.

If a buddy is suffering from anxiety and confusion, you may need to disarm him to prevent him from shooting one of the good guys in error.

Have an evacuation plan in the pre-planning stage. Number all windows for ease of location. Dragging is the fastest way to get a person out of danger. You can also carry a victim using the Hawes technique, which is taught in the military. After dragging or carrying, recheck dressings, tourniquets, and airways.

McElroy recommended North American Rescue trauma dressings and chest-seal products. There is a tube that goes through the nose and down the throat to keep an airway clear. Other supplies that are useful in treating wounded victims include gloves, triangular bandages, feminine pads for sopping up blood, Ace bandages, and good-quality duct tape.

Third Day

The final day started with a warm-up on the steel targets. Teachers shot at steel targets using both hands, strong hand, and support hand. They then shot, moving backwards from thirty feet to fifty feet.

This was followed by instruction on gun-retention techniques. Everybody roped their guns, then Benner demonstrated several gun-retention methods. If someone tries to grab your gun while it is still in your holster, force your gun hand down onto his hand and hold it there.

If he grabs your gun while it is in your hand and you fire it, it won't cycle. Pull it back, tap the magazine, and rack the slide as you pull back. You can then shoot your attacker if necessary. You can also push the gun towards him, then twist it hard

John Benner holding his gun in its holster to prevent instructor Chris Wallace from grabbing it.

to the left or right, and pull it back out of his grasp. Everyone practiced these exercises.

The class split into two groups. One group went to the force-on-force house, a two-story building used for indoor scenarios using Airsoft guns.

I went with the other group to the upper range, where a school corridor had been erected out of sheets of plywood. The corridor was sixty-feet long, fifteen-feet wide, and eight-feet high, with two doorways on one side and one on the other. Forrest Sonewald, Gary Hoff, and Deborah Fletcher were our group's instructors.

With guns still roped, teachers negotiated some scenarios where there was action in one of the rooms, and the good guy, starting at the end of the corridor, had to cope with the active killer.

G.B., an administrator at a private Christian school:
"We have eight members on our board, two of whom actually have conceal-and-carry, six that do not. Yes, we are supportive, and after this training we will bring in a policy."

Before they started, Benner gave them some words of advice. He said police officers want to stop and question everyone they meet when searching for the active killer. You cannot afford the time to stop, because you have to find and neutralize the killer.

"If somebody's hiding somewhere, that's not your problem. You have to make that assessment real quick and blow right by them," he said. "You may see bodies, blood trails, trails of bullet casings. Things of that nature may lead you to where you need to go."

You can question people you come across on the way to see if they have any useful information you can use, but don't waste time. If you don't hear any noise coming from a room, pass it up. You don't have time to search every room on your route.

"Can you make a mistake? Yeah, you can, there's no question about it. This is not a perfect science," Benner said.

When you are moving down a hallway, stay in the middle, and if there are two of you, walk side-by-side. The person on the right covers the right side of the hallway, and the person on the left covers that side, Benner said.

If one of you sees a problem and needs to go into a room, your partner probably should pay attention to the problem as well and wait until you have dealt with that problem before moving on, or he may be in your line of fire.

"You just have to use your common sense, and that's the hard part of the whole thing, because sometimes common sense isn't so common," he said.

Stay away from the hallway walls to avoid bouncing bullets. Bullets hitting a hard surface like a wall tend to stay close to the surface when they ricochet.

"The harder the surface, the tighter the bullet will stay to that surface; the softer the surface, the higher the bullet will bounce," Benner said.

Sonewald chipped in: "If you fire a bullet at less than a forty-five degree angle to a hard surface, it will deform, flatten out, and continue along the line of that surface at between one and eight inches. That's a generality, but I should emphasize, stay off the wall!"

Benner said that the teachers would have to make their own decisions about when to draw their guns. For the purpose of the scenarios, the teacher would start with his gun out. But if he thought he was some distance from the shooting, he would leave his gun in its holster. He would draw it when he got close and might hold it in tightly against his body.

"How you deal with your gun is going to be up to you."

If there were a bunch of kids coming down the hall towards him, he would get over to the right side of the hallway to protect his gun, if right-handed. When approaching the scene of the shooting, he would keep the muzzle dipped to avoid muzzling students and staff.

If a group of kids is running past you to get away, look at their hands. They will tell you who the shooter is, Benner said.

"Once you've shot this guy down, check and make sure there isn't anybody else that needs to be shot. There is a 2 percent chance that you'll have multiple shooters," he said.

Benner advised teachers not to leave the scene unless they hear more shooting, in which case they should continue and head for the sound of the gunfire.

"My suggestion to you is to stay right where you are. If I thought I needed to have my gun out, I would solicit one or two people to watch for the police."

When the shooter is down, move so you are behind him and either cover him from behind or approach him from behind to take his gun.

It may look good in the movies, but never kick the gun away from the killer, as the gun may go off. You don't know the condition of the gun. Even if it doesn't fire, some kid may pick it up, and then you have a problem. It may be safer to keep the gunman covered than to disarm him. Be aware that there is a 75 percent chance the killer will have other guns on him, but don't search him for them.

"We don't want you going up and winding up in a wrestling match with somebody and get yourself killed. You're better off holding your gun on him from a distance until you get some professional help. Let the police take care of stuff like that. They're coming eventually, so let them do their job."

When someone is shot, their blood pressure goes down, which may cause them to lose consciousness. When they fall, it is easier for the heart to pump blood, so the pressure may go up, causing them to regain consciousness and again be a threat.

If the teacher still has a gun on the bad guy when the police arrive, have someone — a student or staff member — stand behind the armed teacher with his hands up and tell the officers that a suspect has been shot and a teacher is holding him at gunpoint. If no one is available, holster your gun, but keep an eye on the downed shooter.

In response to a comment from one of the teachers, Benner said the more armed staff members in the school, the shorter the likely duration of the shooting.

"The more people you have, the less chance you have of this going a long time. If you are spread throughout the building, who knows where in the heck this is going to happen? Is it happening in the lunchroom; is it happening in the library; is it happening in one of the classrooms? There are so many if, ands, or buts, it's an impossible thing to say what you are going to do under what circumstances."

Benner said it is better to make your mistakes in training rather than during the real thing.

With their guns still roped, the teachers did some scenarios where there was action in one of the "rooms" (they only had two or three sides), and the good guy starting at the end of the corridor had to cope with the bad guy or guys. Sonewald debriefed the responder at the end of each scenario and also provided some advice.

J.J., operations manager for a school district:
"I'm very impressed with the training we are receiving.
I think it is realistic."

Scenarios

After lunch, the same group went back to the school corridor set with the same instructors. This time the teachers wore face-masks and used Airsoft guns, which shoot plastic BBs.

The scenarios included:

• A team from another school has arrived for a basketball game. The teams from both sides are milling about and screaming in the end "room" while being shot by an active killer.

• Students in another room are swarming around while being shot by an active killer.

• In another room students are pointing at the active killer, who has shot twice, stopped, and dropped the gun, and is standing behind it with his hands up.

• A teacher with a gun is teaching in one room when he hears shooting and screaming from another classroom across the hall. He has to decide whether to run to the sound of the shooting or stay and protect his own students.

• An active killer commits suicide; when the teacher arrives, gun in hand, he sees that a student has picked up the gun and is holding it by the barrel.

Forrest Sonewald debriefed each responder after each scenario, he asked them to justify each action they took. Rather than make anybody wrong, he would point out other options the teacher could have chosen. Some of the best lessons came out during his debriefings. These are some of them.

Sonewald: "You swung wide; you got effective hits. She tried to engage you. She shot one person, and you already started to put rounds on her, and she tried to shift fire over. Nice job. Now she's down, what's our next concern?"

Responder: "See where the weapon's at?"

Sonewald: "Okay."

Responder: "Seeing the condition they are in. Also checking the room, making sure there is no one else in there."

Sonewald: "Correct. Two percent of the time you've got multiple opponents. So we would move up. You have to check the room. You would continue to swing wide, use your space. Try to check as much of the room as possible — soft corners, from out here in the hallway — and if there is another opponent in there, you try to solve your problem from the hallway before you actually enter that room, which is the danger zone."

"Soft corners" are the corners of the room you can see from outside the room. "Hard corners" are the ones where at least part of your body has to enter the room to see them.

Sonewald went through various options. Do we want to collect that weapon? It depends. One teacher said he would be inclined to take the shooter's gun. Sonewald asked if covering the shooter from where the teacher had cover was an option. He said, if possible, find another responsible person.

A teacher with a roped gun navigating a "school hallway" past two victims. John Benner is in the background.

"Get them to stand out in the hallway with their hands up to receive responding law-enforcement officers. A hands-up position is a universal indication you're not a threat. They need to cut through all the stress and the yelling and screaming to let the law-enforcement responders know that you're there armed — that you're a teacher."

After a scenario in which the active killer was a woman, a teacher asked what he should do if the classroom is empty and there is nobody to cover his back. Should he stay there with his gun drawn covering the shooter?

"That's going to be a personal decision. If she is shot in the doorway, and the gun clatters away from her, and I can clearly see she's not moving, I keep my gun in and tight, close to my body. I may move up to secure the weapon, step back, and then again maintain a cover position. If there's no one there to let responding officers know, again I'm the one in the hallway. Everybody's screaming, and I have a pistol out. The last thing I want after saving the day is to go from hero to zero, because the first responding officer sees me: maybe there's supposed to be one person shot in the hallway; there's blood. He sees me standing there, and he immediately puts a round on me, which is what the officer's supposed to do. So I may choose to get a nice tight angle, so I've got very little area to cover, or move so there's an open area behind the shooter, in case they do come up and try to do something. And then I'll holster the weapon. It's immediately available to me. Important note: that's why it's important to work from the holster, so if I need it, I can immediately come out and put additional rounds on the suspect."

A teacher asked if, after seizing the shooter's weapon, he would pat them down for more guns. Sonewald responded, "Probably not. My concern is the weapon they have on them. Seventy-five percent of the time they have multiple weapons. We're talking rifles, shotguns, or multiple pistols. They have them in jacket pockets, pouches, carry bags, or duffel bags. If the person's down and not moving, my concern is for someone accessing the other firearm. I secure that, so I hold it in a manner that's probably not a threat [by the barrel]."

In debriefing another teacher, Sonnewald said that, if there are two shooters, they will almost certainly stay together. "When you have two shooters, it's incredibly dangerous. And the downside is, to date, statistically, the multiple shooters have never separated, so if there is one, the other one is right with them. It's that mutual-support thing."

When checking a room, he said, "Swing wide on the doorway to catch all the soft corners. Once you've got them checked, then you move up close, and only then you check the hard corners. So now you — or at least part of your body — actually have to enter the room. Once the room is checked, if I know where the bad guy is, I check to see that there're no other people to direct out. Some people may flee, others may hide under the desk — fight, flight, or freeze."

One of the scenarios involved the bad guy firing several shots then putting the gun down. When the good gal entered

Teacher uses an Airsoft pistol to shoot a "bad guy" while a potential victim cowers on the ground.

the room, she watched the hands and saw no one holding a gun, but everybody looking and pointing at the shooter.

Sonewald suggested ordering the bad guy to back up and, while holding him at gunpoint, ordering the children to walk out of the room, without getting between him and the bad guy.

"'You! Lay on the ground.' Now if he follows your instructions, that's good. If he doesn't, that's a red flag. You want to get him away from the pistol. 'Back up and lay down, now. Everybody else — you are in the doorway — come out past me to the right.' Empty the room out. Now the only person in the room is the bad guy, and the gun is on the ground, and you don't have to go in there."

He warned the female teacher not to get too close to a bad guy, if he has not been incapacitated. Many criminals have been shot before, and to them it's no big deal.

Gary Hoff suggested, when getting the guy to back up away from the gun, "one option to consider is: 'turn around; face away from me.' That way he can't see what you are doing, then change position."

Sonewald also suggested to pass your cell phone to a responsible student, tell them to dial 9-1-1 and hold the phone up to you, while you tell the operator who you are, where you are, and what the situation is.

He said if you have a classroom full of kids, and you hear shooting out in the hallway or in another room, you have to make a decision about whether you stay where you are and protect your kids or do you leave the room and hunt for the shooter — ambush or hunt. All the teachers in the group chose to stay in the room where they were, rather than hunt down the shooter.

Sonewald said the decisions you make when the shooting starts are judgment calls where there are few right or wrong answers.

"You're going to have to make a decision. I cannot tell you what to do," he said. "This scenario stuff is the culmination of everything we've practiced up to this point — the weapons handling, the use of space, cutting wide on things. You've got to make a decision based on individual circumstances — whether or not you enter a room; if you are already in the room, as in some of the scenarios, whether or not you set up an ambush or go hunting for the individual. And there are always the after thoughts — do we secure the firearm, do we direct people out, who do we designate to stay with us with their hands up and say we have an armed teacher covering a downed suspect; or if we don't have communication, who do we send to the office?"

Benner added: "Think about this too, folks. If you are involved in a situation, do the best you can. That's all that anybody can ask."

G.K., seventh-grade science teacher:

"The times have changed, and the whole game has changed, and we've got to have people trained. I know law enforcement does a great job, but response time is something else. They have to get there, and usually within two minutes it's over. Two years ago, would I have thought guns would be in schools and teachers would be armed? No. But I would have to say that within a short time we could have teachers that are carrying full time. I would not doubt that will happen."

Force-on-Force House Scenarios

The group moved to the Force-on-Force house. From the outside it looks like a two-story residence, but with fewer windows. Inside, the walls are chipboard. The teachers were put through more scenarios. Chris Wallace did the debriefings.

- The living room downstairs was the library. Students were sitting at tables when the active killer started shooting them. The armed teachers came into the building, but they couldn't see the shooter, who was protected by a corner. Most of the armed teachers made good use of space, keeping well back from the corner when they shot the killer. Most of the time, the killer didn't see the teacher before he/she shot him.

• In the same area, the active killer commits suicide, and a student picks up the gun, holding it by the barrel. Reminding the teachers about what they had learned in the medical class, Wallace said they had to make sure the scene was safe, so the paramedics could come in and tend to the wounded. "Also, what I would do is recover that weapon right away, because if you've got a bunch of panicked kids around or civilians in a shopping mall, who've never seen anybody get shot or whatever, might they not pick up the gun like this guy did? So you want to pick it up and secure it some way. Do not ever kick a gun that you are unfamiliar with, because oftentimes the guns that are bought "off the street" are not in 100 percent tip-top operating condition, and if you kick them and they discharge, you might have another injury." Wallace asked the teacher who had just gone through the scenario, when did you first see the gun the student was holding by the barrel? The teacher said he saw it immediately he came into the room. Wallace suggested: "Could it have been a better idea to say, while you were back there: 'You with the gun in your hand, just slowly reach down, place it on the floor, step away from it, and tell me what's going on here.'" He said it was a non-shoot scenario, but it was complicated. He reminded the teachers that many mass killers commit suicide, so they must be prepared for that.

• An angry father wants to see his kid. The mother has custody, so the two employees at the counter won't let him in. He becomes more and more aggressive and eventually shoots the two at the counter. The armed teacher comes in and shoots the father before he can find the kid.

• An unarmed principal is in his office upstairs, when an active killer comes up the stairs to shoot a group of students hanging around outside the office. As the gunman passes the principal's door, the principal comes out armed with a foam "baseball bat," beats the killer on the head, and takes him down. Jim Irvine was the killer and was taken down quite aggressively several times. In his debriefing, Wallace said there are lots of weapons in a school or even a classroom. "You just have to have imagination to recognize them as weapons. There are a lot of things you are authorized to have in your classroom that can easily be turned into a lethal weapon." He mentioned a claw hammer, a large screwdriver, a baseball bat, and even a laptop computer. "I'd like for you to go back, look in your respective work areas, and start looking at objects — instead of as what the manufacturer intended their use — as what you could want them to do in this scenario," Wallace said. "That's what we wanted to bring out here, is that you are not defeated if you do not have a firearm wherever you are. Not necessarily. But if you can have a firearm, that's the absolute best-case scenario."

Qualification

The two groups of teachers assembled back at the range for their last ordeal: the Ohio peace-officers' firearms qualification course. The peace-officers' qualification is actually twenty-five rounds fired from different distances from four to fifty feet. Benner has added an advancing stage of three rounds and requires twenty-seven hits in the large vital area. The vital area includes the head and chest, tapering down to two large circles representing the pelvic bones.

Stages
• Two in the body, one in the head, at nine feet.
• Right hand four rounds; left hand four rounds; range twelve feet.

- With two rounds in the magazine and one in the chamber, fire three rounds, reload, and shoot three more rounds. Time nine seconds; range twenty feet.
- Fire three rounds in five seconds at thirty feet.
- Fire two rounds in five seconds at fifty feet.
- Fire three rounds with strong hand from chest level in four seconds at four feet.
- Fire three rounds starting from twenty feet, while advancing on the target.

After shooting, one young woman said proudly she had scored twenty-seven out of twenty-eight, "and that's more than my husband, and he's in law enforcement."

R.K., school nurse:

"I feel like it was very organized. They treat you with respect. It's a very positive environment where there isn't negativity; it's only positive reinforcement. They have made sure that if anyone is not real sure of themselves, making sure that they have the confidence to move forward. There has been a lot of improvement in people that came with no confidence and are leaving with a great deal."

The teachers went to the classroom where Benner asked Sonewald and Wallace how they had done on the scenarios.

Forrest Sonewald: "A lot of stuff that was done wasn't necessarily wrong. We talked about different alternatives; you're going to have to make a decision based on the totality of what's going on and what works best for you. We gave you a lot of different choices to make, things to think about for the future. Awesome job."

Chris Wallace: "Even if you don't have a firearm, if you have tactics you may well survive the encounter, as some people found out much to the chagrin of Jim Irvine."

Benner talked to them and shook their hands. He presented each of them a course-completion certificate and, for all but

A "principal" armed with a "baseball bat" emerges from his office and attacks the active killer.

one, a certificate of passing the Ohio state peace-officer's firearms qualification course.

Sharing the Program

Benner said it had taken one year to go from one armed teacher in one school district in Ohio to more than thirty districts by March 2014.

"It's really come a long way in a short time. But we've got a lot of districts here, and some of them will never get armed, I'm sure. But the more that we can get, the better off we're going to be."

Benner said he is willing to share his program with other instructors in Ohio and other states.

"If they want us to share information with them, we are happy to do that, to the point that we'll give them the power-point lesson plan, everything. And we urge other instructors to come down here. Certain ones that we feel are competent, we literally give them the program free."

Chapter 7

ADVANCED TRAINING FOR TEACHERS: FASTER II & III

*"I just feel that I'm a better shooter than when I got here.
I feel I have a better concept of what I need to do
in an emergency situation."*
— R.Z., math teacher and FASTER II student

After putting on three-day training courses for educators, John Benner of Tactical Defense Institute and Jim Irvine of the Buckeye Firearms Foundation decided to take the training to the next level, thus FASTER II was born. It consists of the same three-day format at TDI, with twenty-four people from Ohio school districts, including teachers, superintendents, and custodians. In the class I observed six were women. All of the participants had completed the Level I FASTER class previously. The Level II course was part refresher and part new material. While the FASTER I course I monitored was in weather well-below freezing, with snow as an additive, the advanced course was in the heat of summer with extra humidity.

Day One
The course started in the classroom with Benner introducing his seven other instructors. He talked about the Sandy Hook shooting using information from the investigation done by the Connecticut State's Attorney General.

"The time-line that came out of that, to me, was by far the single most interesting thing," he said. Some people in law enforcement have accepted the reality that they are unlikely to be able to stop an active killer while he is murdering students and teachers.

"In other words, by the time they get there, this thing is over. They're taking reports, they're doing crime scenes, and they're doing all this other stuff, but the chances of them engaging the active killer are actually pretty slim."

Dispatch time varies. It can take two or three minutes from the 9-1-1 call until officers are dispatched. At Sandy Hook, the dispatch time from the first 9-1-1 call was very quick, Benner said.

"They had three officers there by three minutes and thirteen seconds. And that's where things fell apart. Because they waited outside — hearing shots fired inside an elementary school — for five minutes and forty-seven seconds. The guys with the guns waited outside, while the school principal and the school teachers were fighting a guy with a rifle with their bare hands, or trying to. So think about that."

Benner said it is important that the teachers think about that time-line during the training.

"That is why you are so important, because you are there, and it is critical that you do your job."

They must also realize that there will be casualties they can't do anything about. They should not blame themselves for not being able to save everyone, unless in the unlikely event that the shooting starts right in front of them, and they can stop it before it escalates.

The teachers migrated to the range. Their first exercise was to draw and fire one shot at fifty feet. The targets were head-and-shoulders steel plates. The first shot is the most important and must be a hit, Benner said.

The teachers formed up in two lines and were timed individually. The average time seemed to be about 2.8 seconds.

Benner said there had been quite a few misses and urged the teachers to take the slack out of the trigger before they fired the shot.

"If you haven't thought about slack-out when you worked your trigger while you've been off, you are remiss in what you're doing."

He said if you miss that first shot at fifty feet, you are not practicing enough.

Benner had the teachers shoot at the three-inch dots, some from the holster, some from the ready position. They fired one shot at a time, then two, then three.

After watching the teachers shoot, Benner was critical of their weapon handling.

"If you're not practicing what you were taught, you're never going to be a good weapon handler, and we're seeing quite a bit of what we would call sloppy weapon handling. Not necessarily sloppy safety, but just sloppy weapon handling. In other words whenever people are drawing from the holster, this hand (the support hand) is hanging here like it's dead, until we get the gun up, and then we somehow manage to get the gun up with our hand. That's unacceptable. There's no reason for that."

Benner showed that the support hand starts on the chest, while the gun hand gets a good grip and lifts the gun up to chest height and rotates the gun towards the target, which is where the support hand takes up its grip.

Forrest Sonewald demonstrated while Benner explained. "He's going to come up underneath that gun — comes underneath, and he hits that, rolls his thumb in, and simply pushes the gun forward, gets his line of sight, takes the slack out, and presses the trigger, nice and smooth. Then the gun is going to cycle, and he's going to reset that trigger."

He is then ready to shoot again, because it may take more than one shot to put the bad guy down. Benner said after shooting, the finger comes off the trigger and lies against

Instructor Deborah Fletcher instructs a teacher on the firing line.

the frame. Some people were holding their trigger fingers low against the trigger guard instead of alongside the frame.

"If we can see that finger from the opposite side of the frame, it is too low."

If the finger is low and the shooter is startled, the finger will bend involuntarily, slip inside the trigger guard, and jerk the trigger.

To reholster, bring the gun back and scan, which he refers to as "check your world," then do the draw sequence in reverse.

Benner: "These are all skills you must take home and practice and get good at. It's absolutely critical that you do. I can't stress that enough, especially with what you guys are doing. You have got to be good, safe weapon handlers, and you need to be able to hit the target, and I think most of you can do that."

After more shooting on the steel, Benner told the teachers to reload at eye level. Bring the gun back towards the face, and bring the magazine up to the gun. This enables you to keep an eye on the target and anything else that might be going on.

The teachers practiced shooting one-handed and practiced shooting on the move. Starting at fifteen yards, they advanced to seven yards while shooting, then moved sideways, then finally backed up to fifteen yards. They had to change magazines while moving.

After lunch, the teachers learned how to dip their guns so as not to muzzle people who may be running away from the gunman. They learned this technique during the first FASTER class.

The clouds cleared, and the sun shone down, driving the temperature up into the mid-nineties. The humidity made it feel hotter. The instructors urged the teachers to drink plenty of water and stay hydrated.

The teachers used the drop-out to practice shooting from behind cover. The cover was two plastic barrels, one on top of the other, and they practiced shooting at three steel targets as they came into view. The targets had been spray-painted different colors — red, green, and yellow. They

Instructor Forrest Sonewald demonstrates shooting while backing up. Instructors Chris Wallace and John Motil have their hands up to stop him.

then advanced from the cover, shooting at the targets. Each teacher did this twice with better results the second time.

"That was much better," Benner said.

He gave them homework, telling them to dry fire in front of a mirror in their hotel rooms and watch for movement of the muzzle.

J.S., superintendent of a small rural school district.

He was monitoring the class because he had already taken both FASTER classes. "I have four of my people here today. Any time I'm out here listening to John and the rest of the instructors, I always pick up something. That's why I'm in education. I want to be a life-long learner and same thing here. I always pick up information and stuff that maybe I didn't hear the first time when I was actually training, because of the stress, but I pick it up later and take it back, and we practice that."

J.S. said they have multiple teachers who carry guns in his school district. It includes preschool through high school.

After Sandy Hook, a group of parents approached him and wanted to know if they could start a safety committee for the school district. J.S. agreed.

"We met religiously for about four months. It was the largest group of parents, volunteers, I've had in twelve years as superintendent.

"Some out of that group came to me and said: 'We know the board can authorize people to carry firearms. We want that.' I said: 'I'll set you up with the board at the board meeting, open session, and you can talk to them.' And they did. They did an absolutely fabulous job. They came to the board meeting that night, there were four parents — three females — and they had all their facts straight. They spoke very well, got their point across. We waited to see if there would be any push-back from the community — none. And then June of that year [2012], we authorized people to carry.

"And you know what? We're like any other school district in the United States; if people have problems, they come to board meetings and complain — like they should. Not one person in three years has ever mentioned it. It's a non-issue in our district right now."

J.S. thinks his district was the second in Ohio to approve school employees carrying concealed handguns. The police chief and the county sheriff are in favor of what they are doing and have helped with training.

"Without their support we wouldn't be doing what we are doing."

The teachers roped their guns, were split into two groups of twelve, and went to the Live-Fire Houses. I went to the second house, where Chris Wallace was the primary instructor.

The group was divided into one responder and one or two bad guys or gals; the rest were victims of the bad guys. The responders and bad guys were changed after each scenario, so everyone got a turn. As soon as the responder entered the house, he or she could expect to come across active killers as they moved from room to room.

Wallace reiterated his mantra: Never shoot someone from inside a room if you can shoot them from outside the room. The teachers acting as responders were instructed to use as much space and cover as they could.

He talked about coping with a bunch of panicked kids running towards you as you are trying to close with the killer.

"They're potential victims, or they wouldn't be running away. The shooter is not going to be running away. He's going to be shooting. You've got a lot of very panicked people, both students and staff members. When people get around actual acts of violence, if they've never seen this stuff before, a lot of times they will panic, which is natural. That is going to happen. So you, being the responder, have

The bad guy on the right has shot two victims and is aiming at a third. Teacher, followed by instructor Chris Wallace, moves to confront the killer. Both have their guns roped.

to realize that is going to happen, and you have to do something to mitigate it."

He recommended moving along a wall on your right side if you are right-handed. That way you can shield your gun, because it is between you and the wall. Wallace picked a large teacher to demonstrate what he called off-angling.

"I'm going to show you that, even though he's much stronger than I am, this doesn't take any strength."

They stood facing each other, and Wallace tried to push the teacher backwards. He wasn't able to do so.

"I can't move him. So if you are trying to move people away by pushing them in the center of the chest, squaring up on them, even somebody who's not as strong as you, it's hard to do. And you've got to do this quickly, because you've got to get past them to get to where the action is."

With his left arm straight, Wallace pushed the teacher's left shoulder, turning him out of the way.

"So as you're going down the hall, and you've got your gun in hand, you don't need to do anything but that. And let them ride the arm."

Wallace was holding his gun back with the barrel horizontal against his side, between him and the wall. His left arm was straight-forward at shoulder height.

"All I'm doing is pushing on that pocket (the pocket of the shoulder where a long-gun butt would rest), and he's just going to rotate on that axis. I can stay focused on my potential threat, and I can protect my gun."

Teachers started in the first room inside the Live-Fire House. They turned right to go through a doorway into a second room. They had to check that room for a threat, moving forward along the wall on their right until they could see the hard corner to their left. If there was no threat in that room, they advanced, keeping to the wall on the right as they approached the doorway into the last room on the left, where there often was a threat. Checking that room for threats, as for the previous room, they would enter. Several teachers went forward into the doorway, instead of staying outside the room to check most of it before advancing. There was one more room on the right of the house. The doorway into that room was partway down the wall they had been following. Most of the teachers advanced along the wall to the doorway, instead of making use of the space available to check the last room from a distance.

The teachers took turns to run through the scenarios, which changed frequently. Wallace told one teacher to slow down as he neared the shooter and make better use of space and cover.

M.E. teaches third-grade English at an elementary school.
Her purpose in attending the FASTER II course was "to be more educated on protecting our children, and being able to do the right thing in a situation that might occur, and to have that proper training to be able to take care of whatever it is that needs taking care of."

She doesn't get to carry at school yet, but they are waiting on permission. Some members of the school board are being persuaded, and she is hopeful that they will be able to carry at the start of the school year. She is not sure how she will carry, but it will be in a holster. She is concerned that when the young children hug her they not feel the gun. Already fifteen members of her school district have been trained in the FASTER I class.

"*I was approached by our superintendent, and he is very pro gun.*"

He wanted to get a group of teachers trained before he went to the board for permission. The administrators already carry, and now they are seeking permission for the teachers to do so.

Day Two

The second day started on the range at fifty feet, firing one shot from the holster at the head-and-shoulders steel targets.

"Better than yesterday, but still not good enough," was Benner's reaction.

If the killer is down the hallway, and he is on his own, accuracy is important but not vital. If there are other people beyond him, you can't afford to miss.

"Slack out, get your sights, press, nice and slow. Especially at forty-five feet, there is no hurry. You've got to make that shot."

The teachers moved forward to seven yards, where they practiced draw-and-fire one, two, and three shots at the steel. They moved back to about thirty-six feet to continue with draw-and-fire practice, followed by more at fifty feet.

After a break, the teachers roped their guns, then learned some hand-to-hand moves, with Sonewald doing most of the teaching. He taught a double palm-heel strike for occasions

Teachers practice double palm-heel strikes.

when you are surprised or are too close to the opponent to have time to draw your handgun.

"Some people may have a combative background in traditional martial arts. I'm one of them, and I'm used to closed-fist striking, but I don't do it anymore. The reason is, for twenty-five years in law enforcement, I've seen too many broken hands."

Hitting someone in the head with a closed fist is an invitation to broken hand bones, because the head is all hard bone, Sonewald said.

To demonstrate, he hit a six-by-six wooden post that supports the roof of the open-sided building behind part of the range.

"That's about as hard as I can punch it. I'm really feeling the pain, because it's right on top of the knuckles here. You saw how hard I was punching it. Now, I'm going to use the palm-heel — the heel of the palm in line with the bones of my forearm."

He hit the post, making much more noise than with the clenched fist and hitting it with both palm-heels much harder.

"How much more force was I able to generate?"

Before striking, square your shoulders to your opponent. You should be leaning forward into the strike — head forward of the shoulders; shoulders forward of the hips. Hands and fingers should be together; step in towards your opponent, and use all your power, Sonewald said.

"Now, we're not saying you have to do this. If you've got the third-degree black belt in Aikido, Karate, Taekwondo, if you're a UFC fighter, it's all good folks, it's all good. But we're showing you something that, if you don't have a combative background, will fill the bill."

The teachers practiced with the receiver holding up a martial arts pad in front of his face. They learned that even a small woman could make a much larger man step backwards when she hit him with the double palm-heel strike.

Sonewald taught a technique to keep the bad guy's gun in its holster by preventing him from drawing it. However, Benner pointed out that usually bad guys don't wear holsters. The most common position for them is in the waistband in the appendix position. The next most common is in a pocket, and third in the small of the back.

Sonewald told the teachers to do anything they can to put the hurt on the other guy to stop him getting the pistol out. Knees, stomp, shovel-kick.

"If the gun comes out, I'm in a world of hurt."

Sonewald demonstrated a technique to prevent the other guy from stopping your draw.

"He may not have formal training, but he's going to do everything he can to prevent my drawing my weapon."

Sonewald demonstrated how one staff member comes to the aid of another, who is fighting with the bad guy. He urged teachers to push the gun into the bad guy, pull it back, and press the trigger. He said it is vital to ensure that when you fire into the attacker the bullet does not pass through the suspect and hit the other staff member.

Benner interjected: "If one of your armed personnel is fighting with somebody, they can say: 'Shoot 'em; he's trying to get my gun; shoot him.' That's all well and good, but what happens if you've got two kids involved? One of them is the active shooter, and another stepped up to the plate and grabbed the gun, and now they're fighting over it."

The staff member is not going to know which of them is the bad guy.

"It may be a lot more difficult in that particular instance. It's something to think about. You certainly don't want to shoot the wrong one."

The teachers broke into groups of four — a good guy, a bad guy, a responder, and an observer. They practiced responding to two people fighting over a gun.

Day Two, Afternoon

John Benner told the teachers they would be going to the Live-Fire Houses.

"We've got the houses set up. You're going to do some live fire, where you're going to have to make the decision regarding who is the shooter. There's going to be a bunch of targets in there; you're going to have to go through, and you're going to have to eliminate the correct individual.

"Then tomorrow we're going to be doing scenarios all day. We're going to run all kinds of scenarios tomorrow, and some of them are going to be pretty complex. In other words, you may have to follow completely through, including giving first aid, directing people, doing all kinds of different stuff. So we want to talk a little bit about the aftermath."

Live-Fire

Benner sent the teachers to the Live-Fire Houses. The group I was with started in Live-Fire House 1 (LFH1), which was run by Forrest Sonewald, assisted by Wyatt Roush and Deborah Fletcher.

Teacher is about to enter a doorway in Live-Fire House 1 at the start of a scenario. Instructors Deborah Fletcher and Forrest Sonewald look on.

I followed M.E. as she went through the first scenario. The figure targets were all in the last room on the right. The first figure she saw was a black man holding a flashlight. Correctly, she did not shoot him. The killer was partly behind a female figure and was facing away from her, with his gun extended towards the figure of a young man. M.E. shot him, hitting him high in the arm, with the bullet likely to penetrate into the lungs and perhaps the heart.

Sonewald asked her what she would do next. She said she would call for help and get somebody to call 9-1-1 and tell the operator that the shooter is down. She assigned this task to Sonewald.

M.E.: "I want you to stay here while you call, and I want somebody else to stay with me and make sure they know I'm not the shooter."

Sonewald: "Tell them what to do."

M.E.: "Wyatt, you're going to stay with me."

Wyatt Roush: "Okay."

M.E.: "I need to make sure the shooter's down, so you're going to stay with me with your hands up in this position. If somebody comes in, tell them I'm not the shooter. I'm here to check everybody and make sure everything's okay, and the shooter is down, but make sure you keep your hands up."

She positioned Roush behind her, where she assumed the police would be coming from.

Sonewald congratulated her on a good shot through the arm and into the torso.

"That's incapacitating; he's down and out — traversing lung, heart, lung, done. So he's probably done, or if he's not, he's incapable of further movement. Even if he's still alive, he's over there gurgling on the floor. Another option would be, if you've got people ambulatory, move them out. Otherwise, ambulatory individuals should pick up the wounded or disabled and pull them off into another area. Options. I'm not saying you did anything wrong. The only thing I would have changed is, rather than the officers coming in to be confronted by Wyatt, put him in a position somewhere out in the hallway or by the doorway. Give yourself a little bit more space. That way he can actually see the officers coming down the hallway, and he can flag them, saying: 'Over here, over here. The shooter is down, the shooter is down. I have an armed staff member here behind me. We're treating victims right now. We need medical crews here and officers.' You didn't do wrong by having him here, but it probably would have been a bit better option to have him further down the hall."

It took her twenty-two seconds to navigate the building and shoot the active killer. Hers was the fastest time. Sonewald thought it should take about thirty seconds, but other responders took up to fifty seconds to complete the scenario. He told other responders not to go through the scenario so fast that they could not process what they were seeing.

He suggested to the teachers that they keep their guns holstered until they get close to the action. Clues that they are getting close include shell casings, blood on the floor, people screaming, moaning, and the sound of shooting.

Several teachers said they would secure the gun used by the gunman, but were somewhat vague about how to do it. Sonewald asked one responder how he would secure the firearm.

Responder: "If it was on the ground, I would kick it to the side."

Sonewald: "That's why I asked the question. Good idea or bad idea to kick a firearm?"

Responder: "Bad idea to kick a firearm."

Sonewald: "Why?"

Responder: "It could go off."

Sonewald: "Correct. We don't know what they've done to it. I'm not familiar with all weapons systems. The other thing is, not only do we not know what has been done to it, but it will move it from my area of control."

He said a better option is to take the firearm and, if possible, unload the weapon: take out the magazine and rack the slide. If it is a handgun, keep it on your person; maybe put it in a pocket.

"I'm not really comfortable with that myself. Another option is to put it in a trash can; put something over it. Put it up on a shelf, if you have one available. Regardless of what you do, you are responsible for that. The only other option would be, if you have another teacher that you know has training, that you have worked with before, have them handle the weapon: 'This is loaded. This is loaded. This is loaded.' Make sure they understand that."

One large, muscular teacher said he would restrain the gunman.

"You're big enough to restrain him, but remember 80 percent, he's got a long-gun, either a rifle or shotgun; 75 percent of the time, he's got multiple weapons, which means not just rifles and shotguns but pistols, knives, brass knuckles; or he may even be wearing an explosive device," Sonewald said.

The teacher suggested patting him down.

"I'd be real careful of that, knowing that he/she may have weapons; it may be a little better tactic to pull around the corner and maintain a cover position."

Sonewald offered three positions: with the gun at eye-level, with the gun at the low-ready, or with the gun holstered. He said holstered is the safest position for not getting shot by responding officers.

Sonewald asked the teacher if he had looked for another shooter. "I shot the shooter down, where's the second one — always looking for more work."

If there are two shooters, they have always been together, but search the immediate area, he added.

Roush debriefed another responder. After he shot the bad guy, Roush asked what he was going to do next.

"Second shooter," said the teacher.

Roush: "There you go. With your gun in your holster?"

Responder: "No, keep it out."

Sonewald: "You said that you would secure the firearm or direct somebody else to. Tell me what you'd do, how would you secure it?"

The responder said he would ask somebody to secure it.

Sonewald: "I'm a reasonably cool, calm, collected high school senior, tell me what to do."

Responder: "Pick up the gun, and bring it to me."

Sonewald: "Errrr. You're asking a high schooler to handle a firearm. That was a total set up, dude."

The responder and other teachers laughed.

Sonewald said the responder had two choices — to secure the firearm or not secure the firearm. But do not get somebody else to secure it. He or she may pick up the gun unsafely or hand it over unsafely without realizing it.

Try to get your gun back into its holster as soon as possible, but not before checking for a second shooter, he added.

The rest of the group went through the scenario. One teacher shot the first figure target to become visible, a young black man holding a flashlight, and then missed when shooting at the active killer. But most completed the scenario satisfactorily and, with a little prompting, went through the check-list of what to do following the shooting of the active killer.

T.R., head of custodians for a rural school district.

"First, I came here. I actually was trying to get the school to let me carry, and they wouldn't let me do it, so I came to the first FASTER class. They were kinda' on board, but they weren't really quite comfortable with that, and our local police chief, he asked me if I would go to OPOTA (Ohio Peace Officer Training Academy) to become a police officer, and then I would be just a police officer in the school. I would still do my normal job, I'd just carry a weapon at school, and I'm the resource officer. I have full arrest powers. I carry open with my badge on my belt. I wear my normal work clothes. Everybody knows who I am.

"It's such a small district, and our sheriff, he's very much on board with arming teachers. They actually give free concealed-carry classes to school employees, the county does that, and he's very much on board with that."

We then moved as a group to Live-Fire House 2, where another scenario awaited the teachers. This was the same house and layout our group had been through the previous day with roped guns and with real people standing in for active killers. Instead of pointing their guns but not shooting, the teachers pointed and shot at figure targets.

The house was divided into two sections by a center wall. The first scenario involved the teachers going up the left side of the house, mostly keeping to the center wall, which would have made it easy for them to protect their guns from fleeing people — if the teachers were right-handed, that is. They progressed through two empty rooms to the last room on the left-hand side, where the figure targets were located. The bad guy, a white guy with black curly hair, wearing a black Kawasaki T-shirt, was pointing a gun with his left hand, while holding a young blonde girl with his right. The girl's head was about at the level of the gunman's stomach, so his chest and head were clear targets. However, several teachers managed to hit the girl in the head while trying to shoot the gunman. John Benner ran the scenarios with help from Chris Wallace and other instructors.

Again M.E. was first to navigate the scenario. Benner said her shooting was okay, though one of her shots was rather close to the little girl's head.

"Think about taking more time. You were really fast, but slow down. You've got to move at a speed that lets you understand what you see."

By moving too fast, she moved too far into the room, without taking advantage of the cover provided by the doorway. She also led with her gun, which might allow a guy on the other side of the doorway to grab it before she could see him. Benner suggested she bring the gun in closer to her body when going through doorways or rounding corners. Most of the teachers didn't follow Wallace's advice to shoot from outside the room; they moved too far into the room before they shot.

After all the teachers had gone through the scenario, we waited outside while the instructors rearranged the targets, moving them from the last room on the left to the last room on the right.

In debriefing one teacher, Benner said: "You did probably the best job I've seen today, as far as using your space. I think you're the first one to fire from outside the room. So, outstanding and also fast. Always think of using your space. Like I said, when you use the angles the way you did, you can pick them up a little bit at a time. You see some people rush into a room, and they stand there like this, going back and forth, trying to figure out whom they're going to shoot. You did a great job."

Benner and Wallace congratulated a female teacher on doing a good job.

After all members of our group had gone through the second scenario in LFH2, we returned to LFH1 for a second scenario there. This time the targets were in the last room on the left, and two of them were active killers with an unarmed woman obscuring one of them.

A teacher had only one round in his pistol. He fired once, realized his gun was empty, and reloaded quite quickly and efficiently.

Sonewald: "You shot; you had only one round. So when you check your pistol, press-check, take the magazine out, look at what's in it. Enough said about that. Shots, I see one in the torso, and I see one in the other guy's throat, and I don't see any in the no-shoots."

Most of the teachers knew what to do after shooting the active killers:

• Search for other gunmen;
• Cover the shooters;
• Secure their guns;
• Instruct someone to call 9-1-1;
• Instruct others to render first aid;
• Instruct one person to stand with their hands up to intercept responding officers, while remaining close enough for the responder to hear when they arrive;
• Holster the gun, if possible.

After members of both groups had gone through four scenarios each in the two Live-Fire Houses, they returned to the range for a session of shooting steel at seven yards.

Day Three

The third day started on the range with teachers firing their first shot from the holster at fifty feet. The instructors also did this. John Benner declared the teachers were better than on their first day. He encouraged the teachers to practice weapon manipulation and dry firing when they got home.

Chris Wallace: "Just remember, when you're shooting, keep in mind everything you do today. If you make a mistake, and it can be an honest mistake, and your mission here, your life as you know it will end the split second you shoot the wrong person. It's not going to matter what your intentions were. Nothing else is going to matter. Your life as you know it will end if you shoot the wrong person, period."

Benner: "But the bottom line is, there isn't anybody here that hasn't failed in the scenarios at different times. So if you fail one, take it to heart. And I know that the ones that I failed in my career are the ones that really taught me something. Okay, I made that mistake. That sticks with you a lot better than the ones that you really do well on. Do the best you can. That's all anybody can ask."

After more shooting on the steel targets, Jim Irvine gave the teachers a refresher on first aid. He showed them how to put on a tourniquet and how to improvise one. Use compression bandages for junction wounds. With a chest wound do not forget to check for an exit wound. For a sucking chest wound, seal it with a plastic bag or duct tape. The teachers had had a whole evening on first aid in the FASTER I class.

Chris Wallace taught the teachers how to secure a gun from a downed active killer. "We've already talked about how many of them commit suicide, which is usually a head wound, instantly lethal, obvious that they're dead. If you shoot them down and they're unconscious or dead, you've got to recover the weapon. What happens when people shoot themselves in the head is, the gun cycles. It doesn't know they're dead; it's ready to perform again. And I've seen this on the street numerous times, and one of my officers almost got shot in the face recovering a weapon from a dead guy, because the gun cycled, and he went to pull it out of the hand."

People can convulse for several minutes after death, and with a finger on the trigger, they can fire another shot. So to recover a gun from a corpse or somebody who is unconscious, do not approach from the muzzle end, and do not strip it towards your body.

"You see that space behind the trigger? A good way to do this — and what I have used several times on the street to strip guns off corpses — is to take a pen and stick it behind the trigger. There's no way that gun will fire."

If you don't have a pen, you can put a finger or thumb between the back of the trigger and the frame. If you have a 1911-style pistol, you have to get something between the hammer and the back of the slide. To discharge it, that hammer has to get to the firing pin.

B.H., a school-district superintendent for a small district, K through 12, all in one building.

So far, he and a maintenance worker who is a retired police officer are the only staff members to carry.

"The board was very comfortable with us doing it. In fact, our community is very supportive of this I think, but our plan is not public. We have not told the community we are armed. I think long-term we'd like to get more people armed. I've been in the district for eleven years, as a teacher, all the way up, and they obviously knew the retired police officer. So that's what initiated it. We've been carrying at school for two years."

He carries a Smith & Wesson M&P Shield in 9mm concealed every day using a belly band.

"It is a little bit easier for me, because I wear a suit. The majority of times the suit coat covers quite a bit of it. But it's always interesting when little kids in the elementary come running up to you; they want to give you a hug. I always have to remember, because they don't know."

B.H. says he can draw it reasonably quickly, and he practices on his own, though it is not as quick as drawing from an open-belt holster.

"Probably the biggest problem was just getting used to having that on you all day. Even though it's not all that heavy, it has to become part of your normal routine in the morning."

Force-on-Force House

Our group went to the Force-on-Force House in the morning. This was fortunate, because the other group went in the afternoon when it was much hotter. The building is a two-story house, finished inside with unpainted chipboard, which makes it dark inside. It has stairs at each end. It is used for scenarios employing Airsoft guns, which shoot plastic pellets. It has no air conditioning.

Scenario 1

A classroom was set up on the second floor, and the armed staff member or responder was teaching the class. This consisted of about half-a-dozen other teachers sitting in rows facing the responder. Behind the rows of teachers there is an open door, where the responder can see the landing at the top of the stairs. There is an unarmed staff member at the top of the stairs. The active killer climbs the stairs, yelling: "I'll kill everybody in here," and shoots the staff member at the top of the stairs, then turns towards the classroom. The responder attempts to get the students out of the line of fire, then engages the active killer. The group of twelve teachers was divided in half, with six acting as responders, so the course was run six times. Those who didn't act as responders in this scenario were the responders for the next scenario.

The first responder neglected to move his teachers into the safest corner at the back of the classroom, away from the entrance where he had spotted the active killer. He ran forward to the door, through which he could see the killer. He didn't make the best use of space and cover, though he took out the killer. He could have set up an ambush to shoot the killer as he entered the classroom. The second responder had the same problems and would likely have been killed.

Another responder did not herd the students into the safe or hard corner. He asked Wallace how far he should go in tackling the killer.

Wallace: "The problem is, if you are responsible for a classroom, you can't go hunting for him, because if you go out there and get shot, then he just comes in and kills them

In a classroom scenario in the Force-on-Force House, students cower against the wall while the teacher takes on the bad guy.

all. If you are a classroom teacher, you are responsible for that classroom of kids."

If you are a school staff member, you're either a hunter or you're an ambusher. So, if you're a classroom teacher, you're always an ambusher, because you can't leave your kids, Wallace said.

"So the minute you start moving out to hunt this guy, you're shirking your responsibility to protect your kids. If you're an administrator or custodian or something like that, you're a hunter, because you're not responsible for a specific group of kids. You can move around. Your classroom teacher can't."

Scenario 2

The Second Scenario was organized downstairs and involved two active killers. The responding staff member enters the building from outside. He or she can see an area in front of a window where an active killer is shooting unarmed victims. Three of these victims are lying on the floor of the area with white cards on them describing their injuries. One has arterial blood spraying from an arm or

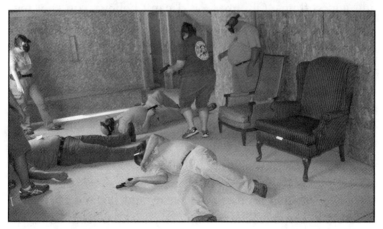

Responding teacher checks for more threats after shooting the two killers on the floor with guns still in their hands.

leg, another has a sucking chest wound, while a third has been shot in the head, and brain matter is visible. The killer has his or her back to the responder. There is a wall angle that provides cover for the responder as he or she advances. Making use of angles and space, the responder is able to shoot the killer in the back. Having shot the active killer, the responder enters the area and has the option of taking the killer's gun or working on the casualties. The second active killer emerges at a doorway at the far end of the area and engages the responder.

"What they're going to have to do is recognize that there's a second shooter in here and figure out how to engage that shooter without getting shot," Wallace said. "When both gunmen are down, the guns are in their hands with their fingers on triggers. The responder is going to have to retrieve both weapons from the downed shooters without discharging them.

"If they improperly strip the weapon, their finger's going to be on that. If they just yank it out, it's going to discharge. One of the others of you who's not wounded will then fall on the floor and say: 'You shot me, you s.o.b.' And start screaming and yelling. 'Oh, my God, I can't believe you shot me. My parents are going to sue you.' And go on like that."

If the responder lays the gun down to attend the one who was shot by accident, another role player who is still standing will pick up the gun and just go: 'Hey, you forgot this.' Bam! The gun will go off again, and another role player will fall down. Then they'll all be yelling at the responder, while he's trying to complete the medical protocol. Tourniquets and other first-aid equipment were there for the responder to use.

"We did this scenario last year, and it's the only time I've ever seen a teacher completely lock up from stress — just become paralyzed."

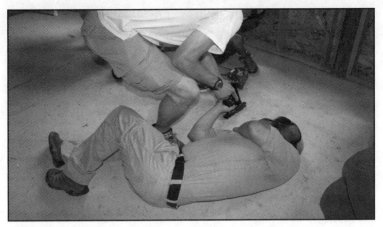

Taking the gun away from a downed gunman.

The first responder shot the first active killer, but didn't take the gun from him, so a student picked it up and "accidentally" shot another student. She also didn't realize there was a second shooter, who would have shot her while she was tending to the wounded.

Wallace: "You've got to recover this weapon right away. It's surprising what can happen. Tactically, on this thing, when he (the second shooter) came out, he'd have just shot you."

The next responder realized there were two shooters and effectively put them down. Wallace said he did a good job at putting the killers down, but he didn't secure the guns immediately. Students tried to secure the guns, and they accidentally discharged, wounding other students.

"Get those weapons right away. We've got two or three extra people who got shot because the weapons weren't secured. But you did a good job in recovering it. I mean you got your finger behind the trigger and pulled it out. That was good."

Several other responders didn't realize there was a second shooter and would have been shot. Wallace recommended asking the other students in the room.

Wallace: "Seriously folks, we're all laughing about this, and we just talked about this on the range, and you saw just how easy it is to forget a little thing like that when you get under stress, and the consequences are that we're getting other people shot, so there is a very serious side to this."

Wallace said the scenario was very complicated. It is rare that somebody gets it 100 percent correct because there is so much going on.

"It's complicated, and it gets very stressful, as some of you have seen."

Scenario 3

This takes place downstairs in the area where the previous scenario was set up. Several bodies were scattered around with their wound-description cards. At the far end, the active killer is standing just outside the doorway, where the second killer emerged in Scenario 2. As the responder entered the room, the killer put his pistol to his head and committed suicide, falling back so his body was hidden behind a partition. His feet were still visible.

The correct course of action for the responder was to check for a second shooter, secure the gun, and treat the wounded, while directing one onlooker to call 9-1-1 and sending another, with hands up, towards where the police would arrive, to explain the situation.

The first responder to go through the scenario did well. He didn't ask whether there was a second shooter, but when Wallace asked what else he could have done, he said he could ask about another shooter.

Wallace praised another responder for doing a good job.

"That was an excellent job, very good, very clear understanding of what was going on; good job stripping the weapon, obviously suicide, right? Good approach on him. Got that weapon recovered and secured it. And very calmly took care of the rest of it. I liked that you used the commanding tone in your voice — that was very helpful — and that the correct medical protocol was applied. So that was a very nice job."

Wallace asked him what else he could have done, and again the responder replied he should have asked if there were any other shooters.

The next responder did ask if there were any more shooters.

Wallace: "The only problem I saw is to remember that down is not necessarily out. You came over here, looked at him, and turned your back on him. If it's clear that he has a serious head wound, and you've got brain matter on the floor, you'd probably get away with that. If he shot himself in the chest, we want to make sure he's dead first."

The last responder also turned his back on the shooter.

Wallace: "The tactical response started out really good. Obviously, if he shoots himself in the head and falls behind the wall, you can't see the gun. You came 'round here, using your space, but then you came in and turned your back on him. And that's when he got the gun up and shot you."

He continued: "Sometimes people will get shot, and they'll go down. When they're prone, their blood pressure comes back up to the brain, and they'll regain consciousness, and then they're dangerous. So if you've got a guy down, and it looks like he's unconscious, get that gun right away."

Day Three, Afternoon
After lunch our group moved to the upper range, where the school hallway with three doorways off it was located.

D.B., who with his wife J.B. is on a church safety committee. Their situation is complicated, because a school meets at the church, so they have to be approved by both church and school to carry.

"I think the most important thing I have learned today is the importance of the priority system they've given for dealing with the scene immediately after the fact. Take care of the threat, secure the area, be darned sure of that, then deal with the rest of the things that they gave us: get people notified, get people posted, and take care of medical — all that's secondary to the threat. Then secure the scene — make sure the children aren't in a panic, try to get the guns, make sure that you know where the guns are, not turn your back on any guns that are still in the hands of anybody who might do you harm if they came to…if they were able to do something. That was eye-opening, because I hadn't had to practice that. I'd never even thought of it in reality."

Scenario 1

The responder is in the school office on the far side of the hallway when an active killer starts shooting in the school parking lot. The responder runs out of the office and down the hallway to the doorway into the parking lot, where he or she takes on the killer, shoots him down, then goes through the check list.

Forrest Sonewald did the debriefing. "Nobody's perfect. When you mess something up, consider it a teaching moment — learn from it."

When responders came down the hallway, he saw different approaches to the door into the parking lot.

"I watched some people swing wide in the interior (of the hallway) across the door, scanning the parking lot. Very nice. I saw others come right up to the opening: not as good. Think, if I can solve the problem from that other area, if I've got a clear shot at the bad guy out here, and if I'm reasonably confident in my skill that I can make the shot. Better to do it in that area than to enter the bad person's world, which is the parking lot."

When the responder enters the parking lot, he should do it as though he is entering a room, checking the hard corners before emerging. Sonewald said he heard responders ask whether there was another gunman.

"A lot of good questions being asked; nicely done. Then the chaos. What do we prioritize? This scenario was set up to be spread out; it's a mess."

The dead and wounded are scattered among the vehicles. The first priority is to secure the shooter's weapon. Having taken it away from the killer, what to do with it? One possibility is to find a responsible adult who is not freaking out and tell him to stand guard over it.

"I wouldn't necessarily hand it to him, because I don't know the firearm's capability, but I'd slide it under the nearest part of a car, near a tire or something like that, and say: 'You can't leave. I don't care if somebody is injured or not, you can't leave. You're responsible for that.'"

Then the responder is freed to organize calling 9-1-1, to post someone to anticipate the arrival of law enforcement, and to supervise the application of medical aid to the wounded.

Sonewald said he had seen some tourniquets applied incorrectly and explained the right way to apply them. He encouraged the teachers to practice with them, so correct application becomes routine.

"You've got to take these out more than once a year for your annual training. Play with them."

Scenario 2

In one of the "classrooms," two guys are struggling with the active killer to get the gun away from him, while he is holding it at arm's length above his head. The responder has to decide who the killer is and deal with him. The responder neutralizes the killer and goes through the checklist, including coping with the wounded.

Again, Sonewald debriefs the responders who went through Scenario 2.

"This is a tough one, because people were turning. You had a bunch of hands on a pistol — three sets. And the hardest thing was determining who was the bad guy. The thing that followed that was people asking the question, which was good: 'Who's the bad guy? Who's the bad guy?'"

Most of the responders heard somebody say it was the guy in the white shirt, and they shot him. Nobody else was hit.

"Good, good. The first thing we need to do after we get rid of the bad guy is what? Secure the weapon, okay. We had a weapon that was handed out to somebody. They were told to stand on it, and not do anything else. What happened? They picked it up, figuring holding it is probably safer than standing on it, and they promptly shot themselves — worst-case scenario.

"Think about securing it. When you've got that many people milling around, don't pass the weapon to someone else unless you personally know their firearms handling skills."

In this scenario, you have three people twisting around. Make sure that when you shoot the bad guy you don't do it if somebody is in line behind the target and will get hit if the bullet passes through the bad guy.

R.Z., a junior-high and high-school math teacher at a small private school.

When she gets back to her school, she said she may set up her room "just a tad bit differently, just to keep my kids a little safer, a little bit more organized, maybe move my first-aid supplies to a different location than where I've got them now in my room. And I will be sharing so much with our principal about what I have learned."

Scenario 3

The parking lot is the scene of a sports rally. One of the students pulls a gun and starts killing others. The responder takes on the killer and shoots him or her down, gets somebody to call 9-1-1, and starts coping with the wounded. A sheriff's deputy, played by Cameron McElroy, arrives with his gun drawn, and the responder follows orders. Eventually the deputy helps cope with the wounded.

Sonewald: "You guys did pretty good. In the previous group, we had three people shot because they tried to draw on an officer. Cameron's yelling: 'Police, get on the ground.' He's wearing an armored-plate carrier that says Sheriff across the front, and he's already got his gun out."

He told the teachers not to assume anybody is proficient at handling firearms or has any medical knowledge.

"Do what you're doing, but go over and check to make sure everything's okay. If you had to move somebody, what do you do after you move them? Recheck the tourniquet; recheck their bandages to make sure they're not messed up and haven't been pulled out of position."

Sonewald talked about stationing a student to intercept police. When the officers arrive, they may yell and scream at him.

"If he locks up, you don't get the warning, or he doesn't convey the right information. I'm not trying to sow seeds of doubt in your mind, but try to hedge your bets. You know law enforcement is coming. If you can free someone up, stand them out there, hands up. Tell them: 'As soon as you see a police officer, don't wait, start yelling: shooter's down, shooter's down, an armed staff member is in the room and we've got wounded' — whatever you want to direct them to yell, but make it simple and tell them to be loud."

Sonewald said don't give an active killer a warning by telling him to drop his gun. You may give him the opportunity to shoot at you, and you may become a casualty.

"So, when you have the opportunity, if it's clear that's the shooter, no verbal warning, pop him, okay. That may be the only opportunity you get, because the gun may be coming your way."

Scenario 4

A man armed with a handgun and carrying what appears to be a bomb is in the hallway. The responder shoots him down, then attends to the wounded without getting them away from the bomb.

Sonewald said the responder will not know what is going to trigger the bomb. It is possible the killer may have a "dead-man's switch" to set off the explosion. A dead-man's switch is a device that will detonate the bomb when the killer relaxes his grip on it. It's like holding a grenade with the pin out. However, dead-man switches are very rare.

"In the movies, everybody has a dead-man's switch because it sounds that much more dangerous and evil, but the reality is even the bad guys screw up, and often when they try to use those, they blow themselves up."

The bomb might be on a timer, or he might have made the device live when he fell down. It is too hazardous to move it, so we need to evacuate the people.

"How far away is far enough? I would get outside the building and as far away as possible. Most of the blast will be contained inside the building, but it depends on the size of the explosive device. Even outside the building, that over-pressure is going to blow out the windows. Where do you think that glass is going to go? Where were you standing? And I don't have that kind of luck. So if you can't evacuate, barricade in place. Get behind the biggest, heaviest concrete wall you can possibly get behind and hope for the best."

After the fourth scenario, the group returned to the classroom, where they received their certificates.

C.B., who teaches art to grades seven through twelve in a very rural school district.
She took the first FASTER class two years ago. She is taking the second FASTER class: "Because I need to get

better at what I do. It is a very big responsibility, and I don't want to miss my target. I need to get better, and I need to keep in practice."

She carries a Springfield Armory in 9mm caliber in a belly band or on her ankle. She doesn't carry a spare magazine.

"I know the ankle isn't the best place to carry it, but it's difficult to conceal with my build. It depends on the clothes I'm wearing."

What got her into it in the first place?

"I thought I'd find it interesting, and I would like to do that if I could save someone's life. If I didn't do it, and something did happen, and kids were killed, and I didn't do anything to try to prevent it, or I didn't know how to prevent it when I could have, that would really make me feel terrible."

FASTER III

The next step in the training of school staff by Tactical Defense Institute is for instructors to go to the schools and work with armed staff members, unarmed staff members, and with local law enforcement. They train the unarmed staff in coping with the wounded and supporting the armed staff. The armed school staff members get to work with local law-enforcement officers, John Benner said.

"It's really interesting to watch the bonding that occurs between them."

TDI put on a FASTER III in the fall of 2015. The law-enforcement officers included the local sheriff's deputies, members of the Ohio State Highway Patrol, and local police officers.

The class lasts two days. They start with an initial talk about the program, mainly for the law-enforcement officers and the unarmed school staff who have not been exposed to the earlier FASTER courses. Paramedics teach the unarmed school staff emergency medical care for coping with the wounded. The armed staff and law-enforcement officers are paired up together.

"We don't let the policemen run with the policemen. We pair them up with the school staff, so they are all interacting. And now they bond. They get to know one another. So now if I'm the policeman responding in here, I've worked with you guys, I know who you are. Coming in here, now I have no fear of shooting the wrong person."

They run force-on-force scenarios using the Airsoft guns. Each officer and school staff member gets the chance to be the good guy, the bad guy, and the victim.

"We use everybody in every different role," Benner said.

The law-enforcement officers see how the armed school staff members operate.

"They see how well the school staff performs, so it really develops confidence in the law-enforcement officers."

He says it really works out well. By the end of the two days, all the law-enforcement officers supported the program.

Benner said that one of the School Resource Officers, a police officer, came to him and said: "When I came in here, I was adamantly opposed to this. I did not believe in it; I was really, really upset by it. Now I am on board. I thought I could protect them, but now I see that I need help."

In November 2015, Benner, Jim Irvine, and Dick Caster attended the Ohio School Board Association annual meeting. Caster, one of TDI's instructors, moderated a panel of three administrators from armed school districts. The event was packed.

Benner said about forty-five school districts in Ohio had armed teachers and staff. He expects more school districts to arm staff as a result of that meeting. He said there are other Ohio school districts that have passed a policy to arm school staff. However, some of these require armed school employees to have only a concealed-carry permit. Benner said that is not enough, but he can offer them free training thanks to the Buckeye Foundation.

Chapter 8

ALICE TRAINING: THE UNARMED RESPONSE

"I think the Gun Free Zone thing is ridiculous."
— Greg Crane, ALICE Training Institute

When Columbine happened in 1999, Greg Crane was a police officer and SWAT team member in the police department of North Richmond Hills, a suburb of Fort Worth in Texas. His wife Lisa was principal of an elementary school in the Burleson Independent School District, just south of Fort Worth.

On December 24, 2000, Crane, his family, and a fellow SWAT team member's family were having Christmas Eve dinner together. They were watching the six-o'clock news when they saw a report that Aubrey Hawkins, a police officer with the Irving Police Department, had been killed in the line of duty. Irving is another suburb in the Dallas-Fort Worth Metroplex. Hawkins was shot and killed responding to a robbery-in-progress by seven prison escapees at a sporting-goods store. About a month later, six of them were caught and the seventh committed suicide. All six were tried, found guilty, and sentenced to death.

"It was a sobering moment, Christmas Eve, to know that a father and a husband had been taken away in such a brutal manner. But it started a discussion 'round the dinner table about the dangers of our jobs," Crane said.

As police officers, Crane and his SWAT team colleague were aware of the dangers they faced daily, but referring to the school shootings of the mid- to late-1990s, Crane pointed out to his wife that schools were not as safe as they used to be.

"I asked her a question I'd never asked anybody in the civilian world: 'What are you guys doing before we can get there?'"

"Her response was their Code Red plan, which was a Lockdown plan. 'We all sit in a corner and wait for you guys to get there.'"

Crane said he could understand securing in place, but gunmen have broken into supposedly secure areas, and second, what about areas that can't be secured, like the Columbine library or the Thurston cafeteria?

"I said: 'What are you telling people to do if they are in that kind of environment? They can't even get a locked door, or the locked door is now defeated?' And she just looked at me with a blank stare, and she said: 'Greg, nobody has ever told us anything about any of those scenarios.'"

"So I went out, like most cops, and tried to steal somebody else's work, and I couldn't find it," he said.

So Crane built a program for his wife's school, and the ALICE training program was born. ALICE stands for Alert, Lockdown, Inform, Counter, Evacuate, not necessarily in that order. The program was launched under the name Response Options but it became better known under the acronym, so it morphed into "ALICE Training Institute" (ATI).

Initially, Crane and a couple of other instructors traveled the country doing training for the schools directly.

"There was one year I think I was home for six weeks out of the whole year."

He realized they had to come up with a better way to deliver the program. So in 2007 he started the instructor program to teach local school-resource officers as instructors, and they would teach the program.

"That immediately became just a phenomenon, and the program grew exponentially with the local police officers taking the program to their local schools themselves.

"It did two things: one, I could teach a class of thirty, and that thirty could then teach thousands. Also, when you had the local police officer coming back saying, 'Hey, I went to this program. This is what we have to do instead of Lockdown,' it carries a lot more weight with local school officials than me coming to them saying, 'Hey, I want to challenge your Lockdown program.'"

After Sandy Hook the program grew again to the point where it became very difficult to administer. Crane teamed up with a businessman from the Cleveland area of Ohio, where the administrative side of the business — the sales team and the office — are located, though Crane and his wife still live in Texas.

"It has grown from me driving the truck pulling the RV with Lisa, my wife, in the back seat as the secretary, the scheduler, the bookkeeper, and all that, to now when we have a full-time staff of about twenty-five with about eighteen to nineteen working in the Cleveland office full-time," he said.

He left police work and did some contract work overseas. When he came back he taught Criminal Justice for Burleson ISD for a while. Burleson was the first school district to implement ALICE.

They trained the staff at all thirteen campuses and the freshman high-school class. They were in the process of negotiating a contract to train tenth, eleventh, and twelfth grades, with ongoing training for new staff and new students. Then came the Amish school shooting (see Chapter 3) and the Platte Canyon High School incident in Bailey, Colorado, where a fifty-three-year-old man took seven girls hostage, sexually assaulted all of them, and shot and killed one before killing himself.

"Local Dallas/Fort Worth media got wind of what Burleson was doing different from everybody else in the country," Crane said.

It resulted in national and even international publicity. "We were on the front page of the *Beijing Times*: These crazy Texans teaching their kids to fight back against shooters."

Crane was on all the national TV shows. "For the most part, once I got to talk to the media, and they understood what we were doing, we really got very little push back. In fact the media has been very friendly over the years."

He did a Google search and found more than eighteen hundred news stories written about ALICE in twelve months. More than 90 percent of them were positive, about 6 or 7 percent were neutral, and about 2 percent were negative.

"The vast majority of our local reporting is very positive, supportive of the schools and what they are doing, supportive of the local police providing the training."

The local police have reported back to him that it improves their relationships with the local schools.

When the publicity about ALICE came out — that Burleson ISD was responding differently to the active killer threat — the school district canceled the contract. Crane found out later that this was because the Burleson police said they could not support what the school district was doing.

"The Burleson thing, while initially it seemed like it was going to be just a huge hurdle to get past, it actually — the press and notoriety we received from it — was just a catapult. We went from nobody knowing our name to suddenly I'm getting invited to places all over the country," he said.

ATI has had people come to its classes from abroad, and they are thinking of teaching internationally. He has had inquiries from Kenya, and the second-in-command administrator of the state university system attended a training Crane put on in Grapevine, Texas, last year. He told the class that in his country they had just had an attack on a university where 130 students were killed. He said they needed something like ATI training.

ALICE Instructor Course
So what is ALICE training?

Greg Crane kindly allowed me to take the two-day ALICE Advanced Training course. It was held in March 2015 at Oklahoma City Community College and was sponsored by the college's police department. The instructor was Kenny Mayberry, a lieutenant with Southeast Missouri State University Police Department. He had a metal prosthesis instead of a right hand. I asked him how he lost his hand, assuming he had been in Iraq or Afghanistan, but he said he had been born that way. Later I asked Crane about Mayberry.

"You want to see something phenomenal: watch that guy load magazines — unbelievable — reload his gun, reload his magazines," Crane said.

The class consisted of twenty-one participants including fourteen law-enforcement officers, five educators from schools and colleges (including one elementary-school principal and a local school-district assistant superintendent), and me. There was also the executive director of an Episcopal church camp and conference center in Granbury, Texas, that is affiliated with the Episcopal diocese of Fort Worth. They have six hundred kids during the summer-camp season.

"We do get a lot of both business people and educators come through the class, but the vast majority — probably 70, 75 percent, I think is the number right now, for the instructor-level class — is local law enforcement, because they're the ones the schools ask," Crane said. "A lot of times the schools will pay for the local law enforcement to come. It's a collaboration, and that's always how I wanted it to be."

I have referred to the ALICE class participants generally as "trainees," because they will return to their home bases as educators who will provide instruction to law-enforcement officers, school teachers, administrators, and others — multiplying the reach and impact of the program manyfold.

Day One

We spent the whole of the first day in an interior classroom with no windows. It had three rows of tables and chairs that were more comfortable than those found in fast-food restaurants.

Mayberry started by reciting the mantra: Alert, Lockdown, Inform, Counter, Evacuate. He defined ALICE as comprehensive preparedness training for a violent-shooter event, using infrastructure, technology, and human actions to increase your survivability rate.

"This program has one primary focus and that is survival — to increase the survivability of those who are under attack," he said. "That's what we want to get into everybody's minds: you have got to survive."

Mayberry outlined how Greg Crane came to start ATI, after asking his wife, a school teacher, what she would do when faced with an active killer. He questioned whether Lockdown was the best response in all circumstances.

During his instruction, Mayberry asked a lot of rhetorical questions to encourage class participation. I have not changed his direct quotes, but I have changed many of his questions into statements for easier reading.

Suddenly, we heard a recorded, rather tinny voice call a Lockdown, and most of the trainees dove under their tables. The voice encouraged us to lock the doors and turn out the lights. A couple of people followed the orders, and we were in the dark.

"This is what we're teaching kids, guys," Mayberry said after turning on the lights. He asked the trainees what was the violent intruder strategy at their schools or colleges. The standard instructions for the kids is Lockdown: "Do not attack the shooter, just get down on the ground and cower," he said.

Mayberry demonstrated how easy it is for an active killer to shoot people hiding under desks or tables. He went from one trainee to the next and simulated shooting them.

"How silly is it to get down on the ground and just wait for some son-of-a-gun to come by and pop you in the back? It goes against all your fiber to stay there. How many of you police officers here have told your kids: No matter what the protocol is at your school, you get the hell out of Dodge?"

He asked them to raise their hands, and several hands went up.

"Then why are we accepting it nationally for kids to get down, get in the corner? Why is that accepted nationally?"

Mayberry said there were other alternatives, such as getting out of the area or barricading the door.

"But if you don't have that thought process going, what are you going to do? You're going to die. You're going to stay underneath that table and wait for us in our white knight's hats riding big white horses to save the day. I have trained my entire career as a police officer to be there if an active-shooter event occurs, as I'm sure most of you in law enforcement here have done. But you are kidding yourself and kidding others if you're going to tell them you are going to be there to save them.

"Even if you guys are on campus right here and the shooting starts happening at the other end of this building, can you save those people at the other end of the building? Sure, you're going to try; you can make a good effort; but once that action initiates, who is the true first responder? They are. So we have got to give them some type of knowledge other than just getting down and getting shot. To do something, anything, beats nothing, guys."

A single strategy, like Lockdown, cannot address all situations, Mayberry said. The teachers and students in the classroom have to be given a range of options.

"ALICE gives you a lot of tools for your toolbox. We're not just going to give you a crescent wrench; we're going to give you a whole host of tools to use, okay?"

Accountability versus Survivability

In the "old days" law enforcement told citizens not to fight their attackers. Now law enforcement advises victims not to allow themselves to be put in a car — fight. After 9/11 airline passengers fought hijackers. Things have changed.

"Are the recommendations passive in those instances? No. Then why should we have passive recommendations for an active-killer event?" Mayberry said. "Can account-ability, responsibility, or liability trump survivability?"

The schools are responsible for the kids, kindergarten through Grade 12, from the time they step onto the school bus in the morning to when they step off it in the afternoon. Teachers and administrators have been drilled that they are accountable for those kids and must keep control of them.

"During an active-shooter event, does your accountabil-ity trump their survivability?"

When someone is shooting, those kids are going to get out of the school any way they can, and it will not be in an orderly line chaperoned by a teacher. "We can account for them later," he said.

The average response time for law enforcement is five or six minutes, and that is after the people on the scene have realized what they are hearing is gunfire, not a car backfir-ing or a construction nail-gun. It is from the time of the first 9-1-1 call to arrival of officers on the scene.

Mayberry asked the law-enforcement members in the class what their department's policy was in response to an active-killer event. Do they team up in groups of four or go in alone? Many said they used the single-officer response.

The ALICE course had a lot of crossover with John Benner's armed-teacher training course. Mayberry, like Benner, pointed out the inadequacy of the responses at Columbine and Virginia Tech.

"Sandy Hook shook all of us ATI instructors and everyone in education and in law enforcement to the core."

A couple of weeks before Sandy Hook, ATI conducted a class at a local school of all the teachers from kindergarten through Grade 12. When they went back to follow up, putting the teachers through scenarios after Sandy Hook, the principal of the elementary school said he needed to apologize, because when they were teaching the class he thought: who would do this to an elementary school. He didn't take the class seriously. After Sandy Hook, he did.

Since Columbine, law-enforcement tactics have changed, but many schools have the same philosophy of Lockdown. They need to get the ALICE philosophy to the school boards and superintendents, Mayberry said.

He compared Columbine, Virginia Tech, and Sandy Hook to show that sixteen years of Lockdown have not improved survivability.

He told us to think like a potential target or victim. Think like a twelve-year-old, he said. It is important for superintendents to give teachers and students the authority to break rules and have a series of options when under attack in order to survive.

When Mayberry started teaching ALICE, his oldest son was six. "I started telling him at six-years-of-age to break the window out and run across the field. Get out of there if you had to get out of there. At six I gave him the authority. I gave him the authority in front of the principal."

Mayberry asked the principal what the procedure was in the event of an active-killer incident? The principal said they Lockdown and have the students huddle in a corner and wait for law enforcement. Mayberry asked his son what he would do, and he said he would break out a window and run across the field. The principal started to protest: "You can't...."

"Yes, I can. I can come back to the school and say I'm sorry that my son broke out a window and ran away from here. I can buy you a new window, but I can't replace that kid. I can't replace my son. He's getting out of there, and I have given him the authority to do so."

He said that command, control, and convenience are not the first priority. Survival, not accountability, has to be the priority.

Mayberry urged the class members to go to town hall or school-board meetings to explain the program and say: "If your son or daughter is in that building, I would much rather talk to you and say: 'I don't know where your son is, but he's not in that building.'"

If an event occurs where they have to flee, whether it's at a mall, church, or school, your kid needs to know where they need to go; who they need to contact; what they need to do.

Lockdown is widely used in schools and colleges in the event of an active-killer incident. It usually means that classroom doors are locked, if possible, and the occupants huddle under desks or in a corner of the room. Originally Lockdown was instituted for the convenience of law enforcement. If everybody was instructed to be down on the ground, the only person standing was likely to be the active killer. It is convenient for administrators, because students are locked up and can be accounted for. It is much less convenient for the students.

Mayberry said active killers are not well-trained assassins. Typically the active killer is one guy. In the unlikely event that there are two they will stay together.

"They planned this together; they have fantasized about this together; they want to be together when this happens."

How much time is it going to take for a four-man tactical team to get together when the active killer is shooting people?

"If those people are properly trained without a firearm, take your pen and shove it in his ear. But you have to have the mindset. It can't be the first time you're thinking about it, and that's what this class does."

ALICE just provided us with more tools and other ways to think about the active-killer events, he said.

"We don't care why they're doing it; we just know they're doing it. But we need to know who they are; what they're doing; where they're at; when they're doing it; and how they're doing it."

Mayberry asked how many educators have studied active killers. None. So what gives educators or business professionals the ability to construct the response to active killers? Most police officers tell their own kids to flee, to get out of the building, in case of an active killer in the building.

"In the last fifty years, how many deaths (in schools) have been caused due to fire? None." However, there are lots of safety precautions against fire in schools. There are sprinklers, fire extinguishers, and fire drills. These precautions are recommended or stipulated by the local fire department.

"So why aren't we (in law enforcement) telling kids at this age what to do if the bad man comes to do bad things?"

In a handout that outlined the course, it listed school-associated violent deaths between 1992 and 2010 at 468, of which 348 were shootings.

Lockdown

Lockdown does not interfere with the shooter's or terrorist's objectives and does not affect the skill level needed to achieve them. In fact, it provides some advantages. It provides the killer with a high profile and plenty of publicity for his cause. It does not diminish the number of potential targets, but it ensures little or no resistance from those targets. Locked doors are not a high level of resistance. Lockdown also results in little chance of a killer's plan failing.

"Low to no resistance. That's the key. We've got a lot of people in one area, and there is low to no resistance," Mayberry said.

What are the benefits of Lockdown? It is good for police and administrators.

Command: one word — Lockdown — can initiate the procedure.

Control: they know where everybody is located.

Convenience: it is easily administered and easily followed. "Because we are sheep, right?" Mayberry added.

Police and administrators keep you in place for your safety.

However it is also good for the gunman or terrorist.

Command: mere exhibition of intent forces command change to Lockdown. What has that done for the killer? One act by the killer enables him to control the whole facility. "How easily can somebody control a facility with our current Lockdown situation?" Mayberry said.

Control: procedure requires everyone to remain in place.

Convenience: minimal action achieves the most difficult objective (containment of a large, complicated structure).

Lockdown keeps you in so the shooter can kill you.

Lockdown bases survival on the inability of the bad guys to reach innocent people before police contact. Historically there have been four possible endings:

• Police intervention.

- Killer suicide.
- Killer's weapon malfunctions.
- Civilian intervention.

"We've had more deaths with police resolution than with victim resolution," Mayberry said.

From a table in a handout, courtesy of the late Bill Barchers:

- Victims resolved two and a half times the incidents that police did.
- Police-resolved incidents resulted in 25 percent more fatalities than victim-resolved incidents.
- Police-resolved incidents resulted in 30 percent more non-fatal casualties than victim-resolved incidents.
- Victim-resolved incidents resulted in almost three times fewer fatalities than shooter-resolved incidents.
- Police-resolved incidents resulted in 16 percent more casualties than shooter-resolved incidents.

Based on those statistics, we should be trying to cultivate the civilian option in order to mitigate casualties, Mayberry said. There are three human reactions to a violent encounter: fight, flight, or freeze. Lockdown most closely resembles freeze.

He played the 9-1-1 tape from the female teacher who had been hit by glass at Columbine. Patti Neilson says she originally thought the shooting was students making a video. When one of the killers shot at her, she realized it was a serious situation. She was hit by glass when the shot broke a window. She told the 9-1-1 operator she was in the library and several times that she had all the students down under the tables. See Chapter 3 for more details of that 9-1-1 call.

Mayberry had a plan of the Columbine library up on his Power Point screen as he analyzed the call.

"You heard the 9-1-1 operator ask: 'is there any way you can get the doors? Is there any way you can get them out?'

Patti was doing what she was trained to do. She told them: 'get down, get down.'

"For five minutes and twenty-three seconds, these two yahoos were out here causing their mayhem. She's telling everybody to get down. Again, nothing against her; she was doing what she was told and how she had been trained. But look at all these exit routes."

He pointed to all the windows and doors through which the students could have escaped. Although the library is on the second floor, because of the rising ground on which it was built, there was no significant drop from the windows.

"How far and how fast could those kids have run in five minutes and twenty-three seconds, if given the authority to do so ahead of time? That is the thing: tell these kids it is okay to do what you have to do to save your life."

Mayberry predicted that if the trainees had not had a talk with their kids or family members' kids about what they should do in case of an active-killer incident, they would do so when they got home after the course. That was a benefit of taking the ALICE course, he added.

"We want to make sure our kids know what they're supposed to do. We want to make sure people that are in authority know what they need to do to save their lives — to increase their survivability chances."

At both the Amish School shooting and the Platte Canyon High School incident, law enforcement waited before going in, he said.

At Virginia Tech, it was the classrooms where the students cowered under desks that had the highest numbers killed and wounded, Mayberry said. See Chapter 4 for details.

In one room, the killer reloaded three times. Many people do not know much about firearms, so he suggested demonstrating to students how handguns are reloaded, because that is when a gunman is most vulnerable. He also suggested showing students what it means if the slide on a semi-automatic is locked back or if the magazine is not in the gun. People think that the guy with the gun has the power, but that is not always true, he said.

"We want to give everybody options; we don't want to give them mandates," Mayberry said.

He listed seven school attacks that were stopped by unarmed educators or students:

- Thurston High School, Springfield, Oregon, 1998: Jake Ryker, seventeen, led the charge in tackling the gunman and knocked him to the ground.
- South Orangetown Middle School, New York, 2009: Superintendent Ken Mitchell tackled a distraught parent with a gun and disarmed him. No one was injured.
- Hillsdale High School, San Mateo, California, 2009: a former student returned to the school armed with ten pipe bombs. After setting off two and attempting to flee, he was tackled by English teacher Kennet Santana and held until police arrived. No one was injured.
- University of Alabama-Huntsville, 2010: a forty-four-year-old biology professor was attending a faculty meeting, when she pulled a 9mm handgun and started shooting at her colleagues. She killed three and wounded three before her gun either jammed or clicked on empty. Debra Moriarity, dean of the graduate program, led the rush that pushed the shooter out of the room and barred the door. Moriarity is credited with saving the lives of others in the meeting.
- Deer Creek Middle School, Colorado, 2010: a thirty-two-year-old man armed with a high-powered rifle shot and wounded two students before being tackled by math teacher David Benke, a six-foot-five former college-basketball player, who led two others in disarming the suspect and holding him for police.
- Snohomish High School, Washington, 2011: a fifteen-year-old female student attacked two fourteen-year-old

girls in a school bathroom, stabbing them many times. Three football players intervened and stopped the attack.

- Chardon High School, Ohio, 2012: a seven-teen-year-old student opened fire on other students with a .22-caliber Ruger semi-automatic handgun killing three and wounding three before being chased out of the building by teacher Frank Hall.

Alert

"In Any School USA, if we hear 'Lockdown. Lockdown. Lockdown,' what do we know? We know something bad is happening, but we don't know exactly what," Mayberry said.

In one class he taught, there was a teacher who had a Lockdown at her school. Their policy was to put everyone down. She started pushing her students out of the window. The administrators asked her what she was doing. She said something bad was happening, so her students were escaping. They told her all they were doing was bringing around a drug dog.

Mayberry said it is important that as much information as possible about the reason for the Lockdown is given, so teachers can choose what course of action to take — particularly the location of any shooting. It is also important to use plain language rather than codes, which may confuse people under stress. Those close to the scene of the shooting may be better off to barricade the door and stay in place, but others further away have the opportunity to escape from the building and flee.

There is no point in withholding information so the shooter doesn't hear it. "There is no cloak and dagger to this anymore. They know what they are doing, so why are we holding it [information] away from everybody else? There are no secrets in this now. If we know it's Jimmy Smith, we get on the PA and go: 'Jimmy Smith is killing people in the front office.'"

They can now prepare. The people closest to the shooting are in the Crisis Zone. People further away are in the Hot Zone. People in the Crisis Zone will Lockdown, barricade the doors, and prepare for the shooter to make entry into their room. People actually in the office where the gunman is, "they have got to do something to save their lives."

People in the Hot Zone know to evacuate, and if they know where the gunman is they will flee in the other direction.

One trainee asked: "Are 9-1-1 operators now advising people to evacuate?"

"Most are telling people three things: run, hide, fight," Mayberry replied.

Homeland Security has come out with run, hide, fight. "That's pretty much across the nation now. Nobody is telling anybody to get down and just wait."

In giving the Alert, information is the key to making good decisions. The more information we have, the better decisions we can make. Mayberry suggested using as many different methods of communication as possible, such as social media (Facebook and Twitter), messaging boards, intercoms, PA systems, and cell phones.

"Resources should focus on providing real-time information to those under attack."

Information needs to go in all directions — to and from the administration, to and from students, and to staff at the scene. Administration notifies law enforcement, which then takes action.

Mayberry said ATI supports Lockdown as a tool. It is a good starting point. He recommended that classroom doors should be locked while the teacher is in there teaching because it increases survivability.

He said that at Sandy Hook, the killer walked past two closed doors that had construction paper over the windows in the doors, because they had had a Lockdown drill in the weeks before. Given the option, the killer will follow the path of least resistance.

If you have to stay where you are, barricade the door. Pile desks, chairs, and cabinets in front of it. A wedge under the door will hold it closed if it opens inward. If it opens outward, and it has a hydraulic door closer at the top, tie the two arms of the closer together so it can't be opened. Use a belt, shoe-laces, even a bra. If you tie it tightly, the door won't open more than a crack.

"Don't rely on the lock," he said and gave an example. A fourteen-year-old middle-school student armed with a gun broke into three classrooms, smashing the glass of the locked doors to get inside. He ran out of a back door before being apprehended without further incident. Just because the door's locked doesn't mean he can't get in.

Can infrastructure design and security measures guarantee safety? No. But if school and other building designers were to ask law enforcement for input in design, it could improve survivability. Infrastructure can provide options that can increase safety. More doors and exits from the building improve safety when people are trying to evacuate. Upgrading infrastructure should address movement and escape, because preventing entry of a determined attacker is unlikely, Mayberry said.

Inform

Continue the Alert by providing real-time information that allows for good decision-making.

Confuse and frustrate the attacker, Mayberry said. Talk to him over the PA system. If you know who the shooter is, talk to him by name. Ask him why he is killing people in the school. If you can get him to look at the surveillance camera, he is not killing somebody. Yell at him. Tell him he is a loser. Play for time. Redirect his focus and his anger, but the killer is very unlikely to negotiate. He just wants to increase his number killed.

In Arizona a student in the playground shoots a kid. A teacher who is a combat veteran, "walks up to the shooter and says: 'Give me the gun. Why are you doing this?'" The student shoots him.

You need to be able to "flip the switch" from looking at the student as a kid who is there to learn, to a bad guy intent on killing as many people as he can before he is stopped, Mayberry said.

"This is a bad guy; he's still a kid. We need to be able to try to get this through to them — that you've got to be able to flip that switch. He's not here for an educational purpose any more; he's here to kill."

Counter

Mayberry said the program provided educators and students with a range of options. The program never tells people to leave what they believe is a safe area and go track down the killer and take him out "because that's fighting. That is not countering."

I suspect the program is playing semantics. If you are defending yourself against a determined attacker who is trying to kill you, you are fighting for your life. But children have been brainwashed at school to believe that fighting is unacceptable. "Countering" is a word that is more politically acceptable to the educational establishment.

Take advantage of the attacker's fragile psychological state. "This is the most fragile they've ever been in their life. They've planned this thing, planned this thing, planned this thing, and now they've finally decided to pull that trigger. It's not that hard to redirect them, to throw them into a state

Trainees hiding under tables after Lockdown was called. Instructor Kenny Mayberry standing near the door.

of confusion," Mayberry said. "We want to make as much commotion as we can."

When they know the opposition is coming, they will often commit suicide, because their ultimate power is to control when they die, he said.

Police usually have a higher skill level with firearms, but their hit rate in a confrontation is only 20 to 30 percent. Active killers usually have a low level of weapons skill, but their hit ratio is 50 percent plus. Why?

Active killers are shooting static targets, while in a gunfight the officer is often moving, and so is his target. We have to change the killer's hit ratio by introducing stimuli that will make it more difficult for him to shoot accurately. Noise, movement, distance, and distractions all help to do this. Shout and throw things at the shooter: books, laptop computers, chairs, desks, pocket change. They will prevent him from acquiring his target, from his sight alignment, sight picture, trigger control, breathing — all things needed to shoot accurately. Interrupt his OODA (observe, orient, decide, act) Loop. Contact with the gunman is the worst-case scenario, but sometimes it can't be helped. Hit him with distractions, noise, and movement, then swarm him.

Mayberry set up a scenario where two trainees threw soft, red, rubber balls at the head of a "gunman" trainee with a blue plastic gun, who was trying to shoot them. We watched the "gunman" flinch and move the direction his gun pointed — away from the ball throwers.

Moments later, when the "gunman" wasn't expecting it, Mayberry roared, threw balls at his head, and charged him. The gunman, quite discombobulated, was unable to get a "shot" off before Mayberry overwhelmed him.

Take back control by applying stimuli to the killer and by swarming him. Swarming is a technique where all the "victims" rush the killer and overcome him by sheer force of numbers.

Mayberry showed a video of a *Fox & Friends* interview with Greg Crane. He has a classroom set up for a demo. A teacher is at the front of the class, and he has just dismissed the students. A gunman comes in, points a gun at the

After the two trainees threw the balls at the "killer's" head, Mayberry attacks him. Two rubber balls are on the floor.

teacher, and is swarmed by students. One student gets the gun away from the gunman.

When the gunman is down, and you have got the gun away from him, what do you do with it, particularly as you can't count on knowing enough about guns to handle it safely? You don't want to be holding the gun when law enforcement enters the room, or you could be shot in error. Mayberry recommended putting the gun in a small trash can and holding it to your chest. Hug the trash can.

He then showed the video of the black and white teams throwing a ball among them, and the audience is asked how many times one of the teams passes. During this a man dressed as a bear walks onto and off the stage. Who noticed the bear? It is easy to miss something you are not looking for. This is a problem with eyewitnesses.

Evacuate

Provide students and staff with the ability and authority to evacuate. The kids want to know what to do. They want to do what they're told. They don't want to go against authority. This is true of most kids, but particularly in the lower grades.

"It's okay for them to get out of here. They're not going to be breaking any rules and regulations; because, again, we're not just talking high school, we're talking elementary. That it's okay for that six-year-old to run over the hill and to the oak tree, where you had taken him earlier with their picnic," Mayberry said.

The teachers should take their kids away from the school buildings to two or three predetermined locations, where they can gather if they have to evacuate. It is important that the kids know prior to any emergency where they're going to run to. The locations should not be across a major highway or thoroughfare, if possible.

Evacuation means removing as many potential targets as possible. If we get the kids away from the scene, they can't be shot. However, ATI provides options, not requirements.

"If we can get the kids out, get 'em out. If you can gain distance, that's the main thing. We don't give these kids enough credit."

Mayberry has trained his own kids to get out if they can. They know to barricade the door if they can't get out.

Evacuation removes the need for family/friends to come to the scene. It also follows a threatened person's natural response. Whether planned or not, a mass evacuation will occur during an active-killer event.

"With high-school kids, they're going to get out; they're going to evacuate. Whether you want it or not, it's going to happen."

Flee on foot. Don't get into vehicles, because they will cause a traffic jam, which means they can't get out, and first responders may not be able to get in. Few resources are required, but accurate information is required.

Having taken the ALICE program, the law-enforcement officers and educators are now sheepdogs, Mayberry said, using the analogy explained by Lieutenant Colonel Dave Grossman, author of *On Killing* and *On Combat*. Humans are divided into sheep (followers), wolves (predators), and sheepdogs (protectors).

"You are not a sheep. You are not following along. You will take control, and you will take care of that wolf."

Referring to Virginia Tech, Mayberry said when law enforcement reached Norris Hall, they couldn't get through the doors because the killer had chained them. They eventually found a door they could open with a shotgun-breaching round. But while searching for a door they could use, they bypassed windows they could have broken to get in. A girl who had to finish her paper got into Norris Hall through a window.

"She thought outside the box," Mayberry said. "But in law enforcement we're so geared to one thing. So we need to start thinking outside the box as well."

While looking for a door they could use, time was passing, and what the students on the second floor did not have was time.

Mayberry said one of the problems in getting school administrators to incorporate ALICE into school emergency plans is fear of liability and "paralysis through analysis."

If there is a mass shooting at any school, there will be lawsuits, don't doubt it. What sort of defense do you want to offer when your organization and you are sued? "We mandated through policy that the occupants sit passively and wait for help. Or, we provided a range of options and communications in order for students to make decisions as to the best action to take, given the circumstances they faced," he asked.

If they talk about liability, you can tell them that this is not just some private company, but its recommendations are supported and matched by the Department of Justice, the Department of Homeland Security, the Federal Bureau of Investigation, Health and Human Services, the Department of Energy, the U.S. Department of Education, the New York Police Department, and Ohio Attorney General.

- The Department of Homeland Security (DHS) in its video, "Active Shooter, How to Respond: Support for Proactive Response, Strategies and Options," recommends the Three-Outs Program: Get Out, Hide Out, Take Out. It is dated 2008.
- International Association of Chiefs of Police (IACP) Recommendations, October 2009: "Do not have a one-size fits all plan; teachers to choose Evacuate or Lockdown. Active resistance is an option."

- Ohio Attorney General and Safety Task Force Recommendations, June 2013: "Lockdown does not mean a stand-alone defensive strategy of securing in place. Evacuate, barricade, counter, for staff and students."
- U.S. Department of Education Recommendations, June 2013: "Has to be the end of Lockdown as the only response plan for schools. Recommends that all options — evacuation, barricade, and counter or run, hide, fight — be part of both policy and training for staff and students."

DHS defines an active killer as an individual actively engaged in killing or attempting to kill people in a confined populated area.

"What does an active shooter look like? You're not going to be able to pick them out of a crowd. They're normal kids, normal looking kids," Mayberry said.

He showed us a video of an active shooter in a workplace, put together by DHS.

The narrator states: "If you ever find yourself in the middle of an active-shooter event, your survival may depend on whether or not you have a plan. The plan doesn't have to be complicated. There are three things you could do that make a difference: run, hide, fight."

First and foremost, if you can get out, do so. Encourage others to leave with you, but don't let them slow you down with indecision.

The narrator continues: "Remember what's important: it's not your stuff. Leave your belongings behind, and try to find a way to get out safely. Trying to get yourself out of harm's way needs to be your number one priority. Once you are out of the line of fire, try to prevent others from walking into the danger zone, and call 9-1-1.

"If you can't get out safely, you need to find a place to hide. Quickly and quietly try to secure your hiding place the best you can. Turn out lights, and if possible remember to lock doors. Silence your ringer and vibration mode on your cell phone. And if you can't find a safe room or closet, try to conceal yourself behind large objects that may protect you.

"As a last resort, whether you are alone or working together as a group, fight. Attack with aggression and improvised weapons and commit to taking the shooter down, no matter what."

Like Chris Wallace at Tactical Defense Institute, Mayberry encouraged class members to look around their schools and classrooms for anything that can be used for a weapon.

"We're saying counter if you have to," he said. "And you've got to remember this: people in schools have policies and procedures they have to follow."

You have to get around the policies. They can get away with having things like hornet spray and fire extinguishers. Use a fire extinguisher to hit him with or to spray him with. The school could have a perpetual canned food drive and keep cans of food in their classrooms — anything that can be used as an improvised weapon.

Mayberry described a brick program at his wife's school district. After they had taught an ALICE course at the school, one of the teachers went to the superintendent, who ordered about 240 unfired bricks and sent them back to the school. At the school, they gave them to the elementary kids. They all pulled a name out of the hat of a teacher or custodian, and the kids got to decorate the bricks and made holes in them for holding pens and pencils. They dry-kilned them, and then they gave those bricks to those teachers, and those bricks are on every teacher's desk, with little pens or pencils sticking out of them with fuzzy hair and googly eyes, he said.

"But what is that brick really? It is a weapon. It's an empowerment tool. When they're sitting there thinking, 'what would I really do' and just kinda' glance at that. My wife has one on her desk. They glance at that, and they realize: okay, I can do what I have to do to save my kids.

And people just look at it; it's just something to hold pens. Nobody really knows what it is."

"You Comply, You Die"

If an active killer gets into your building, he will try to kill you.

"There is no talking to these people. They are not there to make any kind of plans to deal with you. They're interested in making the highest body count as fast as they can get, because they know what? The Stopwatch of Death has started. They know it is going to get stopped. They know law enforcement is coming to stop it," Mayberry said. "Compliance is dangerous. We cannot comply: you comply, you die."

These attacks are happening everywhere: the Amish school, movie theaters, political functions. Not just at major colleges. Most of the deaths and woundings happen in the first few minutes, when law enforcement is racing to get there or assessing the situation from the outside. Examples include Columbine library, Virginia Tech's Norris Hall, and Northern Illinois University.

Mayberry again went through the lessons from the classrooms in Norris Hall, Virginia Tech. He discussed barricading doors.

He showed a very realistic Columbine library shooting reenactment, then discussed what it showed.

Mayberry divided us into three groups of seven, and we prepared for teach-back sessions the following morning.

Day Two

On the second day, Mayberry had an assistant instructor, David Dickinson from Moore, Oklahoma. He has been a school officer for five years and has trained eighteen hundred people in ALICE techniques in his school district.

"Once they started it they couldn't get enough of it." He said the training is all about empowerment. He added that he learned a lot from teachers.

Mayberry showed us a video of the attempt on President Reagan's life. His Secret Service protection detail didn't fire a shot, but they swarmed the shooter. That is, they rushed him and overwhelmed him.

He reviewed what we had learned the previous day.

One at a time we did our "teach-backs," where each person took a topic and elaborated on it for a few minutes. We covered such topics as: an introduction to ALICE; the role of mental conditioning in survival; ALICE concepts; counter strategies; implementing ALICE in your local organizations; and possible opposition to ALICE and answers.

I provided an example of Run, Hide, Fight from the Tucson shooting. One of Gabby Giffords's staffers ran across the square to a bank on the other side of the shopping center. A second one took cover behind one of the stone pillars that supported the hip roof over the gathering in front of the grocery store. Three or four people tackled the gunman, disarmed him, and held him until law enforcement arrived.

The other trainees each took a part of the above topics and gave us a five-minute lesson on it. Generally they showed a good understanding of their subjects and spoke well.

Chelsey Jones of the U.S. Air Force Security Police performing a teach-back.

Captain Roger McCardle of Fort Sill Police Department as the "killer" involved in a teach-back demonstration. Note the rubber ball that has been thrown at him.

Special-needs kids are going to have difficulty evacuating. Mayberry told a story about one such kid at a school in southeast Missouri. She was in a wheelchair, but she was in regular classes for tenth or eleventh grade. She was there when they did the ALICE presentation to the class. At the end she said, "Can I say something real quick?" She looked over at the rest of the class, and she said: "If this happens, you guys get out of here. Don't worry about me, get out of here." And one of the good guys got up and said: "Oh no. You're going to wrap your arms around my neck, and we're running the heck out of here."

"Just remember people want to help. They want to be able to help," he said.

Some school districts are installing eye-bolts into the concrete beside the doors, so that the handle of the door can be tied to the eye-bolt, making it much harder to get the classroom door open.

Scenarios

In the afternoon, we were subjected to various scenarios in the main college building. We followed our instructors for what seemed like miles of wide hallways, eventually climbing stairs to the third floor. We congregated in one classroom where we were kitted out with face-masks and throat protectors. We were assigned three other classrooms for the scenarios. Two of the classrooms were on one side of a corridor and one on the other, in a triangle formation. We split into our three groups, and one trainee was designated as the active killer. He was equipped with an Airsoft pistol, which shot little plastic BBs that stung when they hit on bare skin.

The first scenario was a traditional Lockdown. When Lockdown was called, our six turned off the lights and huddled under the tables. The shooter came in; he turned on the lights and started shooting people. One of the women in our classroom picked up a chair and charged him. Of the nineteen people in three classrooms, the gunman hit twelve.

The second scenario was Lockdown plus barricading the two doors to our classroom. The gunman only managed to hit Captain Roger McCardle of Fort Sill Police Department in the forearm as he was barricading our door. However the gunman never got into our classroom.

The next scenario had us fleeing from the gunman out of the furthest door and running to the stairs down from the third floor. No one was hit. Mayberry responded by saying: "'I don't know where your kid is,' is better than: 'your kid is dead.'"

Mayberry came into the classroom with the gunman and started talking to us. Suddenly, the shooter brings up his gun

In the Lockdown scenario, a trainee attacks the "killer" with a chair. Note the position of the killer's gun.

and is attacked instantly by the nearest trainee, followed by three more. They swarmed him.

In the final scenario, the three groups played musical classrooms. We were supposed to move from one classroom to the next. On our second move, the gunman appeared. One trainee had an open bottle of water in his hand. He threw the water, not the bottle, at the shooter, then

Barricading the door with a table and chair. Note the arms of the door closer have been tied.

Evacuation.

two other trainees piled on. The rather wet gunman didn't get off a shot before being taken down.

We returned to the first classroom, where we turned in our helmets and throat protectors, while Mayberry commented on the scenarios, then handed us each a certificate of completion.

Thoughts on Armed Teachers

In an interview after the course, I asked Greg Crane what he thought about arming teachers.

"I think the gun-free zone thing is ridiculous. Why should I be okay walking on the street outside your school — I'm not a threat to society — but if I come in your building, now I'm a threat to society? I never have agreed with the gun-free zone thing. If I do what you require of me, I've passed the background check, I've done everything the law

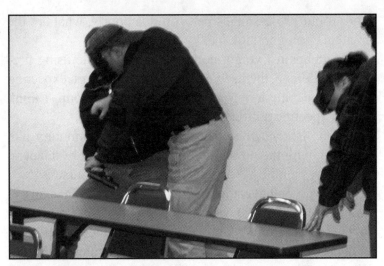

The beginning of a swarm.

requires of me to carry concealed, I should be able to carry concealed wherever I am."

He appears to have no problem with teachers carrying concealed handguns in the classroom to defend themselves and their students. He does have a problem with training teachers to hunt down an active killer.

"If the gunman came into that room, should that teacher have the ability to defend him- or herself? I say absolutely. I just say there's a huge difference between training someone in use of a firearm for self-defense purposes versus training them to become basically a hunter of another human being — being offensive instead of defensive. That is a hugely different level of training and mindset, and it requires a totally different skill-set. I just don't know that by putting a gun in someone's hand and having them run up and down a range for three or four days…. I still train police officers, and I'm completely dismayed at the number of police officers who perform so woefully poorly when you introduce the least little bit of stress. When I'm watching this I'm thinking: my

God, if our professionals perform this poorly, what are the amateurs going to look like?

"And again I've got nothing against people using fire-arms to defend themselves, but when we start expecting them to become a *de facto* armed-response group, I think that's expecting a little bit too much."

Crane is concerned that in a crowded community like a school, with the possibility of many innocent bystanders, some may be hit by "friendly" fire, which of course isn't.

"When you have a lot of friendlies in a confined space, how much lead do we want flying around? Every round has to go somewhere. We know that probably about 70 percent of the rounds at least are not going to hit the intended target. Where are those rounds going?"

The Jake Ryker Award

When Crane was looking into the school shootings and trying to assess how to prepare citizens to respond to active killers, he researched the Thurston High School incident in Springfield, Oregon, on May 21, 1998. A fifteen-year-old student murdered his parents before going to school, where he used a sawed-down .22-caliber rifle to kill two students and wound twenty-three. He was tackled by Jake Ryker and several other students. See Chapter 2.

"Here was a horrific tragedy, and yet a seventeen-year-old, very-young man stepped up in a moment of need," he said. "What Jake did took great bravery, but it didn't take a lot of physical skill. Moving on someone, taking control of a limb, putting them on the ground. That's stuff that kids on the football field do every day. How do you hope to cultivate people like Jake, who have that mindset and have that will to survive?"

Crane said that if one person starts the attack on the gunman, others will follow. But it is important to train the whole group, so everybody knows what is happening.

Jake Ryker receives the inaugural Jake Ryker Award from Greg Crane at the National Association of Resource Officers annual meeting in 2015. (Photo courtesy ALICE Training Institute.)

"Whoever is going to be the first one that's up and doing something, that should trigger a quicker mental process in everybody else, because they've been trained the same way. It will start an overwhelming counter strategy as quickly as it can be done, and that's always been my goal. We can't guarantee zero casualties, but the way we mitigate the casualties to the smallest number is by stopping it as quickly as possible, and that will always be done by the people on the scene already, not those trying to get to the scene."

Once Crane found Jake Ryker's story, he used to recount it to people who doubted that ALICE training would work.

"He was always my counter argument years ago. When people would tell me citizens can't do this, I would say: 'Jake Ryker did.' So it's not a question of whether they can or cannot, it's a question of will they or will they not, and that is all related to what is their mindset based on what has their training been."

So Crane conceived of an annual award named the Jake Ryker Award. The first award was made to Jack Ryker at the National Association of Resource Officers annual conference in Orlando in July 2015.

"The award is going to be given to any K-12 staff or student who in any kind of critical incident — doesn't have to be active shooter, can be a medical situation, bullying, fire, whatever the critical incident is — where a staff member, a student, steps up and interacts in a way that is deemed to have mitigated the casualty number or the severity of the situation. The schools' resource officers will nominate that person for the annual award, and then there will be a committee of us that ranks the nominees, applying a number from one to ten, something along those lines, and whoever scores the highest score will be the annual recipient."

Chapter 9

LUBY'S CAFETERIA:
THE SURGE OF CONCEALED CARRY

"The Second Amendment is not about duck hunting. And, I know I'm not going to make very many friends saying this, but it's about our rights — all of our rights — to be able to protect ourselves from all of you guys up there."
— Suzanna Gratia Hupp, testifying in Washington, D.C., before a House of Representatives committee

It was a sunny fall day in central Texas when Dr. Suzanna Gratia walked into the Luby's Cafeteria in Killeen, Texas, with her mother and father. As they entered the restaurant, Gratia had no inkling that she would be the only one of them to leave there alive.

October 16, 1991, was Bosses' Day, and the cafeteria was packed with employees taking their employers to lunch. Gratia, then thirty-two, was a chiropractor in nearby Copperas Cove. She

Suzanna Gratia Hupp.

and her parents were waiting for her friend, the restaurant manager, to return to their table. They had just finished eating and were dawdling over coffee.

The pleasant atmosphere was shattered when a pickup truck burst through the window into the restaurant, smashing into customers and showering them with broken glass.

At first, Gratia thought it was an accident. She started to go over to help the people knocked down by the pickup.

Then she heard a flurry of gunshots.

Immediately, Gratia and her father tipped over their table and, with her mother, took cover behind it. Gratia decided it must be a robbery, but the shooting continued. Then she thought maybe it was a hit. Perhaps someone important was in the restaurant because it was Bosses' Day. But the driver of the pickup was walking unhurriedly from one person to another shooting them.

"It took a good forty-five seconds, which is a long time, to figure out that the guy was just going to walk around and shoot people," Gratia said. "You kept waiting for him to stop and give some sort of explanation, but he didn't."

By this time, the gunman was standing at the right-front fender of his truck, about fifteen feet from Gratia, still shooting people.

"I thought, I got this turkey. I reached for my purse. I had a perfect place to prop my arm; everybody in the restaurant was down; he was up. Then I realized that a few months earlier I had made the stupidest decision of my life. My gun was one hundred yards away, in my car, completely useless to me. I had made the decision to begin leaving it in my car, because I was concerned about losing my license to practice chiropractic."

Gratia was appalled. She groped for something to do to stop the carnage. She thought about throwing her purse at the gunman. She eyed the sugar container and the butter knife, but the killer had two semi-automatic handguns and was in complete control of the situation. Any attack would be suicide.

Meanwhile, Gratia's father, Al Gratia, was getting increasingly frustrated.

"I've got to do something. I've got to do something. He's going to kill everybody in here," Gratia remembers her father saying, as he started to rise to his feet.

Suzanna grabbed him by the shirt collar and jerked him down, cursing at him and saying: "If you go at him, he's going to kill you, too." But he shook her off and, when he thought he had a chance, tried to rush the killer.

"I remember ducking down because I already knew what was going to happen. He didn't have a chance. The guy could see him coming a mile away. Dad probably covered half the space, and the guy turned and shot him in the chest. My dad went down in the aisle. He was still alive and still semi-conscious, but he was maybe eight feet from me. I saw the wound and, as horrible as it sounds, I basically wrote him off at that point."

After shooting Gratia's father, the gunman changed direction away from her and her mother. For the first time she looked at the gunman's face.

"You think the stupidest things. I remember looking at this guy, thinking, this is a good-looking guy — with a new truck. What could possibly be so wrong in this guy's life that he's doing this?"

The killer reached the wall and fortunately turned away from Gratia. She and her mother were in the front part of the restaurant and were trapped until somebody broke a window near the back. Her first thought on hearing the crash of the breaking glass was that the gunman was not alone. Perhaps it was a terrorist attack. But she saw people escaping through the broken window and knew it was their only chance to get out.

Gratia kept peeking around the table, where she and her mother were crouched, until she saw an opportunity. She stood up with her back to the gunman who was still shooting people, expecting at any moment to be shot.

"I remember standing with my back to the guy, and I kept hearing the gunshots. I kept waiting to feel the impact. I remember feeling that so vividly."

Gratia grabbed her mother by the shirt, pulling her to her feet. "Come on, come on, we've got to run; we've got to get out of here," she urged.

Her feet grew wings, and she ran, not stopping until she was through the window and outside in the sunshine. The restaurant manager, Mark Kopenhafer, met her outside and asked if she was all right.

"I said, 'Yeah, but Dad's been shot.' And I turned around to say something about Mom or something to Mom, and she wasn't there."

Her mother had not followed her out of the restaurant. Gratia learned afterwards from the police what had happened. When they arrived on the scene, the officers knew a man was inside the restaurant shooting people. Earlier, while the gunman had been systematically executing people, everybody was hugging the floor, and it was quiet except for the sound of the gunshots. But when the police arrived, people were scrambling to get out, and pandemonium reigned. The officers could not see who was doing the shooting.

"My mother, according to them, had crawled out into the open where my father was and was cradling him until the gunman got back around to her.

"According to the one cop, he didn't realize who the man was at that point, and he saw the guy look down at my Mom. He said, she looked up at him, put her head down, and then he put the gun to her head and pulled the trigger.

"My parents had had their forty-seventh wedding anniversary a week and a half before, and she just wasn't going anywhere."

The active killer murdered twenty-three people and wounded another thirty-three before he put one of his pistols to his own head and pulled the trigger.

Concealed Carry

In October 1991 Texas had no concealed-handgun law. Only law-enforcement officers could carry concealed handguns legally in the state. At the time only seventeen states were classified as "right-to-carry states." They could also be called "shall-issue states," where if you met the qualifications, you had to be issued a concealed-carry license or permit. There was one exception, and that was Vermont which required no permit to carry a concealed handgun.

The qualifications usually included that the applicant have no criminal record, be at least twenty-one years old (it was eighteen in a few states), not be mentally ill, and qualify under federal and state law to possess a handgun. Most of those states included a list of places where even a permit holder could not carry. These usually listed courthouses, schools, colleges, and private property that was posted. In addition some states such as New York, Maryland, Massachusetts, and California issued concealed-carry licenses at the discretion of the issuing authority.

This resulted in licenses being issued to political cronies, movie stars, wealthy businessmen, other pillars of the community, and sometimes jewelers or people who routinely carried large sums of cash. It did not include single mothers being threatened by former spouses or ordinary citizens threatened by drug traffickers. The obvious conclusion is that officialdom put more value on property than on the lives of its residents. It also appeared to value some lives more than others.

The Florida Legislature passed a shall-issue concealed-carry law that went into effect October 1, 1987. At the time, a dozen other states effectively had shall-issue laws. But Florida created a firestorm. The national media went berserk, calling Florida the "Gunshine" state and predicting that every fender-bender would make the streets run with blood. None of the predicted carnage came to pass. Robbers started picking on people driving rental cars because they were less likely to be armed.

After the Luby's Cafeteria shooting, concealed-carry laws spread like blood from a head wound. Between 1994 and 1996 fourteen more states, including Texas, passed shall-issue laws. Suzanna Gratia, now Suzanna Gratia Hupp since her marriage, helped push these along.

Right after the shooting, she started speaking out. She was a much sought-after guest on radio and television talk shows, because she told the media what they did not expect to hear, and she wasn't afraid to speak out. She said she did not blame the killer, likening him to a rabid dog, and she did not blame the guns he used, calling them pieces of machinery that don't pull their own triggers.

When she balked at going on particularly sleazy programs, she was advised by the late Neal Knox, an NRA board member, to go on all the shows she could. Where else could she get such national attention? And she would get the opportunity to tell her story and give her opinions on the Second Amendment and gun rights. So she accepted most offers appearing on everything from Geraldo Rivera's show to *America's Most Wanted*. She was never paid anything but expenses for any of these appearances.

She created quite a stir when she testified before a Congressional committee about banning military-style semi-automatic weapons. The committee included then Representative — now Senator — Charles Schumer, one of the most anti-gun politicians in the nation. Hupp was scheduled to testify early in the hearing, but was pushed back to later in the day when most of the news media had left. Fortunately, there was at least one camera still running. The video is still floating around on the Internet. After telling her story of the Luby's shooting, she brought up the Second Amendment.

"I've been sitting here getting more and more fed up with all of this talk about these pieces of machinery having no legitimate sporting purpose, no legitimate hunting purpose. People, that is not the point of the Second Amendment. The Second Amendment is not about duck hunting. And I know I'm not going to make very many friends saying this, but it's about our right —— all of our rights — to be able to protect ourselves from all of you guys up there."

At the 1995 session of the Texas Legislature, Senator Jerry Patterson was sponsoring a concealed-handgun bill for the state. He asked her to testify before a Senate committee in favor of the bill. She told her story at the hearing and asked permission to get up and demonstrate. With television cameras rolling, she went around the table pointing her finger like a gun at the senators, showing them how easy it was for the shooter at Luby's to murder the diners. She reached Royce West, a large black Democrat senator from inner-city Dallas, who was leading the charge to keep Texans defenseless. When she pointed her finger at him, he yelled at her to "get that finger out of my face!"

Hupp apologized to the chairman, then asked West: "At that point, Senator, don't you wish you, or someone around you, had a gun and knew how to use it?"

It is interesting that one of the leaders of concealed-carry legislation in the House was Representative Ron Wilson, a black Democrat from inner-city Houston. His wife had been attacked and stabbed by a would-be rapist. Most blacks, particularly Democrat politicians, have been brainwashed to believe that guns in the hands of ordinary people are to blame for violent crime. It is like blaming cars for traffic accidents. They also forget history, when their own firearms were the only things standing between blacks and the fiery crosses of the Ku Klux Klan.

Hupp says she supports concealed-carry licensing because she is a pragmatist, but she feels that citizens should not have to apply for government licenses to practice a Constitutional right.

She says the Texas concealed-handgun law is a big step in the right direction. However, she criticizes it for its cost. She says the inner-city poor — mostly blacks and Hispanics — who live in the highest crime areas can't afford licenses. They are the ones who need them the most. A Texas concealed-handgun license costs $140.

"I think our permitting system is discriminatory at best and racist at worst," Hupp says. "At the very least, we should get rid of the fees."

Hupp likens the cost of the license to the poll tax. For the first half of the twentieth century, Texans had to pay a poll tax for registering to vote. This effectively kept most blacks and Hispanics from voting.

"They are taxing me to be able to exercise a right, and I think that is fundamentally wrong," she says.

Hupp estimates she has testified for concealed carry in front of about twenty state legislatures, some more than once, from Hawaii to Virginia, California to Georgia, Michigan to Missouri. She is acknowledged to be one of the most compelling witnesses in the gun-control/gun-rights debate.

"I'm not a crack shot, but I can definitely hit what I'm pointing at," she says.

When legislators ask her what would have happened if she had shot at the gunman in Luby's and missed, she answers: "It's possible, but if nothing else, it sure would have changed the odds, wouldn't it? Because, as it was, I can't begin to get across to you or anybody else what it's like to sit there and wait for it to be your turn. I get very angry right now even thinking about that. Can you imagine not being able to fight back?"

Hupp has written a book about her experiences: *From Luby's to the Legislature: One Woman's Fight Against Gun Control.* (See the Bibliography.)

Since the mid-1990s, the number of concealed-carry permit holders has surged, particularly since President Obama was elected. Coincidentally, this is mirrored by an increased distrust of government. In the first edition of my book, *The Concealed Handgun Manual,* I estimated the number of people with concealed-handgun licenses or permits at 2.4 million. According to the report *Concealed Carry Permit Holders across the United States* by John Lott's Crime Prevention Research Center, it increased to 4.6 million in 2007 then took off to 12.8 million in 2015.

A couple of Supreme Court cases increased acceptance of using firearms for self-defense both inside and outside the home. In 2008 several justices of the U.S. Supreme Court actually read and understood the Second Amendment of the Bill of Rights. It is quite clear: "A well regulated Militia, being necessary to the security of a free State, the right of the people to keep and bear Arms, shall not be infringed."

Dick Heller was a security guard who carried a gun in his job at the Federal Judicial Center where he protected judges and other federal employees. He sued after his request for a permit to keep his gun at his home was rejected by the District of Columbia. The case produced massive interest and sixty-seven *amicus* or friend-of-the-court briefs, two of which quoted from *The Concealed Handgun Manual.*

It was a landmark case. After years of nibbling away at the "right to keep and bear arms" by the courts and politicians, the decision that found for Heller reestablished that the right to keep guns and carry them for self-defense was constitutional. While it allowed some regulation of the right, it said that Washington's blanket denial of the right to its residents was unconstitutional. The catch was that it did not apply to the states, only to Washington, D.C., and other federal enclaves.

Two years later in *McDonald versus Chicago*, the same majority of Supreme Court justices ruled that their Heller decision also applied to the states. This has resulted in a flurry of lawsuits, mostly backed by the NRA and the Second Amendment Foundation, that are grabbing back the right of the people to be armed.

It was these two cases that indirectly resulted in Illinois, the last state without some form of civilian concealed-carry, to be dragged, whining and protesting, into line with other shall-issue states. As of August 2015 Illinois had issued 130,442 permits statewide and even 34,364 in Cook County, which includes the City of Chicago.

This is essential because armed citizens, including teachers, are vital to discourage and control active killers who would initiate incidents of rapid mass murder on unarmed citizens in public or semi-public places. Without concealed-carry, there almost certainly would be no teachers or ordinary citizens carrying guns for protection.

Unfortunately, along with the increase of citizens carrying handguns for protection, there has also been an increase in so-called Gun-Free Zones. In the same way that in the military, Friendly Fire isn't, Gun-Free Zones aren't. The only thing gun-free about such areas is that law-abiding, legally armed citizens are not there to intervene.

From an Aurora, Colorado, movie theater to Columbine, and from Fort Hood to Virginia Tech, there have been horrendous results because active killers have mostly chosen locations where members of the public are not legally allowed to be armed. Tucson was one exception, where one citizen had a gun but did not have to use it.

In early December 2015, a husband and wife team of Muslim terrorists hit a county social-services building in San Bernardino, California, killing fourteen people and wounding twenty-one. (See Chapter 13.) When the police arrived and entered the building, the terrorists had escaped. The county building was, of course, a Gun-Free Zone.

On the other side of the country, nearly three thousand miles away the sheriff of Ulster County, New York, was tired of hearing about such incidents. Ulster County is about ninety miles north of New York City and includes part of the Catskill Mountains. It is a popular tourist destination. "Every time we read about one of these shootings that go on, there's never anybody with a weapon. And I would love it if something happened to have somebody with a weapon there," said Sheriff Paul Van Blarcum.

So in December he put a statement on his official Facebook page addressed to licensed handgun owners. "In light of recent events that have occurred in the United States and around the world, I want to encourage citizens of Ulster County who are licensed to carry a firearm to PLEASE DO SO.

"I urge you to responsibly take advantage of your legal right to carry a firearm. To ensure the safety of yourself and others, make sure you are comfortable and proficient with your weapon and knowledgeable of the laws in New York State with regards to carrying a weapon and when it is legal to use it."

The statement went on to encourage all peace officers to carry whether on duty or not. As if he had pulled the tail of a tiger, Van Blarcum got more response than he expected.

"It drummed up a lot of controversy, but that was not what I was looking for. I was really only talking to the people here in my county. The media took it and blew it way out of proportion."

He got about three hundred responses from all over the country and even Canada. Eighty-five percent of the responses were positive, he said.

"But the 15 percent that I got that was not positive, most of them were downright nasty." However, the responses he got from San Bernardino and California were all positive.

"I didn't get one from California that did not agree that maybe things would have been different if somebody had had a handgun."

Many sheriffs in New York State supported Van Blarcum's position, but one law-enforcement official who didn't was New York Police Department Commissioner William Bratton. Van Blarcum said sheriffs are accountable to the voters of the county — they have to get elected. But police chiefs, like Bratton, have to pander to the mayor or the city council.

"I had a little bit of a pissing match with the New York City Chief of Police Bratton. Bratton made some off-the-cuff comment after he heard about what I had said. So when they asked me what I thought about Bratton's comment, I said 'Bratton's not allowed to have an opinion. His opinion is whatever the mayor tells him his opinion is.' Which is true. Elected sheriffs, they can say what they feel."

Sheriffs in other states supported Sheriff Van Blarcum's position with statements to their own citizens.

Sheriff Michael Helwig of Boone County in Kentucky reminded current and retired deputies to carry their handguns off-duty and stated on his Facebook page: "I would also like to remind the people who have applied, been trained, and issued a license to Carry a Concealed Deadly Weapon (CCDW) that they also have a responsibility to carry their firearm, which they are proficient with, for the safety of themselves and others."

Several sheriffs in Florida also agreed with Sheriff Van Blarcum. Marion County Sheriff Chris Blair said: "If you are certified to carry a gun, I would like to encourage you to do so. Those who carry firearms responsibly and are confident in their ability, can and should. They are the first line of defense in an active-shooter situation. A lot can happen in the minutes it may take us to respond to those in need, and to have someone there to bring the fight to the attacker will help to save lives."

Brevard County Sheriff Wayne Ivey echoed NRA Executive Vice President Wayne La Pierre in saying: "The only thing that stops a bad guy with a gun is a good guy with a gun. If you are a person who is legally licensed to carry a firearm, now is the time more than ever to realize that you and you alone may very well be the first line of defense for you, your family, and others around you in a terrorist or active shooter-based scenario."

Sheriff Paul Van Blarcum said he recommends people in an active-killer situation to run, hide, or fight.

"We encourage everybody to run, but if you have a weapon…."

He tells people that whether they take on the killer or not is a personal decision.

"You don't have to carry just because I'm asking you to; it's a personal decision. And also a personal decision whether you can fire that weapon."

Run, hide, fight is a mantra that is finally being adopted by officialdom, including the Department of Homeland Security. But much of officialdom, including the federal government, fudges on recommending arming ordinary citizens.

We have come a long way in the nearly thirty years since Florida passed its concealed-carry law. Then only a handful of states had shall-issue laws, but now all states have some form of concealed-carry law, and many law-enforcement officials are encouraging their residents to carry guns as the first line of defense against active killers.

Chapter 10

CHURCHES: SANCTUARIES OR KILLING ZONES

"How do that many people get shot?
The guy, my understanding is, reloaded his gun five times,
and nobody had a gun to stop him."
— Pastor Terry Howell, speaking about
the Emanuel A.M.E. Church shooting in Charleston

Emanuel African Methodist Episcopal Church

For centuries churches have been regarded as places of sanctuary and safety. If somebody accused of a crime in Medieval Europe could reach a church, he was safe and could not be seized by the secular authorities. He had forty days in which to decide to face his accusers or accept permanent exile from the country he was in.

This sense of sanctuary has persisted to the present day. When states passed concealed-carry laws, more than a dozen of them banned handguns from churches or other places of worship. This was in addition to the universal stipulation that private businesses, including churches, could ban guns from their buildings by posting signs. Unfortunately, this has led many churches to be so-called "gun-free zones" and target-rich environments for inadequate and unbalanced individuals to vent their rage against society by committing rapid mass murders.

In addition to schools and colleges, churches are favorite targets for active killers to murder innocent victims. They are where large numbers of mostly unarmed men, women, and children are gathered to worship. The last thing on the minds of most is having to defend themselves in God's house.

South Carolina is one of the states that bans possession of concealed handguns within its churches. Its concealed-carry law states that permit holders are not authorized to carry in a "church or other established religious sanctuary unless express permission is given by the appropriate church official or governing body."

One church in downtown Charleston where such permission had not been given, nor was ever likely to be given, was Emanuel African Methodist Episcopal Church. The church has a long and distinguished history. It was founded in 1816 by blacks who split from Charleston's Methodist Episcopal Church. One of its founders, Denmark Vesey, was involved in a slave revolt in 1822, and along with other supposed conspirators was tried in secret and hanged. Whites burned down the original church, so the congregation met secretly until a new church was built after the Civil War.

Church leaders have a tradition of involvement in politics as well as spiritual matters. This was the case with the pastor in June 2015. Reverend Clementa C. Pinckney had been a member of the South Carolina Senate since 2000. He was a charismatic figure in the Charleston community and was committed to gun control.

On June 17, 2015, shortly after 8 p.m., he was conducting a Bible-study and prayer session in the church, when a twenty-one-year-old white man entered the church through the back door and joined the group. The young man was dressed in jeans and a grey sweatshirt and was wearing a fanny pack.

According to contemporary news reports, he was welcomed and sat down beside Pinckney. After spending about an hour with the group, he became argumentative. When the group started praying, he stood up and pulled a Glock .45-caliber pistol from his fanny pack and pointed the gun at eighty-seven-year-old Susan Jackson. Her grand-nephew, Tywanza Sanders, 26, tried to talk the gunman out of shooting members of the church group. But the young man apparently said he had to do it because blacks were raping white women and taking over the country. He was quoted as saying he was there to shoot black people. When he made it clear he intended to shoot all of those present, Sanders dived in front of Jackson and was first to be shot.

The son of one of the victims was quoted as saying Reverend Daniel Simmons, a seventy-four-year-old retired pastor, tried to grapple with the killer. He was shot and later died at a nearby hospital. Police said the gunman carried eight magazines loaded with hollow-point rounds and changed magazines five times. An avowed white supremacist, he shouted racial slurs during the massacre.

After he stopped shooting, the killer told one woman he was leaving her alive to report on what he had done. He then put the gun to his head and pressed the trigger. The only result was a click because the gun was empty. He fled through the church office and out of the back door.

The gunman killed nine of the dozen people, aged twenty-six to eighty-seven, at the session — six women and three men. All were black, and all were hit multiple times by .45-caliber bullets fired at close range. One woman and her eleven-year-old granddaughter played dead and, along with another woman, survived the massacre.

When the gunman fled from the church, he took off in his black Hyundai heading for North Carolina. About 10:30 the following morning, Debbie Dills, 51, was driving to work at a florist store, when she saw a black Hyundai driven by someone who might be the suspect. The man was driving on U.S. 74 towards Kings Mountain. She pulled over and phoned her boss at the store to ask him what she should do. He phoned the police, who stopped the suspect and arrested him in Shelby. According to documents released by police, the suspect admitted he was involved in the shooting. He waived extradition and was returned to Charleston. At the time of writing the suspect faces nine counts of murder, three counts of attempted murder, and a gun charge.

As was to be expected, almost as soon as the gun smoke cleared from the church, politicians and others weighed in for more gun control. President Barack Obama lost no time in blaming the gun for the shooting.

"I've had to make comments like this too many times. Communities like this have had to endure tragedies like this too many times. We don't have all the facts, but we do know that, once again, innocent people were killed in part because someone who wanted to inflict harm had no trouble getting their hands on a gun," he said.

FBI Director James Comey admitted that the background check system should have prevented the gunman from buying the gun he used, but failed. So even the much-touted background check that gun-control advocates want to expand to cover sales among private individuals has feet of clay.

Charleston's long-time mayor Joe Riley, a Democrat, urged more gun control. He told CNN: "It is insane — the number of guns and the ease of getting guns in America. It just doesn't fit with the other achievements of this country."

Without naming the NRA, he said: "It is a small, really small group, well-funded, that keeps this issue from being appropriately addressed."

Gun-rights advocates shot back at Obama. Erich Pratt, director of communications for Gun Owners of America wrote: "The President wants to blame an inanimate object — the gun. But that just deflects blame away from the real culprit: gun-control policies that leave people defenseless in the face of evil perpetrators, who are never effectively prevented from acquiring weapons."

Noting that people with concealed-carry licenses can carry in South Carolina churches, but only with permission, Pratt said: "Unfortunately, the pastor was an anti-gun activist. As a state senator, the pastor had voted against concealed carry. But the President completely misses all of this. He ignores the fact that this was yet another example where a massacre took place in a Gun-Free Zone."

He said that in 2014, Pinckney, as a state senator, had voted against bill S308 that would have expanded concealed-carry to allow license holders to carry in restaurants that serve alcohol. The bill passed and was signed by Governor Nikki Haley.

Charles Cotton, NRA board member and former executive director of the Texas State Rifle Association, was more blunt. He seemed to blame Pinckney for the deaths at the church, writing in a post on the Internet, that the pastor voted against concealed carry.

"Eight of his church members, who might be alive if he had expressly allowed members to carry handguns in church, are dead. Innocent people died because of his position on a political issue."

While only one person is responsible for the murders — the gunman — the point is made. It is another example of a gun-free zone being a liability. There is no guarantee that, even if someone in the church had had a gun, he or she could have stopped the shooting and survived. But as Suzanna Hupp put it after the 1991 Luby's Cafeteria shooting, "It sure would have changed the odds, wouldn't it?"

On *Fox & Friends*, Bishop E.W. Jackson, a Virginia pastor and Republican politician who is black, urged pastors to defend themselves and their congregations.

"It's sad, but I think that we've got to arm ourselves. At least have some people in the church who are prepared to defend the church when women and children are attacked."

He was asked by co-host Brian Kilmeade if he personally would defend himself and his congregation with a gun.

The former U.S. Marine corporal replied: "I'm a pastor. It's absolutely something that I would do to protect the people whom God has given me charge over."

Co-host Steve Doocy opined that, if somebody in the church had had a gun, he or she would probably have been able to stop the massacre, particularly as the gunman apparently reloaded five times.

"If you take the time to reload five times, if somebody was there, they would have had the opportunity to pull out their weapon and take him out," he said.

Living Water Fellowship Church

Less than six months before the Charleston incident, another shooting took place in a church in Florida that had a very different outcome — because the intended victims fought back and the pastor had a gun.

On Tuesday, December 30, 2014, Pastor Terry Howell, 61, had an unpleasant duty to perform: he had to fire his church's maintenance man.

Howell had started the Living Water Fellowship Church in 2000 in Kissimmee, a suburb on the south side of Orlando.

Terry Howell, pastor of Living Water Fellowship Church.

The congregation had grown to about fifteen hundred and included a preschool.

About 8 a.m. Howell was in his office upstairs in the church. He was seated behind his desk with the forty-seven-year-old maintenance man seated across from him. Howell's daughter Kristy and the church's administrator, a woman, were also in the room.

Howell started carrying a gun in April 2014. A group,

mostly pastors, decided to get concealed-weapons permits. Howell had read accounts of shootings and thought
getting a permit might be a good idea.

"Most of the pastors that I know carry, especially in
south Florida."

There was no particular incident that prompted him to
get the permit.

"I don't think that when you get a concealed-weapons
permit, even though you might carry a weapon, I don't think
that anyone would ever think they're going to use it."

After getting his license he went to the range to practice
many times.

That morning Howell was carrying a Springfield XDS
semi-automatic in 9mm caliber in a belt holster concealed
on his right hip. The maintenance man was legally carrying
a .45-caliber semi-automatic, Howell said.

The maintenance man had worked at the church for
nine years.

"Probably in the last four, he didn't really agree with
our policies or with me — didn't like me. But he did a good
job, so we can work with that."

Then the employee got involved in attempting to steal
some items from the church, Howell said.

"It all happened within probably three or four minutes.
We were just talking about the incident and he's like: 'Are
you going to fire me over this?'

"And I said: 'Yes.'

"And at that point, he's like: 'F--- you.'

"And he pulls the gun out, aims it at my face, and pulls
the trigger. There's no talking about it; there's no threatening. He just pulls his gun and fires it."

Incredibly, the bullet missed, hitting the wall behind
Howell, but close enough that the pastor got powder burns
causing bleeding on his face. Fortunately, he was wearing
glasses, which protected his eyes. The gunman fired twice.

"He fired once at me, and my daughter grabbed his arm and pulled, and he fired the second shot in the side wall."

Howell credited his daughter with probably saving his life.

"Both of the women thought I was shot. He probably thought I was shot too. I mean, how do you miss that? So they jumped him. They jumped on his back," the pastor said. "You know in most of these shootings, people just sit there and wait to be picked off. I read somewhere there's a list of things that you do, and one of them is that you attack the attacker. He can't shoot everybody. Everybody's afraid to do anything, so everybody gets shot. And so they jumped him and, of course, I jumped in and grabbed him. They ran out of the room once I had him cornered. Then I don't remember much. At that point we were out of the inner-office into the bigger part of the office, I'm on the floor. I shoot from the floor."

Howell was wrestling with his attacker on the floor, then the gunman was up and heading for the door. The pastor was able to get his gun out and fired at him three times, though he remembers firing only twice. He remembers seeing the sights on his gun, at least on the two occasions when he hit his attacker.

"He's moving, fifteen feet away from me. My understanding is I shot him in the chest. I don't know how that happened. I don't remember looking at him. Once I went into that mode, I'm looking at a figure. It's almost blocked out. Apparently I fired a shot and missed, but I remember aiming twice."

Howell thinks he also hit the gunman in the side. Despite his wounds, the attacker took off running. Despite blood all over the place, the pastor thought perhaps he had missed him. The gunman ran down a flight of steps along the outside of the building for about two hundred feet before turning and entering the church through the front door. He collapsed just inside the front door.

"When he was inside the front door, I wasn't chasing him actually. I ran down through the inside of the pre-school to head him off, so if he came down the hallway, I'm going to head him off. So far as I know at that point, he still has the gun. So I run down the hallway and come around the corner, and he's lying on the floor. He ran the same direction but outside the building; I'm inside the building. I'm trying to cut him off to get the school on Lockdown."

Meanwhile, Kristy and the administrator had run down the stairs and out of the building. There were several female office staff working on the ground floor, and Howell's wife Debra had ushered them out of the building.

"They were all downstairs working. So she [Debra] had emptied the office. She probably saved the day," the pastor said.

The young women, including Howell's daughter, fled from the building and got into a van belonging to a construction worker who was working in the church.

"The construction worker looked out, saw everybody screaming and running to his van, so he ran out to the van," Howell said.

The construction worker drove off with the women while Kristy called 9-1-1.

"We have an employee with a gun, and he's just shot our pastor."

The 9-1-1 operator asked for the location, and Kristy told her Living Water Fellowship Church. The operator asked if she was at the church.

Kristy: "No, we got in the van and ran."

Operator: "Where's the suspect now?"

Kristy: "I don't know. We ran out; we left."

Operator: "And who is it?"

Kristy: "It's our maintenance man."

She said, there is a school in the building. The operator asked if the suspect was still at the church.

Kristy replied sounding frantic and crying: "I don't know. We left; we ran. I don't know. It's my Dad; I don't know if he's okay. Please hurry; please hurry."

Operator: "We're sending help; we're sending help. What's your name?"

Kristy: "He's upstairs in the office."

Operator: "Okay, who is?"

Kristy: "My Dad, my Dad, my Dad."

Operator: "Your Dad, and he was the one who was shot?"

Kristy: "Yes, the pastor."

Operator: "Okay."

Kristy (after a pause): "We had to get out guys. We gave the order for everybody to get out or we were next."

The Operator asked what the suspect was wearing?

Kristy told her he was wearing a black shirt with blue jeans and that he was a Filipino. Kristy expressed concern about her mother, who had not come with them.

Somebody in the van: "We need to go back."

Operator: "No, do not go back; do not go back."

Kristy: "Are they there?"

Operator: "Do not go back to the church. We are sending deputies and an ambulance on the way now.

The operator asked where they were, and Kristy said they were in a housing development.

Kristy: "Is pastor okay?"

Operator: "Yes, ma'am, our deputies are with the pastor now, and someone will come out there and meet you, don't go back to the church. Stay there."

Kristy breaks down crying and hysterical.

Howell said listening to his daughter on the 9-1-1 call was distressing.

"The phone call messed me up more than the shooting messed me up."

Back at the church, Howell approached the gunman lying in a pool of blood.

"When I ran around the corner and saw him down, I looked for the gun. The gun's not there. Then, when I determined he's not a threat, I put the gun back in the holster, called 9-1-1."

While he was waiting for the officers to arrive, Howell took his gun out of its holster and put it in a drawer.

"So I don't physically have it on me when they come in the door."

The time from the beginning of the 9-1-1 phone call to when the operator said the deputies were with the pastor was just more than 2½ minutes.

"It felt like eternity," Howell said.

When the deputies arrived, they handcuffed Howell, not knowing he was the pastor they had been told was the one who was shot.

"They came in the door, I mean holy cow, every gun in the county was pointed at me," the pastor said.

"I had my hands up when they came in the door. And I said: 'I shot him, and I can't believe I'm not dead,' something like that."

The officers asked him if he had a gun on him. He told them the gun was in a drawer in the pre-school office, which was close to the door. The officers found the maintenance man's gun in the upstairs outer office where Howell had shot him.

The maintenance man was taken to Osceola Regional Medical Center in critical condition. He was charged with Aggravated Assault with Intent to Kill. He was later transferred to Osceola County Jail. However, Howell said the attacker was later released on a $50,000 bond without an ankle monitor while awaiting trial.

After the shooting, the pastor received some negative feedback from some members of the church, and he said his congregation dropped about 10 percent. However, he also received a lot of support. The Sunday following the attack, Howell had the district superintendent preach for him.

"When I walked on the platform, the church gave me a standing ovation."

There have been a couple of incidents where he has reacted to loud noises. One occasion was when the church music started with drums playing really loudly.

"Me and my daughter were standing there, when the drums hit we both screamed. We make fun of it now; it wasn't fun then," Howell said.

On another occasion, one of his security-team members came over and tapped the front of the platform. He jumped back and again made a joke about it.

He said there have been occasions when he has become emotional when he didn't expect it. He hasn't dreamed about the incident or relived it.

"For me I feel like I stopped the threat. I haven't really personalized it or internalized it, I guess, because I don't feel a whole lot. I don't feel good I did it, and I don't feel bad I did it. I feel like I did what I had to do, and if I hadn't done what I done, then other people could possibly be dead. It's only a miracle. Nobody, in any of these reports of mass shootings, nobody goes in and shoots one person. They just start shooting, right?"

Howell said he wasn't trying to hurt the shooter, he was just trying to get the gun away from him.

"I knew that if I didn't do something, somebody else would get hurt."

Kristy felt guilty about leaving him, he said. She doesn't remember the struggle or getting out of the room.

His memory of the incident is somewhat different from what the evidence showed. The investigators told him he fired three times.

"I don't remember firing three times. I told the police he fired three times and I fired twice. I don't remember missing."

The officers took Howell's gun and were holding it as evidence until after the trial. In the meantime he bought a

Glock 43, a single stack 9mm. However the Springfield is still his favorite, in part because of the safety features. It has a grip safety in addition to a trigger safety.

Pastor Howell keeps a gun handy at home, he said.

"When I'm at home, I don't have my gun more than two feet away from me."

Howell doesn't carry at the church everyday. His gun was in his truck as we spoke. The pastor has security at the church on Sundays, but not during the week. His security officers are usually retired peace officers, military, or civilians with concealed-weapons licenses. This predated the shooting. Although some of his security officers have suggested putting up no-gun signs at the church, he has resisted and does not have a policy.

"We certainly don't need the wild, wild West, but I think that when we make rules that take guns away from law-abiding citizens — there is a saying that 'when police are minutes away, seconds matter.'"

He finds it difficult to understand how the killer in the Charleston church killed nine people while reloading five times.

"How do that many people get shot? The guy, my understanding is, reloaded his gun five times, and nobody had a gun to stop him."

Howell tends to meet a lot more people that admit carrying guns.

"They're a little more open with me about it than before. I'm surprised at the number of women that carry guns in their purses."

He goes to a District Council which represents 360 churches where they talked about the shooting from the platform. After the service was over, many of the pastors came up to him. Many of them said they carried guns, some only since his incident. "The only person who wasn't carrying was me."

New Life Church

Another incident where somebody with a gun stopped a shooting happened in a church in Colorado Springs.

When Jeanne Assam awoke at 5 a.m., she was hungry. She was on the last day of a three-day religious fast, but the hunger pangs were not excessive. The first day was always the worst. She was fasting in the hope of discovering what God wanted her to do with the rest of her life. Before the day was over, He would give her a hint.

She sat up in bed and started to read her bible. Normally on a Sunday she would go to New Life Church, where she was a member and also a volunteer security officer. She was having doubts about whether to continue in law enforcement or try something else. She had been a police officer in Minneapolis for five years, then moved to Colorado, where she had held several law-enforcement jobs. She was qualified as a police officer in the state, though she was not working for a police agency at the time.

Assam had decided to stay in her apartment this Sunday, December 9, 2007, to contemplate her maker and her future and not to go to the church with its cafeteria, where she might be tempted to break her fast.

About 8:30, she decided she needed a break from the scriptures and, still in her pajamas, got out of bed and went to her computer. She went to the MSN home page, and in the top-right-hand corner immediately saw a story about a shooting in Arvada, a Denver suburb about seventy-five miles north of her Colorado Springs apartment.

The story said two people had been killed and two more wounded at a Christian missionary-training school called Youth with a Mission or YWAM. The gunman, who was not named, was still on the loose. His description was vague: white male in his twenties, possibly wearing a skullcap and glasses, maybe a beard — no height or weight.

"I knew in my gut that he was going to come to New Life. I just was certain. I don't know how I knew other than it was God telling me: get to church," she said.

She phoned the head of the security team and told him she was coming to the church. Then she got into the shower. "When I was showering, I knew that there was a chance that I might not be coming home that day. I mean I just knew it. This is how certain I was that he was coming to that church. I just thought: either I'm going to come home, or I'm not going to come home; I'll be killed."

To that point in her life she had not felt anything as compelling as the feeling she was going to confront that gunman. She felt she couldn't warn the security team, because other than this premonition, she had no evidence that the gunman was going to the New Life Church.

"I was just like, I've got an assignment: he's coming, and I'm going to take him out," Assam said.

She dressed in jeans, a short-sleeved sweater, and a black blazer to cover her gun. The gun was the Beretta 92FS that she had carried when she was a police officer in Minneapolis. It was loaded with fifteen rounds of 9mm hollow-points in the magazine and one in the chamber. She did not carry any spare magazines, as she didn't feel she would need them.

"I just knew God was going to be with me. I didn't know what the outcome was going to be, because you never know what God is going to do. But I felt I've got enough here, I've got my gun and my rounds, and I've got God."

She got into her car and drove the mile to New Life Church. The morning was bright and cold. There was snow on the ground, but the sky was clear. The blizzard that had been predicted had not materialized, but it was twenty degrees Fahrenheit. As she drove, Assam recited scripture from memory.

The church has more than ten thousand members and is located on a property of thirty-five acres on the north side of Colorado Springs. Assam arrived about 10:15. She was the only female member of the church's volunteer security team. In addition to the volunteer security officers, four Colorado Springs police officers in uniform were present. Two of them patrolled the extensive parking lot in their patrol cars, and two were stationed in the buildings.

Normally Assam would be assigned to protect the pastor during the second service, but because she was armed and a qualified police officer, she was posted in the lobby outside the huge sanctuary and in the long hallway that led to it.

The second service let out late, at about 12:40. Normally it would let out at about 12:20, but there was a guest speaker, so there were more people present than usual.

"The cop next to me looked at his watch, it showed 12:45, and said: 'I'm out of here.'"

There were still hundreds of people milling about. The volunteer security team would not leave until almost all the members had left.

Meanwhile, a troubled twenty-four-year-old was sitting in his red Toyota Camry in the parking lot. The previous evening, he had turned up at the Youth with a Mission training center in Arvada and asked to stay the night. After making some cell-phone calls, he was asked to leave by staff member Tiffany Johnson. He pulled a handgun and began shooting, killing Johnson and Philip Crouse and wounding two others. The gunman went home, but left the next morning for the New Life Church in Colorado Springs.

He waited in his car until he saw the four uniformed Colorado Springs police officers leave the church parking lot in their patrol cars. He apparently drove around the church setting off at least two smoke bombs, then he parked in the northeast parking lot.

About one o'clock a volunteer at the information booth in the lobby caught Assam's attention. He pointed towards the front doors and told her that a church member had said something weird was going on outside. Assam approached the man and asked him what was happening. He said a smoke grenade or smoke bomb had been set off outside the front doors.

She went outside to investigate. An usher who was driving by joined her. They found what looked about the size of a stick of dynamite, but light blue or light grey in color with commercial writing on it. Dense white smoke was pouring from it. Assam didn't want to get too close to it, because she didn't know if the smoke was poisonous or if the device might explode.

"People were so naive that they were walking through this smoke like it was nothing," she said.

Assam directed people away from the smoke. She was trying to decide what to do next, when suddenly the smoke stopped. She tried to find out who had set off the devices and got two different accounts.

"One witness said it was a white male in a red car, and the other witness said it was three white males in a white car. As a cop I know you get really different witness information like that all the time, so I was going to write both down."

She went back inside the church to write down the witnesses' names before she forgot them, because she would have to make a report.

"I wasn't thinking, oh my God, the gunman's here. I was just thinking this is weird."

The same volunteer in the information booth said there was another smoke grenade outside at the cafeteria doors, which were some way from where Assam was standing.

In the parking lot, the twenty-four-year-old got out of his car carrying a Bushmaster AR-15 semi-automatic rifle. He was carrying two semi-automatic handguns — a .40-caliber

Beretta PX4 Storm, fully loaded in a right thigh holster and a Springfield Armory, model XD9, 9mm. He was wearing a black ammo vest and had loaded spare magazines for all three weapons.

David Works, 51, his wife Marie, and their four daughters were getting into their white Toyota van in the east parking lot. They had attended the second service and were about to drive home to Denver. His wife was behind the wheel, and three of their daughters were in the back seats — Stephanie and her twin Laurie, both eighteen, and eleven-year-old Grace. Rachel, sixteen-years-old, was about to get into the back through the sliding door on the passenger side.

David Works had just gotten into the front passenger seat and was fastening his seatbelt when he heard a popping sound. He looked up and saw a man twenty or thirty yards away shooting at a white truck that was driving by. When the truck had gone past, the shooter looked at Works. He later told police that they made eye contact. The shooter raised his rifle and started shooting at the van. David Works yelled at his daughters to get down, then heard Rachel cry out in pain. He ducked down as the gunman fired several more shots. One hit Stephanie in the chest, killing her. David got out of the van to help Rachael, who was lying on the ground beside the open door. The gunman was walking towards the front of the van in an arc. Works felt a burning pain in his stomach and fell beside Rachael. He was hit twice, once in the lower abdomen and once in the groin. He lay on the ground until paramedics arrived some minutes later. Rachel died later that evening at the hospital, but her father survived.

The Purcell family was leaving the east parking lot in their white Toyota Sequoia SUV when a man dressed in black and holding a military-style rifle blocked their way. Matt Purcell, 48, was driving. His wife Judy, 40, was in the front passenger seat, while their daughters, Kayla, 16, and

Kristen, 12, were in the back with a friend, twenty-four-year-old Chelsea York.

Matt Purcell stopped six or eight feet from the gunman. Initially, Kristen thought she recognized the gunman and thought he was holding a paint-ball gun. They realized their mistake when he raised his rifle and started shooting at them. His first shot shattered the windshield and the second ploughed into the hood. Purcell tried to drive off but stalled the vehicle. The gunman walked around to the passenger side of the vehicle and fired several more shots. Mrs. Purcell told police she realized she had been hit when she saw blood on her hands and felt heat on her shoulder. As soon as he restarted the engine, her husband drove off and took her straight to the hospital.

After shooting people in the east parking lot, the gunman headed for the east doors of the main church building, changing magazines on his AR-15 as he went.

Jeanne Assam was still talking to the volunteer in the information booth when she heard a muffled pop, pop, pop, coming from the East Hallway. The hallway is more than a hundred-yards long and is thirty-feet wide. It runs from the east entrance to the lobby of the sanctuary. It is the biggest and the busiest hallway in the complex, with the special-needs ministry and all the children's ministries, including those for the babies and the preschoolers, leading off it.

Assam started walking from the information booth to the hallway. "As I'm walking, I heard the thundering crack of a high-powered rifle, incredibly loud," she said. "This was the loudest gunfire I've ever heard. It's obviously a high-powered rifle, not just a handgun."

She heard several shots fired fast, one after the other, obviously from a semi-automatic rifle. Though she didn't realize it, the gunman wasn't even inside the church at that point. The active killer fired seven shots from outside that hit the glass and steel outer doors.

"I pulled my gun out of the waist of my jeans, and I'm thinking: where is he?"

He was still outside, shooting through the metal and glass double doors.

Hundreds of people were still in the huge hallway, all screaming and running in different directions. Mostly they were running past Assam heading away from the gunfire.

Somebody yelled: "He's got a gun; he's got a gun."

Assam yelled: "Where is he?" She couldn't see him. She is only five-feet five-inches tall and couldn't see over the mass of church members. Another member of the security team, a man over six-feet tall spotted the gunman.

"There he is Jeanne; he's coming in the doors right now," the security officer yelled.

Assam immediately sprinted down the hall towards the doors and the gunman.

"All of a sudden, instantly, everybody's gone. All the people in the hallway have found a place to hide. The best way to describe it is when you turn on a light and there's cockroaches, and they scatter, and they're gone. So no one was left in the hallway except me and the gunman, and I'm walking. I've stopped running, and I'm walking."

She could see the killer dressed all in black with boots and kneepads, looking almost like a SWAT officer, and carrying an AR-15 semi-automatic rifle. He pointed his rifle up as he came through the doors.

"When he pulled open the second and last set of doors, this evil flooded in, into that hallway —— just a huge sense of evil," she said. "The presence of evil was big; it filled the whole hallway, and that hallway is so huge."

Assam felt that presence of evil would have scared a normal person, but because she was on a fast and was trying to find God, she said she was not intimidated.

She thinks the killer saw her before she ducked into a smaller hallway on her right. But he probably thought she was like everyone else, looking for cover and to escape. He probably didn't notice that she had a gun in her hand.

"I'm really calm, my hands were not shaking, my heart was not pounding," she said.

She had cover in the smaller hallway: the gunman couldn't see her, but she couldn't see him. She wanted to make sure he was still heading towards her in the wide East Hallway. She took a peek around the corner of the hallway.

"I looked real quick, then I took some steps back, and I prayed. I took a deep breath and just said: 'God, please be with me.' I needed God, because I knew if I messed this up, people were going to die, and I could die. I put my gun up to the high ready, and I was going to shoot him as soon as he came even with me."

Meanwhile the killer was advancing down the East Hallway, shooting as he came. Assam found out later that he was shooting at the elderly volunteers further down the hallway. They were lying on the ground with bullets hitting all around them, until one of the security guards got them to move out of the line of fire.

He was also shooting at fifty-nine-year-old Larry Bourbonnais and a security officer who were taking cover behind a pillar. Later Bourbonnais told Detective Jeff Strossner he was a Vietnam veteran and had decided long ago that if a Columbine- or Virginia Tech-type of shooting incident occurred he would try to stop it. He was eating a cheeseburger in the cafeteria when the shooting started. He ran towards the sound of gunfire down the East Hallway. He spotted the gunman and took cover behind a large pillar that he thought was made of concrete. The security officer was also behind the pillar, and Bourbonnais tried to persuade the officer to give him his gun, because he had a clear shot. The officer refused, so Bourbonnais stepped out from behind the

262 ☞ Surviving a Mass Killer Rampage

pillar and yelled at the gunman to distract him. The shooter saw him and raised his rifle. Bourbonnais stepped back behind the pillar, and the gunman fired. The pillar apparently was not concrete, because the bullet went through it breaking up, and three bits of shrapnel hit Bourbonnais in the left forearm.

Though Assam had cover and concealment in the smaller hallway, she felt that waiting for the killer was not a good plan. She decided to confront the gunman.

"When I asked God to be with me, and I stepped out from behind cover, I felt an instant presence, a huge, magnificent power of the presence of God, surround me," she said. "I had a shield surrounding me, not just in front of me. It was really powerful. I've never felt anything like that before or since."

Assam took several steps out of cover into the East Hallway and shouted: "Police officer, drop your weapon."

They were sixty feet apart. He turned his body and his weapon towards her to fire. She fired her Beretta 9mm five times rapidly, aiming for "center mass" — the middle of his body.

"He went flying backwards onto his back," Assam said.

The killer sat up as she moved towards him and told him to drop his weapon or she would kill him. He shot at her with his AR-15, so she continued shooting at him, she said.

"He was lying on his back with just his head propped up, and that would have been fine with me. I would just have thought it was over, but then he started to make a movement. As a police officer, when I tell someone not to move, you don't move. I had to shoot him again."

He shot at Assam several times, because there were several bullet marks in the wall behind her.

"So we're shooting at each other, and he missed me, and I hit him," she said. "And I killed him. He did not kill himself."

It was all over. She had confronted the gunman, stopped his killing spree, and had survived.

A few minutes after the shooting stopped, police officers started to arrive at New Life Church. The Colorado Springs Police Department got the call of what police refer to as an active shooter at 1:10 p.m., according to Police Chief Richard Myers. The dispatcher immediately called on the radio to see if any of the officers who had been providing security at the church were still there. Two of the officers, Mark Chacon and Alan Roman, had their radios on and were several blocks away. They immediately turned around and drove back to the church. They learned that the shooter had entered the church by the east doors. An El Paso County Sheriff's sergeant and Colorado Springs Officer Eric Price joined them. In Price's report, he stated that they made a "four-man active-shooter entry team" and entered the building. About twenty yards down the hallway they came across several New Life security officers standing near the downed killer. They were the first police officers to reach the scene. Price had been on traffic duty elsewhere and estimated the time he reached the church parking lot was about 1:20 p.m., according to his report. The first officers may have been on church property within two or three minutes of receiving the call, as Myers claimed, but it was several minutes later before they reached the scene of the shooting. As is frequently the case, by the time they got there it was finished, and the shooter was dead.

Assam is convinced that her shots killed the gunman, so she was shocked and felt betrayed when a few days later the El Paso County coroner issued his autopsy report. It stated that the gunman had committed suicide. Coroner Robert Bux, who conducted the autopsy, said that the killer had put a handgun in his mouth and shot himself.

Bux said that Assam hit the gunman twice in the left thigh with the bullets going through the muscle without hitting bone. In addition, Detective Richard Gysin noted in his report that there were marks on the barrel and the stock of the AR-15 where her bullets had apparently hit. Bux said several superficial wounds on the gunman's left hand and wrist and on his chest were probably caused by shrapnel when those bullets broke up after hitting the rifle. His report stated that a piece of shrapnel was found in the chest wound.

Dr. Alexis Artwohl is a retired police psychologist who works as a behavioral science consultant to law enforcement. She is also on the faculty of Force Science Institute, an organization that does ongoing research in human-performance factors relevant to the use of force in law enforcement.

Artwohl says that decades of research in human psychology have confirmed that it is normal for people to have some incorrect memory details even in everyday life, and this can be amplified in high-stress situations. The research on eyewitness memory shows that honest eyewitnesses often have memories that may be the truth for them, but are not an entirely accurate reflection of what really happened. Memory gaps are normal, and the memories may never come back because they simply aren't there. There are multiple reasons for these gaps, such as people simply being unaware of what's going on around them, or the information never makes into long-term memory storage. Memory retrieval can also be influenced by many factors. Sometimes memories may not surface into conscious awareness until a later time, and memories may also change over time.

"Our brain is wired to remember the gist of the situation, but research shows we often get the details confused or inaccurate. Ordinarily this confusion causes only minor problems like forgetting where we put our car keys, or arguing with a family member about who said or did what. However, if you get tangled up in the criminal justice system, the devil can indeed be in the details. Now the normal memory gaps, false memories, and changing memories may be viewed as signs that you are lying or trying to cover up wrongdoing."

Artwohl has interviewed several hundred law-enforcement officers who have been in shootings. She and other researchers have confirmed that officers, like all humans, often have memory gaps and false memories of an event. This can even include officers at the scene of a shooting having no memory of having fired their weapons.

"I collected cases of officers who discharged their weapons at the scene of a shooting, but later on had no memory of actually firing their weapons. In some cases, they remember rounds going off, but they thought it was the bad guy's gun when, in fact, it was their own gun. That's unusual but it does happen.

"There is now ample research on the importance of sleep cycles for memory consolidation. The brain is very active during sleep. One of the brain's tasks during sleep is to sort through the day's events, consolidate some of those into coherent memories, and help our brain make sense out of what happened. That's why immediately after an event, jumbled and incomplete memories can become more complete and coherent after one or two sleep cycles."

She said some police departments allow officers who have been involved in a shooting the option of a rest period, ranging from a few hours to a few days, before providing a full, detailed formal statement. This is in accordance with the *Officer Involved Shooting Guidelines* published by the Police Psychological Services Section of the International Association of Chiefs of Police.

This does not preclude officers from providing an immediate, brief public-safety statement to help first responders secure the scene, search any additional suspects, and help the investigators perform the initial tasks of the investigation, such as collecting evidence, identifying other eyewitnesses, etc. The recommendations contained in the guidelines are not mandatory, but provide agencies with science-based suggestions to help officers and agencies make the best decisions about how to handle the aftermath of a shooting. Each situation is different and will require thoughtful decision-making. Many of the suggestions in the guidelines can apply to citizens as well, Artwohl said.

The book Dr. Artwohl wrote with Loren Christensen, *Deadly Force Encounters: What Cops Need to Know to Mentally and Physically Prepare for and Survive a Gunfight*, should be read by anyone who carries a gun for self-defense. (See the Bibliography.)

Bourbonnais told Detective Strossner he saw a semi-automatic handgun in the suspect's hand and noticed that the gun had a half-ejected cartridge case stuck in the ejection port. This caused the gun to jam. Bourbonnais said he picked up the gun and racked the slide to clear the case. Assam and the other security officer there told him to put the gun down, which he did. Assam told Detective Mike Happ that she kicked the gun away from the gunman. Police officers arrived shortly afterwards and took possession of the gun.

Detective Gysin documented the positions of eleven spent 9mm casings. Ten all had the same head stamp and were fired by Assam. One, with a different head stamp, was found near the gunman's Springfield Armory 9mm. Gysin said he believed this case was the one cleared by Bourbonnais from the Springfield. It is probable that he was holding the Springfield at the time, because it also showed evidence that it had been hit by a bullet.

Gysin noted four bullets apparently fired by Assam that missed the gunman — three hitting walls and one in an aluminum door-frame.

Assam was interviewed a couple of hours after the shooting by Detective Mike Happ. She said being interviewed so soon after the shooting, she didn't remember everything. She attributed this to "battle fog."

"I could not remember all the details right after this shooting. I had a much clearer image a few days later. I was still in shock. I shouldn't have even given them my statement until later."

Dr. Robert Young, a psychiatrist from New York State and member of Doctors for Responsible Gun Ownership, says faulty memory of a traumatic event and memory-shifting over time are common reactions.

"Assam's experience is a good example of common phenomena after traumatic events. Her conviction about events transpiring in ways that the physical signs don't agree with, and her own memories changing, perhaps becoming clearer, are both very typical experiences. This is documented both in the gun literature and in the psychiatric literature.

"When your mind is focused on survival, and you've got tunnel vision directed at whatever you assume is the greatest threat, not paying attention to anything else, you can't really be sure of everything else."

Whether Assam killed the gunman or not is irrelevant to the outcome. Though heavily out-gunned, she hit him several times, put him down, and eliminated the threat. No one inside the church was killed or wounded except Bourbonnais, who was hit by shrapnel in the forearm.

The gunman had several hundred more rounds of ammunition for his three guns in magazines, and it is likely that, had he not been stopped by Assam, he would have continued his murder rampage.

As Coroner Robert Bux says: "She's a hero, a *bona fide* hero, and because of her courage, there's a whole bunch of people who didn't get killed."

Colorado Springs Police Chief Richard Myers also called her a hero and credited her with saving many lives.

Assam's state-
ment about her
memory of the
incident being
much clearer after
a few days is con-
firmation of the
advice of John
Benner and oth-
ers not to give a
statement to law
enforcement right
after the shooting.
This is why it has
become standard
practice not to
interview an offi-
cer involved in
a shooting for a
day or two after
the event. What is

*Jeanne Assam with
President George W. Bush.*

good for the officer should be good for the public.

Larry Bourbonnais learned another lesson from the
New Life Church shooting. What appears to be a concrete
or stone pillar in a building may not be what it appears and
may not be good cover from fire.

If you want to know more about Jeanne Assam and the
killer and what led them to that fateful meeting at New Life
Church, I recommend Assam's book: *God, the Gunman &
Me.* (See the Bibliography.)

Church Security

Church security is a complicated issue. Churches vary
greatly in size — from small, often rural, churches where

everybody knows everybody else to huge mega-churches with congregations that may number in the tens of thousands. They are located in states that have varying laws about whether ordinary citizens with concealed-handgun licenses can carry in places of worship. However, as mentioned at the beginning of this chapter, in most states that allow concealed carry in churches, the church authorities can ban guns by posting signs or giving other notice. Even in gun-friendly Utah, the Mormon Church has banned guns carried by private citizens from its facilities.

The previous three accounts of church shootings span the gamut. The Emanuel African Methodist Episcopal Church murders in Charleston are at one end of the spectrum — no guns in church, period. The New Life Church in Colorado Springs is in the middle, with a security team, one member of which confronted the killer and ended his rampage. At the other end is Living Water Fellowship Church in Florida, where the pastor, Terry Howell, has a security team but does not prevent parishioners from carrying their own guns concealed.

In 2013 the Mennonite Mutual Insurance Company, which specializes in church insurance, put out a paper of advice for churches. It offers three possible alternatives for church security.

Never allow guns on church property, as in the AME Church in Charleston.

Hire only trained professionals, either off-duty law-enforcement officers or professionally trained security officers.

Have a volunteer security team made up of parishioners with special training.

It then states: "There is one option we have not advocated here — that of allowing just anyone with a concealed-weapon permit to carry a weapon....

"Allowing or encouraging people to carry weapons into church with no written policy or specialized training creates a huge liability issue and should be avoided."

Obviously, the insurance company is concerned about a permit holder making a mistake, or even a member of a church security team shooting the wrong person. They appear more concerned with their liability than the individual parishioner's Second Amendment right to be responsible for his or her own safety.

I spoke to the security supervisor of a Texas mega-church that has a security team of mostly off-duty law-enforcement officers. Although the church does not have signs prohibiting parishioners from carrying their guns, they are told to leave their guns in their vehicles. While this policy is convenient for members of the security team, it does no favors for the parishioners. Members of the security team are less likely to mistake a law-abiding churchgoer for an active killer and shoot the wrong person. However, the victims in the New Life Church shooting in Colorado Springs were shot in the parking lot. When you have to cross several acres of parking lot to get to your car and gun, particularly in the evening, you are as vulnerable as a skinny dipper in a shark tank.

The complaint by law enforcement and security officers that they may shoot the wrong person has been used to disarm ordinary citizens in stores, movie theaters, malls, schools, colleges, and on the street. It hasn't happened, but what has happened is that active killers choose so-called gun-free zones, including churches, to commit their atrocities.

Chapter 11

MASS MURDERS ELSEWHERE: HOSPITALS, MALLS, THEATERS, AND OFFICES

"Gun-free zones are a magnet for deadly attacks."
– Dr. John R. Lott, Jr., President of
the Crime Prevention Research Center

In the first several chapters, we have seen how mass shootings at schools, colleges, and universities have changed law-enforcement response to these active killers. We have seen the rise of SWAT teams and their inadequacy to cope with these incidents where the Stopwatch of Death rules. We have seen that waiting for an *ad hoc* group of four officers also permits too many deaths and have come to the logical conclusion that the first law-enforcement officer has to go in immediately to stop the killer. That is exactly what happened at a nursing home and rehabilitation center in North Carolina in 2009.

Carnage in Carthage

Carthage, North Carolina, is the small town that could have been Detroit. In the late 1800s it was the home of the Tyson Jones Buggy Company, internationally known for building upscale buggies for domestic and foreign clients. In the 1900s Henry Ford wanted to buy the plant to start producing his horseless carriages. The company wouldn't sell, so Ford built his empire in Detroit. The city later declined to be the home of the University of North Carolina. Today with little more than two thousand residents, the town is the seat of government for Moore County.

On Sunday, March 29, 2009, Justin Garner, 25, was the only Carthage police officer on duty. He was qualified as a master police officer and had been with the department since October 2004. Garner started his patrol shift at 5:45 a.m., wearing his blue uniform. He was driving a marked, white Dodge Charger and wearing his issue Glock, Model 22, semi-automatic pistol in .40 caliber. He had fourteen rounds in the magazine and one in the chamber. He was right-handed and carried the gun in a holster on his right hip.

About 7 a.m. Garner stopped at a McDonald's for breakfast of a biscuit and gravy with a bottle of water to wash it down.

Pinelake Health and Rehabilitation Nursing Home is in Carthage and provides long-term care for elderly patients and rehabilitation for some older patients after surgery. In March 2009 the facility housed about one hundred patients cared for by about thirty staff members. One of those staff members was forty-three-year-old Wanda. We won't use her last name for reasons that will become clear. She was working in the Alzheimer's Unit, which was permanently kept locked, because the patients had a propensity for wandering off if not contained.

A couple of weeks previously Wanda had left her forty-five-year-old husband because of his heavy drinking and verbal abuse. He had an anger problem and had threatened her frequently, including pointing a gun at her on at least one occasion.

Michael Cotten, 53, drove into the parking lot at Pinelake Nursing Home shortly before 10 a.m. He was there to visit his aunt, Helen McLeod. He noticed a heavy-set man with a beard and wearing bib overalls. As he was pulling his truck into a parking space, he noticed the man was standing near another vehicle and pointing at him what looked like a shotgun. The gun was actually a .22-caliber Remington Model 597 semi-automatic rifle. Cotten and the heavy-set man stared at each other, then the gunman fired at least three shots at the visitor. One shot broke the driver's side window, and another hit Cotten in the left shoulder.

"I jumped out of my truck and ran inside the nursing home," Cotten said in a statement to Lieutenant C.D. Ritter of the Moore County Sheriff's Office.

He ran to the nursing station and told the nurses to call 9-1-1. Someone asked him if he had been shot. He acknowledged that he had.

"I looked out the front and saw the white male coming toward the building. I ran down the hall."

Near the end of the hall, Cotten met two employees. Together they ran into a patient's room and locked themselves in the bathroom.

"I could hear shots being fired up the hall from where he was. The shots got closer to where we were located."

Captain Bill Mackey, then a lieutenant and one of the investigators, credited Cotten's actions.

"He was in his truck, and the truck was still running. He could've easily pulled it down into drive and run off. But he chose to get out and go in and try to warn the patients and the staff that this guy was out there and was coming."

Shortly before 10 a.m., Michael Lee Gillis, 41, who lived in Carthage, arrived at Pinelake to visit his grandmother, Annie Blue. His mother, his stepfather, his aunt, and his two sons, Matt and Mike, accompanied him. Annie Blue's room, which she shared with Rosa Hubbard, was 211 on the left-hand side at the end of Hallway 200, which stretched away from the nurses' station. The group had just walked into the grandmother's room when Gillis heard a gunshot.

"I could tell that it was a shotgun blast, both from the sound of the shot and from the racking of the slide," Gillis told Special Agent B.T. Sullivan of the North Carolina State Bureau of Investigation, who took his statement.

Gillis stepped out into the hallway to see what was happening. Almost immediately, he heard one of the orderlies, "Spin" McLaughlin, cry out, "He's got a gun."

Over the public address system, they heard, "Lock it down."

Gillis and McLaughlin immediately started moving people into their rooms. McLaughlin moved two wheelchair-bound women into the room across the hallway and shut the door.

Gillis retreated into his grandmother's room as the gunman was walking down the hallway. He closed the door and braced it with his foot, while holding the handle so it could not be turned. Gillis's mother, Rudy Yarborough, called 9-1-1 twice from Hubbard's phone. By the time she had made the second call, the gunman had fired four or five more shots, Gillis said.

They waited tensely as they heard the squeak of the gunman's shoe soles on the floor right outside their room. He turned to head back towards the nurses' station but not before he fired the shotgun into the room next door to them, killing seventy-eight-year-old John Goldston in his wheelchair with a round of buckshot that hit his aorta.

The gunman crossed the hallway to shoot into Room 208, killing eighty-nine-year-old Margaret Johnson. She was hit with one bird-shot round in the abdomen and pelvic area. Gillis said there was a break in the gunfire, which may have been because the gunman was reloading. He could hear the gunman moving down Hallway 200 towards the nurses' station.

"As he moved down the hall — he was almost midway down the hall — I slipped out of my grandmother's room and into the hallway, thinking that perhaps I could take him down," Gillis said.

What he saw was a heavy-set white man about six-feet tall with medium-length dark hair that covered his ears. But what captured Gillis's attention was the Winchester 1300, pump-action, 12-gauge shotgun the man was holding in a port-arms style of carry.

Gillis did not follow the gunman. His mother was tugging at him, trying to get him back into Room 211.

"The shooter turned and looked at me but did not seem to focus. I don't remember seeing if he has any other firearms other than the shotgun. That's a bit foggy to me. The shooter paused by a room with a woman in it but, for some reason, he did not fire at her. This was the same time that he saw me. He actually pointed his weapon at this lady but he did not shoot," Gillis said.

Gillis returned to his grandmother's room, because he was concerned for his mother's safety, as she had followed him out into the hallway. He ushered the members of his family and Rosa Hubbard into the room's bathroom and had them barricade the two access doors.

Gillis went back into the hallway and started moving towards the nurses' station in the middle of the complex. He could no longer see the gunman, who had turned left and entered Hallway 300.

About 10 a.m., Joann Dowdy and Jerry Avant, 39, a registered nurse, and several others were at the nurses' station near the middle of the building.

"I heard somebody yell, 'He's got a gun,' and about a second later I seen a black man come around the corner from the main entrance saying, 'Call 9-1-1; I just been shot,'" Dowdy said in a statement.

Avant picked up the phone and dialed 9-1-1, she said.

Several witnesses said they heard Avant over the public address system telling everybody to lock the doors.

An elderly patient in a wheelchair appealed to Dowdy not to be left where she was, so she wheeled her into Room 201 and closed the door on both of them.

According to Captain Mackey, Avant started pushing patients in wheelchairs into their rooms and shutting the doors.

"When he heard there was a gunman coming in, he was doing everything he could to hide as many patients as he could away from being hit. If he [the gunman] came in and was shooting, he [Avant] was trying to get the patients back in their rooms and get them away from any fire that may be going on within the halls of the nursing home."

The killer chased Avant down a service corridor that led from Hallway 300 to a back door near the kitchen. Michael Gillis found him there on the floor lying against the exit door.

"I could tell he's been shot, and I saw glass shattered on the floor from the windows around the door. I asked Jerry what I could do for him. He said, 'Call 9-1-1.' He was pulling his shirt up, trying to show me where he'd been shot.

"I told him 9-1-1 had already been called. He said, 'I think I'm dying.'

"I tried to comfort him. I told him, 'You're going to be fine.'"

Gillis ran back to the nurses' station to get Avant some medical assistance.

Emergency Medical Services personnel worked on Avant and prepared him for transport to the hospital. He could talk on the way to the hospital, but when he arrived his heart stopped, and he could not be revived. An autopsy determined he had been hit by three or four shotgun rounds.

Mackey added, "I would say, without a doubt, he saved some lives, and he also gave his life, because he never strayed from what he was doing. He stayed on it even to the point where the shooter caught up with him and started shooting at him and pursued him and eventually got him down and killed him.

"I remember speaking with one of the people who got there first and was attempting to help him [Avant]. To show you how much of a person he was, he tried to help everybody — even though he was mortally wounded and dying, he was still telling the people to go help the patients, that he was all right, go help the patients. He wanted to make sure the patients were going to be okay."

In addition to Avant, many members of the staff did what they could for the patients, said Mackey.

"I can't say everybody, but quite a few members of the staff were trying to do everything they could to help the patients, to keep them from getting shot, and after they were shot, trying to do everything they could to help them. I commend the nurses on the staff because it wasn't every man for himself by any means. They were doing everything they could to be there for them."

Wanda was in the Alzheimer's Unit when she heard over the public address system the order to lock all the doors. This was followed by a warning that someone was in the building shooting.

"Somehow I knew right away that it was [my husband]," she told Detective Eric Galloway in her statement.

Immediately she and other nurse assistants started getting all the patients into one room. Once they had all been herded into one room, Wanda toured the facility to make sure all patients had left their rooms and were accounted for. While she was checking the rooms, some of the other nurse assistants said someone was in the building shooting. Wanda hid in a bathroom.

"While I was in there I heard at least three gunshots," she said.

These were most likely the shots that were fired in Hallway 400 hitting three patients, just outside the Alzheimer's Unit.

When she came out of the bathroom, Wanda saw Jesse Musser, 88, lying dead in the hallway outside Room 405. He had been shot in the back with one round of bird-shot while in his wheelchair. Bessie Hedrick, 78, was killed by one round of buckshot while still in bed in Room 404. Tessie Garner, 74, was mortally wounded in Room 403 by a shotgun slug that went through her left arm and into her chest. She was taken to Moore Regional Hospital where she was pronounced dead.

Officer Justin Garner was parked in the parking lot of Carthage Auto Glass when he received the call on his radio to get to Pinelake Rehab as shots had been fired into the building. Engaging his blue emergency lights and siren, he raced the two to three miles to the facility in two to three minutes, he told Special Agent J.A. Cadwallader of the State Bureau of Investigation. As Garner pulled into the driveway of Pinelake, he turned off his siren, and as he parked in front of the building, he deactivated his emergency lights.

Garner advised the dispatcher that he was on the scene. He noticed a red Ford Ranger pickup with the driver's side window shattered in the parking lot. No one was in the vehicle, and the officer could see no one in the parking lot.

Garner got out of his patrol car and walked to the front door of the facility. As he entered the center, he noticed an elderly woman sitting in a wheelchair to the left of the front door. The woman was slumped over and was bleeding. This was Louise Dekler, 92, who had been shot with a buck-shot round in the pelvic area. Correctly, Garner passed the woman by. His job was to find and neutralize the gunman before assisting any of the wounded.

As he continued down the hallway, he said a woman ran towards him and told him someone was shooting, before she ran out of the front door.

Garner continued down the hallway with his gun drawn, looking into the rooms on either side as he passed them. At the end of the hallway was a dining room where he saw a woman. He asked her where the shooter was, and she pointed

Officer Justin Garner, who responded to the call at Pinelake Health & Rehab Nursing Home. (Photo courtesy Carthage Police Department.)

to the hallway that led to the nurses' station. He headed in that direction.

Just before he reached the nurses' station, Garner heard four gunshots in a row, coming from his right, somewhere in the building. He did not see Lillian Dunn, 89, who was dead, still sitting in her wheelchair on the other side of the nurses' station. She had been hit with two rounds of birdshot in the chest and abdomen. However, he did see a man on the other side of the station, who pointed down Hallway 300 in the direction of the gunman. This was Michael Gillis.

In his statement Gillis said he was about halfway up Hallway 200 when he saw Garner in uniform heading towards him from the other side of the nurses' station.

"I waved to him and attracted his attention and then pointed to him that the shooter had gone down Hallway

300. He nodded to me, providing acknowledgment that he understood. He turned down Hallway 300, out of my sight," Gillis said.

He added that Garner was holding his pistol in "a low-ready position with a two-hand grip."

The officer proceeded cautiously past the nurses' station and down Hallway 300 to his right, where Gillis had pointed. As he walked down the hallway, he noticed a mop bucket in the middle of the passage. He looked down to walk around the left side of the bucket.

After passing the bucket, he looked up to see a heavy-set man walking from a hallway to his left into the hallway he was moving along. Garner described the man as a white male, wearing a red shirt, suspenders, and blue jeans. He was holding a shotgun and was feeding rounds into the loading gate from a bag slung across his chest.

Garner told Cadwallader that he pointed his Glock at the man and told him two or three times to "drop the weapon." The man ignored him and continued to reload the shotgun. When he had finished reloading, he pointed the shotgun at Garner, who fired one round from his handgun. The officer said he believed they both fired together, because he never heard the blast of the shotgun, but felt the pellets hit his left leg.

Garner stepped to his left into a room and took a second or two to regroup before he stuck his head out from the door into the hallway. He was not sure if he had hit the man or if the man was coming after him. But the gunman was lying face down on the ground where moments before he had been standing. The shotgun was lying next to him, and he was moaning.

Garner estimated they were about twenty-five feet apart when they exchanged fire. However, Carthage Police Chief Bart Davis said they had measured the distance from the room Garner had stepped into and where his empty casing was found to where the killer fell. It was 142 feet.

"We were amazed at the distance," Davis said.

Garner approached the gunman and told him to put his hands behind his back. The man offered no resistance. As he put the man's hands behind his back, he noticed the gunman was wearing a revolver in a holster on his belt. He removed the gun and laid it on the ground. The man was so large Garner needed both his pairs of handcuffs to secure him. The officer unloaded the .38-caliber Colt Detective Special. The gunman was also carrying a .22-caliber Taurus PT22 semi-automatic pistol.

Garner told Cadwallader the only thing the man said to him was, "Kill me, please, just kill me." He repeated this several times.

Garner notified his dispatch that he had one man in custody and requested EMS, because the man had been shot, and he [Garner] also had been shot. He checked the gunman's wound. It appeared that the bullet had entered the chest cavity under the man's left arm. He could find no exit wound.

Moments later deputies from the Moore County Sheriff's Office arrived and searched the facility for any other suspects, while Garner stayed by the gunman. Subsequent investigation determined the gunman acted alone. He appeared to be looking to kill his wife, Wanda, but his shooting of Michael Cotten in the parking lot and his execution of Louise Dekler as he entered the building indicated he was intent on venting his rage on anybody in his way. Mackey said the gunman went after the patients in his vindictive rage because he knew his wife cared for them.

When backup arrived, Garner turned his gun over to Carthage Police Lieutenant Bickel. Garner told Cadwallader his uniform pants had four pellet holes in the lower left leg and two pellet holes in his left black boot. Two buckshot pellets hit the officer in his lower leg and foot.

The gunman told deputies the .22-caliber rifle he had used in the parking lot was on his black Jeep Cherokee.

Moore County District Attorney Maureen Krueger, at a news conference after the shooting: "The police were called, and Justin Garner, who is an officer with the Carthage Police Department, he acted in nothing short of a heroic way today, and but for his actions we certainly could have had a worse tragedy. The important thing is that we had an officer, a well-trained officer, who performed his job the way he was supposed to and prevented this being even worse than it is now."

Mackey too credited Justin Garner with saving many lives. He said that Wanda usually worked in Hallway 200, which probably was why the gunman went there first. He had fifty-nine assorted rounds of buckshot, slugs, and bird-shot, as well as extra rounds for his Colt Detective Special. He undoubtedly would have continued killing had Garner not stopped him, Mackey said.

The only possible criticism of Justin Garner's actions that day is that perhaps he allowed the gunman too many chances to drop the shotgun before he opened fire, thus allowing the man the opportunity to hit him. Fortunately, the two buckshot pellets that hit him caused only minor wounds.

Mackey said it is important to take into account that Garner had not been on the job very long and was following his training by trying to defuse the situation without resorting to deadly force. However, he conceded that a more experienced officer might have shot the gunman sooner.

While Garner did not hear the boom of the shotgun and surmised both he and the gunman fired at the same time, two witnesses described hearing the shotgun first, followed by the officer's handgun.

Michael Gillis said he heard Garner say in a loud, clear voice, "Put down your weapon."

He said, "I heard a gunshot and then heard pellets rattle down the hallway. I then heard a single shot from the officer."

This perhaps illustrates the conflict between a law-enforcement officer's training to save lives and the necessity to use deadly force on occasion.

We will leave the last word on that with Mackey: "Other than the fact he got shot in the process, you couldn't ask for a better situation for a law-enforcement officer to try to do his job and also try to give the person an opportunity to save himself and surrender."

However, what really saved other lives from being taken was that Garner went in immediately he arrived. Although he was the only Carthage officer on duty, he could have called for backup from Moore County deputies and waited until they arrived before going in. He didn't. He went in immediately and disabled the killer. By doing so he almost certainly saved several patients and staff members from being killed or wounded.

This is how it should work, but often doesn't. It didn't happen that way at Sandy Hook, and it didn't happen that way at San Bernardino. (See Chapter 13.)

Carthage Chief Davis said his officers were trained that in an active-killer situation the first officer to arrive on the scene went in immediately without waiting for backup. So Garner was following his training. He said that prior to the shooting when he was the assistant chief, he and Garner had role-played as the bad guys in active-killer training put on by Moore County Sheriff's Office.

According to call reports, Garner was wounded and the gunman taken down at 10:07 a.m. The first two deputies arrived on the scene at 10:08, while the third deputy arrived ten minutes later at 10:18. If Garner had waited to assemble the traditional team of four officers, he would have given the gunman a further eleven minutes to continue killing.

Mackey pointed out that often there is a time lag between a call and the call-taker typing out the entry, particularly if they are busy. Whatever the time lag, the Stopwatch of Death keeps ticking until the killer is stopped.

In September 2011 the killer was found guilty of eight counts of second-degree murder and several other offenses, including assault with a firearm on a law-enforcement officer. The judge stacked the sentences to run consecutively for between 142 and 179½ years in prison.

Dr. Lee Silverman, Mercy Fitzgerald Wellness Center

Like nursing homes, hospitals are usually so-called "gun-free zones," thus are soft targets for active killers. July 24, 2014, was a warm, dry, partially cloudy afternoon. A forty-nine-year-old patient arrived for his appointment with a psychiatrist on the third floor of the Mercy Fitzgerald Wellness Center. The center is in Yeadon, while the Mercy Fitzgerald Hospital across the street is in Darby. Both are suburbs on the southwest side of Philadelphia.

The psychiatrist, Dr. Lee Silverman, 52, had treated the patient about twenty years before and had recently started seeing him again. The last time the patient had been in the office was six or eight months previously, the psychiatrist said. At the time the patient had been ranting about the gun-free signs on the building.

"He was accusing me of deliberately putting the signs up to keep him out of the building," Silverman told detectives.

He had explained to the patient that he had nothing to do with putting up the signs. But the patient became more agitated, talking over him and interrupting him.

"I said, 'Look, this isn't working; you need to leave my office. I'll write your prescriptions. You go calm down; come back to the next appointment, and we'll work this out.' That was my position. And my boss had to escort him out; he just wouldn't leave."

On July 24 the patient arrived early. His appointment was for 2:45 p.m., but he arrived about 1:30 p.m. according to a police report. Silverman told investigators he had the office secretary contact Theresa Hunt, 53, the patient's case manager, to see if she was available for the appointment. When Hunt arrived, the three of them walked from the reception area down a narrow corridor to Silverman's office. Silverman and Hunt followed the patient into the office, and the doctor sat down behind his desk. Hunt sat down in her usual chair, in front of the desk to Silverman's left. Normally the patient would sit in the chair to the doctor's right, but he didn't sit; he remained standing.

The patient was upset. Silverman thought it was because he was being evicted or had been evicted from his apartment because he didn't pay his bills. He was upset with Hunt, because she worked part-time for the community organization he blamed for his eviction.

"I was trying to reassure him and deescalate the situation," the doctor said.

They had been talking for only a minute or two when the patient, with no warning, pulled out a small revolver, pointed it at the left side of Hunt's head, and fired twice, killing her.

"I remember the shininess of the gun and the flash from the muzzle more so than I remember the bang sound. I remember him smiling when he shot her."

Silverman was startled and recoiled backwards, tipping his chair over and landing on the floor behind the desk. He crouched behind the chair and the desk, while the patient was waving the revolver at him and yelling at him to get up.

"I was sure I was going to die, and then I remembered that I had brought for self-protection a handgun with me," Silverman told the detectives.

The gun was in his pocket, and because he was crouching, it was a struggle to get it out. He had just got it out when the gunman fired a shot that hit him in the head.

"He was pointing towards my head, and I put my hand up, and I believe the bullet went through my thumb."

With blood streaming down his face and coming from his thumb, Silverman thought the bullet had gone into his brain, though he still seemed to be alert. He headed towards the door of his office, but the gunman was in the way. Silverman was still in a crouch when the gunman pointed the revolver at him.

"Just as he was pointing the gun at me, I started firing, and he was firing at me. I squeezed the trigger until it had stopped firing, and I think he ran out of bullets."

The gunman fired two more shots at Silverman from the Iver Johnson top-break, .32-caliber revolver. He had fired two shots at Theresa Hunt and the one shot that hit the doctor in the head. The revolver held only five rounds.

Silverman was shooting an L.W. Seecamp, .32-caliber semi-automatic, which held seven rounds — six in the magazine and one in the chamber. He hit the gunman in the chest and in the arm.

Silverman remembers staggering out of his office into the corridor and screaming for somebody to call an ambulance.

Dr. Jeffrey Dekret, the director of psychiatry for Mercy Fitzgerald, had an office directly across the corridor from Silverman's. About 2 p.m. Dekret had a patient and was closing his door, when he saw Hunt, Silverman, and Silverman's patient about to enter Silverman's office. Dekret continued with his patient's appointment. A few minutes later, Dekret heard male voices shouting.

"Dr. Silverman was shouting, 'No, no, no. Don't do it, Richard, don't do it.'"

John D'Alonzo, a case manager, was in the reception area, when he heard shots being fired. He hastened into the corridor where, he told detectives, he also heard Silverman pleading, "Don't do this; I have a family; I have a wife and children. What are you doing? Don't do this; please don't do this."

Realizing something was wrong, Dekret opened his door and stepped into the corridor. D'Alonzo was already there, and the two of them tried to open Silverman's door, but it was locked. Dekret had a key and unlocked it. D'Alonzo pushed the door open about a foot.

Dekret said he saw the patient's arm and hand holding a silver-colored revolver that he was pointing down at Silverman, who was crouching to the right of his desk. He could not see Hunt, who was out of his line of sight. Dekret and D'Alonzo backed up. Dekret remembered D'Alonzo shouting for somebody to call 9-1-1. The doctor retreated to his office and was wondering what to do to keep his patient safe, when he heard five or six shots, he told detectives.

Dekret and D'Alonzo went back to Silverman's office. Dekret entered the office. He saw Silverman with blood streaming down his face and saw Theresa Hunt.

"I see the case manager, who I think is Theresa, in the chair leaning back with her head back and no color, that gray," Dekret said.

He went over to her and checked for a pulse, but felt none. He attended to Silverman, pulling out his handkerchief and putting it on the head wound.

Meanwhile D'Alonzo saw the gunman coming out of the office.

"He was still holding the gun. I believe it was opening; I think he was trying to reload it. I just knocked his arm down, and I sort of bear hugged him and wrestled him to the ground," D'Alonzo said.

The case manager stayed on top of the gunman, holding him down and securing his right arm while he was squirming and trying to escape. He was threatening to kill Silverman. Dekret joined in and managed to get the revolver, which was open and empty. He got up and put it in a drawer in the desk then returned to the fray.

"I had my knee on the guy's head, ended up I was holding one arm, John was holding the other," Dekret told the detectives.

The two men held the gunman down until police officers arrived and took over. Silverman and the gunman were taken to the local hospital's emergency room, but because of the nature of their wounds, they were transferred to the Hospital of the University of Pennsylvania in Philadelphia, a Level 1 trauma center. Silverman was treated and released a few hours later. The gunman was in critical condition.

Delaware County District Attorney Jack Whelan, who was responsible for prosecuting the gunman, believes that Silverman saved the lives of others as well as his own that afternoon.

"What I was able to observe and then learn from subsequent interviews is that the doctor certainly acted in self-defense. If it wasn't for him possessing the handgun, I have no doubt that he'd be dead today. And I believe that [the gunman], in addition to killing his caseworker, then turned and tried to kill the doctor on his way out of that office. There were other people in the waiting area, and he wouldn't have hesitated to kill them, as well as attempting to kill the police when they arrived."

Whelan said there was evidence from witnesses that the gunman was trying to reload his gun, "Which we believe again to lead to additional shooting, additional attempts to kill."

Silverman did get his gun back, Whelan said.

Later, in a recorded statement, Dekret said Silverman had told him he had a permit to carry a firearm, but he had never seen the psychiatrist's gun. As the Mercy Fitzgerald

Hospital and campus was a gun-free zone, there was some speculation that Silverman might lose his job. However, the hospital issued a statement saying in part: "We are thankful for the swift action of Dr. Lee Silverman, Dr. Jeffrey Dekret, John D'Alonzo, and the other colleagues and visitors who took brave and difficult action during yesterday's tragic event. We extend our condolences to Theresa Hunt's family, and we are praying for Dr. Silverman's speedy recovery. We look forward to Dr. Silverman's return to serving patients at our hospital."

The gunman entered a plea of "guilty but mentally ill" to all three charges in July 2015. He had a long record of firearms offenses and mental illness.

On Sept. 25, 2015, Judge Mary Alice Brennan at Delaware County Court of Common Pleas in Media gave the gunman the mandatory life sentence for the murder of Theresa Hunt. The judge also sentenced him to ten-to-twenty years for the attempted murder of Silverman and five-to-ten years for illegally possessing a firearm. The sentences for the attempted murder and the firearms charge run consecutively.

Dr. John Edeen is a pediatric orthopedic surgeon in San Antonio, Texas, and is a member of Doctors for Responsible Gun Ownership. In an article entitled "The Unthinkable: An Active Shooter in a Hospital" that appeared in the March 2015 edition of *San Antonio Medicine*, he states that if Dr. Silverman's incident had happened in Texas, the doctor could have been charged with a Class A Misdemeanor. If found guilty, he would have been subject to a year in jail, a $4,000 fine, and loss of his concealed-handgun license. At the time he wrote it, this was true. However, due to a change in the law, going armed into a gun-free zone is only a Class C Misdemeanor with a fine of $200. However, if the person is asked to leave and refuses, it is a Class A Misdemeanor.

Edeen has been trying to change the law and hospital culture in Texas to permit staff members with concealed-handgun licenses to carry inside hospitals.

He wrote: "It is immoral to continue the fallacy of 'gun-free zones' in our hospitals, when experience shows that deranged killers go out of their way to select such places to do their mass killing. Accepting this reality will require a culture change among some staff and hospital administration."

Edeen collected almost five hundred signatures supporting concealed carry in hospitals from people in San Antonio's Methodist Hospital and Methodist Children's Hospital. He then got a phone call from the CEO telling him he was violating the hospital's anti-solicitation policy.

"This was followed by a registered letter saying the same thing," Edeen said.

He stopped collecting signatures, but has continued to put pressure on the administration. After the San Bernardino shooting, the administration did increase armed security in the hospital.

"It's still not adequate, because if there is armed security in the ER and the shooting is up on the ninth floor somewhere, by the time the cop from the ER gets there, it's already over," he said.

Meanwhile Edeen is working for changes in the law from the Texas Legislature.

Dark Knight in Aurora

Movie theaters are privately owned businesses and as such are permitted in most states to erect signs prohibiting law-abiding citizens from carrying concealed handguns on their property. Such was the case with Century 16 movie theater in Aurora, Colorado, on the night of July 20, 2012. Aurora is a suburb on the east side of Denver. The theater was owned by Cinemark and was located in the Town Center Mall. It was holding a midnight showing of *The*

Dark Knight Rises, the latest Batman movie. Some of the four hundred members of the audience in Theater Nine were dressed in appropriate costumes.

According to news reports, this is what happened. Sometime before the movie started, a twenty-four-year-old neuroscience graduate student parked his white, two-door Hyundai behind the theater, close to the emergency exit from Theater Nine. The young man, a student at the University of Colorado Denver, entered the theater along with other audience members and sat in the front row.

Before the movie started, he appeared to take a phone call, then left through the emergency exit, leaving it propped open with a plastic tablecloth holder. He returned to his car and changed into black tactical gear, including a gas-mask. About 12:38 a.m. he reentered the theater through the emergency exit. He was carrying a Smith & Wesson M&P 15 semi-automatic rifle with a drum magazine, a Remington 870 Express Tactical shotgun in 12-gauge, and a .40 caliber Glock 22 semi-automatic pistol.

According to witnesses, the student threw two teargas grenades, then walked up and down the aisles shooting people at random. The drum on the rifle held one hundred rounds, but malfunctioned after he had fired sixty-five of them. He switched to the shotgun, firing six rounds, then to the pistol, firing five more, according to police.

Initially, people thought the shooting was all part of the show, but they soon realized it was for real. Starting at 12:39, the police received dozens of 9-1-1 calls reporting the shootings. Twelve people died, and fifty-eight were wounded. Four more were treated for tear-gas inhalation, and eight were injured in the rush for the exits. The police arrived within ninety seconds of the first 9-1-1 call, but the gunman had escaped through the emergency exit.

Police found him near his car, still wearing his tactical gear. For a moment Officer Jason Oviatt thought he was a

SWAT officer, but he realized that only the suspect would have donned a gas-mask. Oviatt and another officer arrested him at gunpoint. Oviatt testified that the gunman put his hands up when ordered and offered no resistance.

He told officers that he had booby-trapped his apartment. Police evacuated the area, and a bomb squad defused several explosives.

The gunman was tried and convicted in 2015. The jury could not agree on sentencing him to death, so he was sentenced to twelve life sentences without parole for the murders plus an additional 3,318 years for attempted murders and for possession of explosives.

Interviewed on radio in April 2014, economist Dr. John Lott, president of the Crime Prevention Research Center, said there were seven movie theaters within a twenty-minute drive of the gunman's apartment. The Aurora Town Center Theater was the only one posted with signs banning concealed handguns.

"He went to the single place where concealed-handgun-permit holders weren't able to go and defend themselves."

Trolley Square Mall

The Trolley Square Mall in Salt Lake City, Utah, was another "gun-free zone."

Fortunately, when Ogden Police Officer Ken Hammond, 33, went to the mall on February 12, 2007, with his pregnant wife Sarita, for an early Valentine's Day dinner, he ignored the gun-free signs. Ogden is a city of about eighty thousand residents forty miles north of Salt Lake City.

About 6:40 p.m. an eighteen-year-old Bosnian-born legal U.S. resident arrived at the mall and parked his vehicle in the parking garage. When he got out of his vehicle, he was carrying a Mossberg pump-action shotgun. He also had a Smith & Wesson .38-caliber revolver and a backpack filled with ammunition.

Still in the parking garage, the gunman shot at Jeffery Walker, 52, and his son Alan, 16, hitting them both with the shotgun. Alan managed to escape, but his father fell and was finished off by the gunman. Then the gunman shot Shaun Munns, 34, with the shotgun at a range of thirty yards. Munns fled and survived his wounds.

The killer entered the mall through the west entrance after shooting at the entrance doors. On the main level of the mall, he shot Vanessa Quinn, 29, twice with the revolver, hitting her in the chest and the head, killing her. He entered a card store called Cabin Fever where he shot five people with his shotgun. He left the store to reload, then returned, shooting three of his victims again, leaving three dead and two seriously wounded.

Meanwhile Ogden Officer Hammond and his wife had been enjoying dinner in the Rodizio Grill on the second floor of the mall. When Hammond heard the killer's gunshots, he looked over the railing down onto the first floor and spotted the gunman. Yelling that he was a police officer, Hammond drew his concealed .45-caliber Kimber pistol. He told his wife to return to the restaurant and call 9-1-1. Sarita Hammond was a police dispatcher and knew the procedure. She called 9-1-1 and told the operator what was happening. She also gave a detailed description of her husband, which the district attorney later said probably saved him from being shot by Salt Lake officers.

Ken Hammond engaged the killer, shooting down from the second floor, and was credited with distracting him and thus saving the lives of more people in the mall. When Salt Lake Sergeant Oblad arrived in the mall from the south entrance a few minutes later, Hammond came down an escalator to join him. The two officers exchanged fire with the killer.

Four Salt Lake SWAT officers entered from the north entrance and challenged the gunman. When he turned around to face them, pointing the shotgun at them, they opened fire on him. Two officers used Heckler & Koch MP5 sub-machine guns, while another used an AR-15 rifle, hitting him thirteen times and ending the fight. The gunman died just inside the entrance to the Pottery Barn store. From the time the gunman killed Jeffery Walker to when he was killed was seven minutes. He killed five people and seriously wounded four.

Westroads Mall

Ten months after the shooting at Trolley Square Mall, another active-killer incident took place at Westroads Mall in Omaha, Nebraska. A nineteen-year-old with a long history of mental illness entered the mall about 1:40 p.m. on December 5, 2007. He walked into the Von Maur department store armed with a stolen AK-47 variant and two thirty-round magazines. He took the elevator to the third floor, where he opened fire, killing eight people and wounding four. Most were store employees, but several were customers. The gunman ended the shooting spree by shooting himself fatally in the head.

The Westroads Mall was also a "gun-free zone." After the shooting, Dr. John Lott of the Crime Prevention Research Center found 2,794 news stories about the incident. However, not one mentioned that the shooting had occurred in a "gun-free zone."

"Surely, with all the reporters who appear at these crime scenes and seemingly interview virtually everyone there, why didn't one simply mention the signs that ban guns from the premises?" Lott wrote.

He said the same thing happened in reporting by the media on the Trolley Square Mall shooting.

The concealed-carry law went into effect in Nebraska on January 3, 2007, so it is possible that some of the shoppers or employees might have been armed and able to cut short the gunman's rampage.

It does appear the news media have a deliberate policy of suppressing that very relevant part of the story. Major media folk generally don't own firearms, don't like anyone who carries a firearm, and hate to give any credit to an armed citizen for doing anything. The idea that gun-free zones and the people who create them might be partly responsible for many deaths is anathema to them.

Washington Navy Yard

Military installations in the United States tend to be target-rich areas for mass killers, because they are largely gun-free zones, which makes absolutely no sense at all. This is where our warriors live and train, but guns on military bases are for training only. Forget about self-defense from active killers. The only people allowed side-arms on military bases in the U.S. are military police and civil police employed by the military. The worst example of the results of this misguided policy was the first attack on Fort Hood. Because it was finally ruled a terrorist incident, I have described it in Chapter 13.

Through the end of 2015, the second deadliest attack in a military installation in the U.S. occurred on September 16, 2013, at the Washington Navy Yard in the nation's capital. The Navy Yard, established in 1799 on the banks of the Anacostia River, is home to the Chief of Naval Operations and headquarters of the Naval Sea Systems Command (NAVSEA). It is a gated facility that houses various other departments of the Navy, some classified, and employs fourteen thousand military personnel and civilians. The facility has its own emergency services, including the Naval District of Washington (NDW) Police.

The largest structure in the complex is Building 197, which houses the headquarters of NAVSEA and employs about three thousand personnel. The building is six hundred thousand square feet of office space on five floors, each one containing a maze of cubicles and offices separated by long, narrow corridors running east-west and north-south across the huge building. Two large open atriums in the middle of the building stretch up through all five floors.

One of the employees in Building 197 was a thirty-four-year-old Navy veteran working as a civilian contractor supplying information-technology support services. He had been working there only about a week.

According to a Washington Metropolitan Police Department (MPD) after-action report and news reports, this is what happened.

In the week before September 16, the contractor went to Sharpshooters, a gun store in Lorton, Virginia, where he bought a 12-gauge Remington Model 870 Express Tactical pump-action shotgun that he modified by cutting off the butt and shortening the barrel. He also bought thirty rounds of double-ought buckshot.

On the morning of Monday, September 16, he drove from his hotel in his rented Toyota Prius to the facility, where his identification was checked at one of the gates. He parked the car in a parking garage and, lugging a backpack containing the shotgun, he walked to Building 197. He entered the building at 8:08 a.m., swiping his identification card at the employee turnstile, and took the elevator to the fourth floor. He walked to the men's restroom, entered a cubicle, removed the shotgun from his backpack, and stuffed his pockets with extra shells.

The contractor emerged from the restroom and walked into a cubicle area near an atrium. At 8:16 he opened fire and killed his first three victims. He shot at a young woman, wounding her in the head and one hand. MPD Chief Cathy Lanier stated in an interview with *60 Minutes* on CBS that the first 9-1-1 call came in to the D.C. Office of Unified

Communications (OUC) one minute thirty-six seconds after the first shot was fired. Some people in the building did not call 9-1-1 but called the base emergency services number.

The first 9-1-1 caller heard what he thought was a large safe being dropped. He stood up and looked over his cubicle partition to see the gunman shooting at a young woman.

"He immediately ducks down, gets under his desk, and uses a metal filing cabinet to conceal his location. He uses his mobile phone to call 9-1-1," the report states.

The caller provided a detailed description of the gunman, but there is some confusion about the location of Building 197, which later delayed the arrival of MPD officers. The civilian communications center dispatched MPD officers to the scene.

About 8:18 someone set off the fire alarm in an attempt to warn other occupants of the building. Subsequently, the alarm would make it much more difficult for responding officers searching for the shooter to ascertain where the shots were coming from. It also made it difficult for officers to hear their radios.

By 8:20, four minutes after opening fire, the active killer had shot and killed eight victims on the fourth floor. He then headed down to the third floor.

"Within the first two minutes on the third floor, [the gunman] fatally shoots two more victims. He has now shot and killed ten people within the first six minutes," the report states.

After emerging from his latest victim's office into the hallway, he fired at a group of employees at the other end of the corridor, but none were hit. The killer spotted a young woman hiding between a metal beam and a filing cabinet.

"He stands directly over her and attempts to fire twice, but the shotgun does not fire. It appears that it is not loaded," the report states.

The killer walked off, while reaching in his pocket for more shells. Police later evacuated the woman.

Moments later the gunman entered a stairwell on the third floor and encountered several employees coming down from the fourth floor. Before they can retreat back up the stairs, he shot one woman, hitting her in the shoulder. The woman was led up to the roof, where a U.S. Park Police helicopter evacuated her.

There were several more encounters on the third and fourth floors, where the gunman fired at groups of employees without effect.

At 8:23 the first MPD officers arrived at the Navy Yard, less than five minutes after being dispatched. According to standing orders, some of the entrance guards had locked the gates and responded to the shooting. This increased the time for MPD officers to enter the facility. When they did get into the base, there was some confusion about finding Building 197. They also received information that the shooting might be in Building 58 and that there might be more than one gunman.

Meanwhile, the gunman had reached the first floor. He approached the main entrance of the building when he encountered a security guard, Richard "Mike" Ridgell, a former Maryland state trooper.

"Before the guard can react, [the gunman] fires at him, hitting the guard and shattering the glass windows of the front entrance. [The gunman] retrieves the sidearm of the mortally wounded guard and proceeds north down the hallway," the report states.

A short time later, the killer encountered a security guard and a Navy military-police officer. They exchanged fire, but no one was hit.

At a stairwell on the west side of the building, the gunman looked out of a door into an alley, where he saw two men. Using the Beretta 9mm pistol he took from Ridgell, he fired at them, killing one. This was the last person he killed. The time was 8:38 a.m.

For another forty-seven minutes, the gunman roamed around the building, exchanging fire with law-enforcement officers on several occasions. He discarded the shotgun at some point during this period, but he still had the Beretta pistol. At least 117 officers from eight different law-enforcement agencies entered Building 197 to search for the killer.

At 9:12 MPD Officers Scott Williams and Emmanuel Smith, along with two agents from the Naval Criminal Investigative Service (NCIS), Brian Kelley and Ed Martin, searched for the gunman and cleared rooms on the third floor. About 9:15 Williams led the other three into a cubicle area where the gunman was hiding.

"As the officers make their way down the narrow pathway running along the bank of cubicles, [the gunman] fires at least one shot from a handgun. The MPD officer who is leading the team down the pathway is struck in both legs. The other MPD officer and two NCIS agents drag the injured officer back out of the area into the main hallway and request the assistance of additional officers," the report states.

The officers and agents spoke briefly to two U.S. Park Police (USPP) officers, Andrew Wong and Carl Hiott, then dragged Williams, the wounded officer, to the stairs and carried him down to seek medical attention. Meanwhile MPD Emergency Response Team Officer Dorian DeSantis joined Wong and Hiott in the hallway. Leaving Wong in the hallway at the south entrance to the cubicle area to provide cover, the other two officers entered the area and started searching the banks of cubicles.

"As they round the partition to the last bank of cubicles, [the gunman] jumps out from under one of the desks and fires upon the MPD officer, who has just rounded the cubicle partition. [The gunman] is approximately five feet from the officer when he fires. Seeing the suspect fire, the MPD officer returns fire, while attempting to move back and laterally away from the shooter. The USPP officer also returns fire. The MPD officer is hit by one round fired by [the gunman], but the round hits his vest," the report states.

At 9:25 a.m. fire from DeSantis and Hiott killed the gunman. Later DeSantis found the bullet fired by the gunman in his bullet-resistant vest.

The gunman killed twelve people and wounded three. All the victims were civilian employees or contractors. After the attack, the FBI determined the gunman was mentally ill and had been suffering from the delusional belief that he was being controlled by extremely low-frequency electromagnetic waves.

As usual President Obama lost no time in advocating for more gun control, even though most of the prohibitions and restrictions demanded by gun-control activists were present in connection with the Navy Yard shooting. The gunman not only passed a background check enabling him to buy the shotgun, but he had a security clearance. The Navy Yard was effectively a "gun-free zone," except, of course, for law-enforcement officers and the killer. The nation's capital itself was a gun-free zone for law-abiding citizens, where many politicians prefer dead victims to dead perpetrators killed by residents in self-defense.

Chapter 12

RAPID MASS MURDERS: TRAINING TO RESPOND

*"Recognize that today's world is a tough place to be
and that the only one responsible
for your personal security is you." –* Ed Lovette

We have covered much in the way of training to stop active-killer rampages in Chapters Six, Seven, and Eight. Much of what is taught to teachers and other school staff is relevant to stopping such incidents, be they in shopping malls, restaurants, or movie theaters or on military bases. So let us return to Tactical Defense Institute in Ohio, where John Benner teaches a three-day course entitled Active Shooter/Killer Course for Civilians. I have attempted not to repeat what was taught in the FASTER classes and instead concentrate on what I have not addressed before.

As a concealed-handgun-license instructor in Texas, I have always advised students not to become involved in third-party disputes. It is a good general rule. You are armed primarily to protect yourself, your family, and perhaps close friends. You are not a police officer.

However, I believe there is at least one exception to that rule. If you are in responding distance of an active-killer rampage and you are armed, you have a choice. Do you head to the sound of the gunfire and try to save some lives by stopping the killer, or do you run in the other direction like everyone else? In most cases the safest course of action is to flee like everyone else. But there will be some people, like Jeanne Assam at the New Life Church or Joe Zamudio at Gabby Giffords's event in Tucson, who will feel obliged to try to stop the killer and save lives. Of course, if you are in the same location when the active killer starts his rampage, your choice is easier. You will be saving your life and perhaps the lives of anybody in the vicinity. That is why you carry a concealed handgun. The course at TDI is designed for those individuals who carry concealed handguns and want to be prepared for anything.

Civilian Training Course

The students on the course were a varied lot, including doctors, medics, fire fighters, and law-enforcement officers, as well as interested civilians. Of the twenty-three students, five were women. Most of the students came from Ohio, but a few came from further afield, including one from Montana. In the FASTER I and II classes, I monitored the courses, but with the Active-Killer course I participated. I actually took this course before monitoring the FASTER classes.

The course started in the TDI classroom with John Benner. After going over the history of mass shootings in the United States, which we have covered in the first five chapters, he described why it is important to have armed citizens anywhere that mass shootings may occur. Current training in enlightened police departments and sheriffs' offices is that the first officer on the scene goes in and confronts the shooter. But even then there is going to be a response time of several minutes during which the Stopwatch of Death is ticking, and people are dying. Benner pointed out that time is the most important factor. Therefore, the best solution to an active shooter or killer is to train civilians, hence the course.

"Seventy-five percent of the time the problem is solved by you guys," Benner said, referring to civilians.

He divided active killers into three groups.

First, there is the single killer who may have several firearms, but acts with minimal planning. Luby's cafeteria in Killeen, Texas — twenty-three killed and twenty wounded — and the shooting at a McDonald's restaurant in San Ysidro, California — twenty-one killed and nineteen wounded — are good examples. Benner said the San Ysidro shooting in 1984 was another example where police contained the scene without going in, while the shooting continued.

"This was the Columbine we should have paid attention to," he said. Another example is the incident at Pinelake Health and Rehabilitation, Carthage, North Carolina, in 2009 — eight dead. There the killer was searching for his estranged wife intending to kill her. When he couldn't find her, he started shooting people at random. Officer Justin Garner went in alone and confronted the gunman, wounding him and getting wounded himself. He did the right thing. He did not wait for backup, which would have been long coming, as he was the only Carthage officer on duty at the time. (See Chapter 11.)

The second type is where one or two people do a lot of prior planning, creating obstacles and possibly improvised explosive devices. Examples are Columbine — thirteen dead and twenty-one injured — and Virginia Tech — thirty-two people dead and twenty-three wounded.

The third level is a terrorist incident. Benner divided these into two groups. First is the single terrorist on a personal jihad, like the shooters at Fort Hood — thirteen killed and thirty wounded — and the Trolley Square Mall in Salt Lake City, Utah. There, off-duty Ogden police officer Ken Hammond confronted the shooter and pinned him down while his wife called police. Hammond had a 1911-style semi-automatic and no spare magazines. "He was out of bullets," Benner said.

The second type of terrorist incident is a well-planned, often state-sponsored, massive attack. A good example is the massacre at Beslan School in south Russia, where 385 people, mostly children, were killed.

"We have no plan to respond to this," Benner said.

Another example is the attack in Mumbai, India, where ten terrorists killed 166 people and wounded another 308. The latest such attack at the time of writing is the attack in Paris, where 130 died and hundreds more were wounded. More about these in the next chapter.

Options

If we are faced with an active killer, Benner suggested these options. If we are unarmed, the first option is escape. Have an escape route in mind and preferably two. Leave your belongings behind unless you have something bullet-resistant to act as a shield. Pick up or carry something to fight with. Move from cover to cover. The second option is to hide. Barricade your hiding place. Lock the door. Silence your cell phone. Have something with which to fight if necessary.

Tony Rose of Dayton, Ohio, shoots around the left side of a barricade.

Finally, as a last resort, when your life is in imminent danger, seize your best opportunity to attack, such as when the shooter is changing magazines. Act with extreme violence.

"Your objective is to kill that person," Benner said. "There are no second chances here."

The unarmed response has been dealt with in detail in the ALICE program in Chapter 8.

If you are armed, it is your choice whether to fight and/or defend others. If you decide not to fight, follow the instructions for unarmed response. Do not have a gun in your hand when confronting law enforcement.

If you decide to engage the shooter, remain calm — practice tactical breathing, deep breaths; use good tactics — do not go so fast that you miss things you ought to see.

"Find your own pace to do it," Benner said.

Be aggressive — speed, surprise, and violence.

Shoot the killer down. Keep shooting until he is no longer a threat.

When safe, holster your gun and await police.

If the killer is actively shooting people, do not order him to drop his gun or challenge him. It just gives him an opportunity to shoot you, Benner said.

After lunch we did some accuracy training on figure targets at distances from five to thirty yards. Then we faced small head-and-shoulders-shaped steel targets, which we shot while moving forwards, sideways, and backwards. We practiced rounding corners and shooting from cover using the "drop-out" technique. A group of us went with David Bowie, a police officer and owner of Bowie Tactical Concepts, to one of the Live-Fire Houses, where we practiced scenarios with empty guns. All this was very similar to the shooting and scenarios done by the educators in the FASTER classes.

Situational Awareness

We started our second day in the classroom. Ed Lovette gave a presentation on developing our situational awareness. Now retired, Lovette has been a firearms instructor for the New Mexico State Police, a CIA officer, and a columnist for *Combat Handguns* magazine. He defined situational awareness as a state of general alertness, which allows you to take the element of surprise away from a threat to your personal security.

"We don't want to be surprised," he said.

It is not enough to tell someone to be alert and stay safe. You must tell them how to be alert and how to recognize the danger signs.

"We have to know what to look for," Lovette said.

The goal is to be able to use your awareness to detect, assess, avoid, evade, counter, and prevail in the encounter.

"Doing this requires a lot of discipline," he said.

It requires mental preparation, and he suggested a reality check. "Recognize that today's world is a tough place to be, and that the only one responsible for your personal security is you."

John Benner (right) introduces Ed Lovette to the class.

You also need to decide before you get into a situation that you will be able to use deadly force if necessary. "Have that conversation with yourself."

Mental conditioning means working exercises into your routine such as the "What If" game. News programs provide a lot of information about incidents in which people are hurt or killed. Spend a few moments thinking what you would do in similar situations. Spend a few minutes a day just sitting and listening to any sound you can hear. Then spend the same amount of time sitting and saying to yourself, what am I feeling? Focus on what is going on around you. It may be in your car before you drive to work.

Another exercise is a game of Xs and Os. Every time someone approaches you without being seen, you score an X. If you see them before they get close, you get an O. Try to minimize the Xs and increase the Os. Mental preparation plus mental conditioning equals situational awareness.

Lovette then went over color codes, which classify our awareness level. The late Colonel Jeff Cooper adapted these from a Marine Corps code. Condition White is a normal non-combative state of mind.

"If we are attacked in Condition White, we are likely to not do too well," Lovette said.

Condition Yellow is a state of relaxed alertness. Condition Orange is a state of alarm. We become a little nervous. We may experience a dry mouth and butterflies in the stomach, and we may need urgently to pee. And Condition Red is defensive combat. We experience a chemical dump that prepares us for fight or flight. It negatively affects our ability to operate firearms. Fingers become flippers as we lose our fine motor skills. We need to make sure we can articulate to the police or a prosecutor why we shot this person.

Danger signs are anything that warns us that we may have a problem. They may be visual, auditory, or intuitive — that is knowing without knowing why.

"Women are a lot better at this [intuition] than the guys," Lovette said. Pay attention if the women with you say something is not right.

Situational signs are also important. If someone tries to force you into a freezer or a car, "this is the one they tell you, if you ever in your life are going to resist, this is the one."

Awareness keeps us from being surprised, which helps us prevent the onset of survival stress. It buys us time, allows us to make a plan, and allows us to use our training. If we are attacked at close range when we are surprised and we believe we are going to die, survival stress kicks in, and we lose our conscious mind. The subconscious mind takes over, and we go into survival mode. The chemical cocktail is dumped into our system, causing a loss of fine motor skills, auditory exclusion, loss of near vision, and tunnel vision. We will react as we have been trained to do, but with about 50 percent efficiency.

When we talk to somebody who has been involved in a situation, he may not have a clear memory of what happened.

We also have to deal with what Lovette calls the Four Deadly Ds.

- Denying — this isn't really happening.
- Deferring — this is not really a danger sign, so I will put off doing anything about it.
- Daydreaming — Often you will be in your car going somewhere familiar, and when you get there you can't remember anything about the journey. We have to fight this all the time.
- Distraction — A pretty woman can be a great distraction, sometimes by intention. A street fight or a traffic accident can distract you from the real threat.

Pay attention to everything going on around you. When you put your gun on in the morning, it should be like turning on the ignition key. You go into Condition Yellow.

Before you enter a convenience store or a restaurant, assess the situation — don't walk in blindly. Be aware of everything inside your twenty-one-foot personal safety zone. Watch all 360 degrees around you. Always know how to get out of where you are, whether you are on foot, in a vehicle, or in an office building or mall.

Protect your back by sitting with your back to a wall. It was failure to do this that cost Wild Bill Hickok his life. Sit where you can see the exits and the cash register. In a vehicle be sure to use your mirrors. Break conventional thought patterns by ascertaining what you are really seeing.

Always keep the edge. Be prepared, have a plan, and do something. "Doing something may be being the best witness you can be."

Surveillance

A mass killer is not likely to have you under surveillance unless you are the target of his anger. You might be a teacher at school or a supervisor at work who he feels treated him badly. You are more likely to be watched prior to a kidnapping, car jacking, home invasion, or even while being stalked. However, Lovette gave us a primer on detecting surveillance. Surveillance detection is one of three interrelated skills, the other two being surveillance and counter-surveillance, he said.

Surveillance can be stationary, on foot, mobile, or technical. Criminal surveillance is likely to be on foot or mobile and amateurish. You will probably be followed either from home or from your office or place of work, so be particularly observant as you leave home or arrive at the office. Frequently ask yourself: Is anything different from usual?

You can detect and confirm surveillance given enough time, distance, change in direction, and change in your environment. But it is much easier to stay off the bad guy's radar screen.

Avoid becoming a target, and don't invite trouble. One way to stay off the radar is not to project a victim aura, as in being in Condition White. How is your posture when you walk? Are you purposeful or detached? Do you limp or is your shirt buttoned incorrectly? Are you wearing a hospital patient band? Are you paying more attention to your cell phone than to your surroundings? Change routes to and from home, and don't let anyone follow you home.

An example of criminals following potential victims home happened in Cheshire, Connecticut, in 2007. Two career burglars followed Jennifer Petit, wife of a prominent doctor, and their eleven-year-old daughter home from the supermarket. In a subsequent home invasion and hostage situation, Dr. Bill Petit was beaten but escaped. His wife was forced to withdraw $15,000 from her bank, then she was raped and murdered. Their two daughters died after the attackers set the house on fire. The two murderers were caught as they attempted to flee. Both were tried, found guilty, and sentenced to death. However, Connecticut abandoned the death penalty in 2015, so they will likely spend the rest of their lives in prison.

"The smoldering char of the Petit house and a suburban street in Cheshire, filled with fire trucks and police cars, was chilling evidence that there is no social contract that protects the good people among us," Lovette said. "Even if you pay your mortgage, mow your lawn, and send your kids to good schools, live as decently and honorably as the Petits; evil can still find you, even while you're sleeping in your own bed."

There are some actions that should alert you to the possibility of being watched.

- Have you seen the same person or persons before?
- Do they "belong" in that location?
- Do they move when you move?
- Do they show up at different locations where you happen to be?
- Do they seem unusually interested in you?

Once you become suspicious, you need to confirm those suspicions. If they are planning to rob or kidnap you, you want them to know you have seen them. Make it obvious.

"When you look them in the eye, that's a gotcha," Lovette said.

If you are on foot, how many do you think are watching you? What do they do when you move? How do they react when you look at them? Did you catch them peeking at you? Is there non-verbal communication between partners?

If you are in a vehicle, what makes you think that car is following you? In criminal cases it is usually one car. The vehicle moves when you move and stops when you stop. It follows you through a red light. It closes up in heavy traffic and backs off in light traffic. It uses another car for cover: it pulls out to check on you then drops back behind another vehicle.

The simplest action is to speed up. Make three right turns, but only if you know the area. Consider changing lanes with signal. If he is still with you, try a lane change without signaling. If you are on a freeway, consider crossing several lanes of traffic to take an off ramp, again, if you know the area. If you are familiar with the area and you are on a road, consider a no-signal left turn at an intersection across traffic or consider a U-turn.

If you are convinced you are being followed, go anywhere with lots of light and/or lots of people — anywhere you might find police, fire, or security personnel.

Be sure you can describe the person or vehicle you think is following you. Get a good description and write it down at the time, John Benner said. If possible, take photos of them.

"Our minds play tricks on us."

A Walmart parking lot is a good place. If you are in a car and you have a cell phone, consider staying in the car and making the phone call from there.

If you call the police while driving, can you tell them where you are?

Live-Fire Houses

In the afternoon, we started on the range, "shooting down an active shooter" as we advanced, aiming for the upper chest circle. David Bowie showed us how it is done. We followed his example, advancing from about ten yards to about three, firing as fast as we could make good hits.

Again we were split into three groups. My group stayed with Bowie at the range for some precision shooting, while the others went to the two Live-Fire Houses nearby.

Later we trooped along to Live-Fire House 1, where we had to identify and shoot down the active shooter in one of the furthest rooms. When it was my turn to take on "the

Instructor David Bowie demonstrates shooting down an active killer.

shooter," I arrived in the doorway of the last room on the right and could see several "people" facing me. The nearest guy was pointing an empty beer bottle at me. It could have been mistaken for a gun. At first glance none appeared armed, but behind the white guy with the beer bottle was a black guy wearing bib overalls whose right hand was not visible. As I moved to the right I saw the gun in his right hand, and I shot him in the chest three times.

I also saw a guy holding a woman in front of him, possibly as a hostage. I shot him in the head three times. This was a mistake, but I could see by the patches on the guy's face that I hadn't been the only one to shoot him. There was no evidence that he was armed.

On my second run, several "people" were in the last room on the left of the shoot house. As I rounded the corner and could see into that last room, I saw a woman pointing a gun in my direction. I shot her three times. Behind her and to one side I saw a "young guy" holding a skateboard. I told him to drop it. He didn't, but I refrained from shooting him.

At the second Live-Fire House, I was standing facing a closed door. Instructor Chris Wallace told me I could hear shooting, to go through the door and solve the problem. I pulled on the door to open it, but it didn't open. I had not noticed that the door hinges were not visible, so I should have pushed the door to enter, not pulled it. I guess I'm just one of those guys who go through life pulling doors marked "push." Going through the door I found myself in an empty room, but I could see through a doorway into a second room. The second room was dark, but I entered and was able to make out the "shooter" behind some other "people." I hit him with my usual three hits to the upper chest. Wallace said I should have had a flashlight with me to light the dark room, and I could have shot the "bad guy" from outside the room instead of following my outstretched gun into the second room and making myself more vulnerable.

After a break for dinner, we returned to the classroom where Greg Ellifritz, a police training officer from Columbus, Ohio, gave the class a session on Combat Casualty Care. This may be useful during or after a shootout or during everyday life. You may get wounded even if you win an armed encounter, so you need to know how to treat yourself or others.

"You may have to take care of yourself for a little while until the medics get there," Ellifritz said.

Day Three

We started our third day on the range. John Benner told us we needed to know how to operate what he called "battlefield pick up weapons," in particular a weapon we might take from the body of a terrorist who had no more use for it, such as an AK-47 or even an AR-15. However, Benner warned that if a police officer or another armed citizen saw us with an AK-47, we might be mistaken for the shooter. Some of the students split off for instruction from David Bowie in how to operate an AK and an AR.

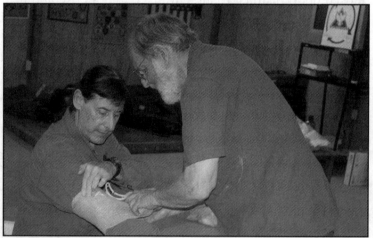

Author puts a pressure bandage on Ernie Husted during the session on Emergency Casualty Care.

Benner explained that if we are heading for the sound of shooting, we may well be heading upstream in a river of panicked victims trying to get away from the shooter. He said he learned that from some school-resource officers. "I never really thought about having two hundred kids rushing at you, and you're trying to move down this hallway."

Or we may be making our way through a group of people frozen in place by surprise at what is happening. When people first hear gunfire they are not going to start running immediately. "That's not going to happen," Benner said.

A lot of people are not going to recognize the noise as gunshots. "This is about action versus reaction. We all have that lag time — that's the time when we see something, our mind processes it, and now we're going to act on it. That takes time. The bigger the surprise is, the longer it takes for us to react to it. You may react quicker because you know what a shot sounds like."

Benner also recommended keeping our guns holstered when heading for the sound of gunfire, in case we were mistaken for the shooter and so no one could snatch our guns. When drawn, weapons should be held close to the body so they are easy to control.

We each practiced pushing through a group of people with our guns empty, verified by being "roped" with yellow tubing inserted through the barrels and magazine wells. Then we practiced with our pistols hot, pushing our way through half-a-dozen chest-high sandbags hanging from the roof, then advancing on a target, shooting rapidly as we closed. We tried these drills several times, with our guns holstered and when holding them.

Scenarios

For the rest of the day we were put through scenarios using Airsoft pistols shooting plastic BBs that sting when they hit you. We started at the two-story Force-on-Force house. I volunteered to go first so I could photograph others going through the scenarios. I had a relatively easy scenario — they seemed to get more complicated as time went on.

I put on a black face-mask to protect head and eyes and picked up the Airsoft pistol that looked like a Glock. I stood outside the house and was told by instructor Chris Wallace that I had just dropped off my kid at the daycare center. At my age that was a bit of a stretch but no matter. I had stepped out of the building when I heard shooting — Go!

With no hesitation, I pushed my way into the "daycare center." I was in a large room with a counter on the far side that separated it from another room. I could see the "bad guy" on the far side of the second room beyond the counter. He was shooting his Airsoft pistol at others in our group, who I assumed were playing children or daycare staff. I raised my gun in both hands and shot the "active killer" in the back several times. Wallace told me I had done okay in shooting the 'killer" as soon as I could see him and what he was doing.

I watched and took photographs as others faced different scenarios. The bottom floor of the house was then converted to a doctor's office. A blonde young woman was the responder and was sitting near the counter waiting for an appointment with "Doctor Smith." The "bad guy" came in, pushed past the receptionist, and was immediately shot by the young woman, who said she shot him as soon as he pulled out a gun. She was praised for being quick off the mark, as the instructors were expecting the "bad guy" to get into the doctor's office and start shooting before she ran after him and shot him.

Another scenario had the "good guy" as an employer upstairs in an office when a "bad guy" comes in intending to kill him. The "good guy" is unarmed except for what might have been a baseball bat. The "good guy" got out of his office with the "bat." As the "bad guy" followed his gun through

Lindy Sherman of Cincinnati pushes through a crowd of sandbags to engage an active killer.

the door to the outer office, the "good guy" ambushed him and whacked his gun arm. Had it been a real baseball bat, the attacker would have been disarmed or worse.

The final scenario had Ernie Husted of Springfield, Ohio, as the "good guy." He was upstairs when a "terrorist," shouting "Allahu Akbar" or "God is great," ran up the stairs. Husted was able to shoot him, but was not aware of another "terrorist" who ran up the stairs at the other end of the building and shot Husted in the back before he knew he was up against two.

Our next stop was a clearing in the trees on the other side of the property known as the Upper Range. Again, I volunteered for the first scenario. Instructor Jeff Lehman kept me in the trees out of sight of the range. When the scenario was ready, I walked up into the clearing for a briefing. The clearing was littered with plastic barrels, a couple of steel pepper popper targets, two old tractor tires, two shot-up old cars and a van, and several people wandering about. Greg Ellifritz told me this was a "Walmart parking lot" with some shoppers going to and from their vehicles. I was to head into the parking lot like I was going to my vehicle.

As I walked towards the vehicles, I saw a guy come out from behind the van and start shooting the "shoppers." I drew my Airsoft pistol and shot the attacker several times. After some prompting from Ellifritz, as in "Take cover," I got down behind the engine block of one of the cars and pretended to be calling 9-1-1. I then put my gun on the hood of the car, because I didn't want to be holding it when the police arrived. In the debriefing, Ellifritz said I should have kept the shooter covered. Again, because I went first I had the easiest scenario. The next student had two shooters to contend with. Often terrorists will work in pairs with the backup one attracting no attention unless the first one meets resistance.

The next scenario involved two terrorists who took AKs out of the back of one of the cars and headed towards the "Walmart store." Two students shot the men, even though they had not shot or even threatened anyone. In the debriefing, Ellifritz said what he would have done was follow the men into the store and shot only if they threatened anyone. He said they might have been returning the rifles to the store after buying them earlier. With AKs this was unlikely, he acknowledged.

The final scenario was with a "bad guy" who was wearing a suicide bomb vest. We had been told earlier that the only way to stop a suicide bomber was to shoot him in the head, and the students did this.

Our last exercise was back at one of the Live-Fire Houses. Previously we had faced only one "bad guy" at a time in the Live-Fire Houses, although we didn't know there was only one until we had completed the exercise. This time we were faced with two terrorist targets, complete with Arafat head-dresses and AK-47s. These guys were easier to identify, so neither of them lived to gloat over the Infidels.

*Student takes on an active killer
in the "Walmart parking lot."*

Feedback

One of the things that impressed me was the number of students who have returned to TDI again and again for training. Only a handful of us had not been to TDI before, and some students had been back a dozen times or more: some described themselves as TDI addicts.

Ernie Husted said this was the tenth time he had been to TDI:

He keeps coming back to keep his skills refreshed. "It's a very fair price for the training you get." It is only a couple of hours from where he lives in Springfield, Ohio. "The quality of the instructors is top notch. I've never seen an instructor down here ever be anything except patient. They never roll their eyes; they never give you that smirk. They'll ask you questions, and they treat you like a commodity in the aspect you're down here to learn, and their job is to make it as good as possible."

He said that tackling an active shooter is an area he was weak in. "My responsibility as a concealed-carry-permit person is to keep my skill set up to the very best of my ability if I'm going to carry a weapon."

Christina Baird was there with her husband:
She said this was her second time at TDI. *"I work in a facility where I have lots of employees. It's not in the best area of town, so I feel this gives me an edge if something were to happen. I was tired of being afraid. So being here gives me that opportunity where I can face my fear head on and learn how to do something about it."* She is fearful every time she locks her building at night. She weighs 110 pounds. *"I have a big building to lock in not the best area, so yes, I am fearful every night when I close our building."* She carries a handgun. *"I figure at my size the best defense for me is to get my carry license and have some protection."*

Melissa Rippe and her twin Lindy Sherman are both from Cincinnati:
They are more interested in shooting than their husbands. *"Our family calls us the tactical twins,"* Rippe said. She and her sister have been coming to TDI for three years. *"We started three years ago with Pistol One, Two, Three and just started coming back every class they had almost."* They have also attended Tactical Shotgun and Tactical Rifle.

"They were phenomenal about teaching us from square one exactly how to do it right, and we had a ball. So every time we feel like cutting loose, we just come out here and play."

"We don't want to get too political, but I think the country is in for some hard times. I do believe we have a radical Islamic problem here. It's coming into this country and across this world. So I acknowledge it, and I think we've got men and women who are fighting for this country overseas, and the least we can do is help defend the country they are fighting for here at home."

Memory Consolidation
At Tactical Defense Institute in the FASTER I and FASTER II courses, John Benner told the students that after

you have been involved in a shooting incident, you have the right to remain silent. He encouraged them to use that right. By that, he did not mean you should literally clam up and say nothing. Rather, you should say you will cooperate fully after you have talked to your attorney. This perhaps needs some elaboration.

Well known gun and self-defense writer and instructor Massad Ayoob advises trying to help the police understand what happened at the scene by telling investigators you were attacked and pointing out evidence and witnesses to them. But there are some caveats.

First responders to the scene will be very concerned with the safety of everyone involved, including themselves. You need to educate yourself about the appropriate manner and timing of securing your weapon and letting the first responders know you are not a threat. You should try to remain as calm as possible and always very carefully attend to and follow any commands that officers will give you. Remember that you are now a suspect in a violent confrontation and should expect to be viewed as such by the first responders.

The first responders will want to identify and collect evidence, identify other eyewitnesses, understand the gist of the situation, direct medical responders to any injured individuals, figure out who is who, and the like.

Dr. Alexis Artwohl, the retired police psychologist, recommends that your first call after the encounter should be to 9-1-1 and the second to your attorney, who should come to your location immediately.

Be aware that the emotional intensity of the situation could result in your making lengthy and emotional statements beyond the brief information relevant to helping the first responders. Your attorney can help calm you down and can assist you with a concise public-safety statement, should you choose to make one. Your immediate statement can help first responders secure the scene and initiate the investigation.

However, you are not obligated to make any statement immediately following the incident, and it is probably best to decline to give police a full, detailed statement then.

Artwohl points out in Chapter 10 that you are likely to get some details wrong and suffer memory lapses in the immediate aftermath of a shooting. If you allow yourself to sleep, it will help you consolidate and perhaps recover some memory details. However, there is always the possibility that your honest memories may not either be an entirely accurate reflection of reality.

You will be asked to provide a full formal statement later to assist investigating officers and possibly others in the criminal-justice system. Artwohl explains that a full formal statement is an in-depth interview during which investigators will be seeking as much detail as possible from the participants in the event to help the investigators understand what occurred.

Remember that your 9-1-1 call will be recorded, and any statements you make at the scene will now be evidence in your case. Prior mental rehearsal of how you will calm yourself down and be disciplined in your statements will help you behave appropriately and help you and the first responders deal with a highly stressful situation.

The time to educate yourself about your legal rights and responsibilities is now, Artwohl said. This includes identifying whom you will call for immediate legal assistance and consulting with them to understand your potential liabilities and what assistance you can expect from them in the event you are involved in an incident.

CHAPTER 13

RADICAL ISLAMIC JIHAD: THE THREATS

*"An armed man will kill an unarmed man
with monotonous regularity."*
— Clint Smith, President of
Thunder Ranch shooting school

President Barack Obama may not want to acknowledge it, but Radical Islam is at war with the United States. The aim of the Islamic jihadis is to destroy the Western way of life and replace it with a worldwide caliphate under Sharia law. As former Republican presidential contender Senator Marco Rubio put it, they want to destroy us because we let women drive and girls go to school.

The major threat in 2016 is the Islamic State (IS), also known as the Islamic State of Iraq and Syria (ISIS), the Islamic State of Iraq and the Levant (ISIL), or Daesh. This organization of mostly Sunni Muslims controls large parts of Syria and Iraq, but has tentacles into Libya, Nigeria, and Afghanistan. Several thousand citizens from European countries and the U.S. have joined ISIS in Iraq and Syria, and some of them have returned to their countries of origin. We must assume some of them are likely to make terrorist attacks here in the U.S. and in Europe.

Radical Islamic terrorist attacks can be divided into two groups. There are the "lone wolf" attacks carried out by individuals or small groups of fanatics, who have been radicalized either through social media or through mosques run by radical clerics. These attacks involve minimal preparation and few people, so are the hardest to prevent. They are organized locally and have not been especially successful in terms of numbers of innocents murdered.

The second type of attack is the highly organized, often state sponsored, strategic attack that results in large numbers of casualties and widespread terror. Most strategic attacks subject the target to several attacks at once. They involve a lot of planning, intelligence gathering, logistics, and training for the terrorists. Examples include the attack on the city of Mumbai (formerly Bombay) in India in 2008 and the more recent attack in Paris in 2015.

Similar strategic attacks have occurred in Central London and Madrid. During the morning rush hour on July 7, 2005, four radical Muslim suicide bombers exploded three bombs on the London Underground and one on a double-decker bus. They killed fifty-two civilians and injured more than seven hundred.

An earlier morning rush hour attack occurred on March 11, 2004, in Madrid, Spain. Ten bombs exploded within minutes of each other on four commuter trains killing 191 people and injuring more than eighteen hundred. Responsibility for the attacks was claimed by Al Qaeda but a judge found no direct link and blamed cells of Islamic extremists influenced through the Internet.

While ISIS appears to be the most dangerous threat in 2016, all terrorist groups — Al Qaeda, Hezbollah, and others — learn from one another.

The only successful strategic attack launched in the United States was conducted by Al Qaeda on September 11, 2001, when four airliners were hijacked: two of them were crashed into the twin towers of the World Trade Center in New York and one into the Pentagon in Washington, D.C. The fourth aircraft did not reach its target: it crashed in a field in Pennsylvania, because the passengers fought back.

According to John Giduck, the terrorism expert whose book on Virginia Tech I have mentioned, Al Qaeda was very good at learning from other terrorist groups and incorporating their techniques into their own attacks.

It took a long time before terrorism experts realized that Al Qaeda strategic attacks always involved four separate incidents, all assaults using the same method, Giduck said.

"Al Qaeda, when it launched strategic-level operations, could never afford a failure. They had to be the one group that always proved they could bring its enemy to its knees, and so they factored failure right into their strategic-level operations. They always anticipated that out of four teams and four different safe-houses, one would get stopped by the target government. They would develop intelligence that they were there, and they would stop them in the safehouse. They always planned that another one might be successfully thwarted by the target victims themselves or the unexpected presence of law enforcement or military. So it always gave them two for success."

On "9/11" Al Qaeda hit three of their four targets, but even if they had hit only two, it would still have been a huge success for the group.

Part of the purpose of strategic-terrorist attacks is to generate maximum news coverage and put pressure on target governments. When bombings did not produce enough casualties, terrorists turned to taking hostages in large numbers and killing many of them. This extended the time-line of the news coverage.

"The terrorists are always stuck in this ratcheting up, endless escalation, of their own accomplishments, because the news media only makes really big deals of those attacks that break an existing record. So the terrorists then have to think of bigger and better ways to do things. Then you started seeing mass hostage seizures," Giduck said.

The next step was for terrorists to use different methods of assault in one strategic attack. These are known as symphonic attacks. Again, it took western experts a while to realize what was happening because these attacks often included a hostage seizure, and the media focused on the hostages and often ignored the ancillary assaults.

Giduck defines a symphonic attack as a group of simultaneous – or near simultaneous – attacks at a variety of targets using at least several different attack methods or tactics. Mumbai in November 2008 was one, while "9/11" was a typical Al Qaeda swarm attack, striking the group's standard four targets simultaneously, but utilizing a single attack method. A symphonic attack is like a symphony orchestra.

"You have a number of different people, all on different instruments, seeming to play different things at different tempos, while a conductor tries to hold that chaos together in a way in which the whole becomes greater than the sum of the parts. Same with symphonic attacks. Lots of different things going on, all at the same time. Not four identical things going on," he said.

Mumbai

In November 2008 at the city of Mumbai on the west coast of India, ten terrorists from neighboring Pakistan carried out a series of synchronized attacks that lasted for four days, in which about 166 people were killed and more than three hundred wounded.

Mumbai is India's largest city with more than eighteen million residents and is the financial and commercial capital of the country. The city is built on what were seven islands, which were artificially connected and now form a peninsula.

The attacks were carried out by members of Lashkar-e-Taiba, a group of Pakistani Muslim extremists, and were controlled by organizers in Pakistan. India is mostly Hindu, while Pakistan is mostly Muslim.

According to news reports and *Wikipedia*, the attacks developed as follows.

On Wednesday, November 26, the attackers left Karachi by boat, traveling about 550 miles before landing aboard inflatable boats on what was the southernmost island, Colaba. The terrorists split up and headed for their different destinations. The first target was the historic railway station — Chhatrapati Shivaji Terminus or CST. Two terrorists attacked the station shortly after 9:20 p.m. local time. They fired their AK-56 rifles indiscriminately into the crowds. In the following ninety minutes, the terrorists killed fifty-eight people and wounded more than one hundred.

The killers headed to the nearby Cama Hospital, killing eight police officers on the way. At the hospital, they shot it out with several members of a police anti-terrorist squad, killing most of them. The pair were stopped at a roadblock and again shot it out with officers. One of the terrorists was killed and the other captured.

About 9:30 terrorists entered the Leopold Café, pulled AKs out of their backpacks, and opened fire, killing about ten people before they left.

Meanwhile two bombs on timers exploded in two taxis, killing both drivers and several passengers. About fifteen other people were injured.

About 9:40 p.m. several terrorists arrived at the Taj Mahal Palace and Tower Hotel. They attacked guests around the swimming pool and in bars and restaurants in the hotel. Six explosions were reported in the hotel: three in restaurants, two in elevators, and one in the hotel lobby. In the early hours of November 27, fires were seen in the hotel's top floors. During that first night, fire fighters using ladder trucks rescued about two hundred staff and guests through windows.

Trade delegates from the European Parliament were staying in the hotel at the time, but all escaped. An assistant to one member of the European Parliament was wounded. About thirty people were killed during the siege that lasted four days.

Shortly before 10 p.m. on the 26th two terrorists attacked the Oberoi-Trident Hotel, entering through the restaurant and opening fire on staff and guests. Forty-four hostages were rescued on the 27th and about thirty-five more on the 28th. Bomb blasts caused fires in the hotel on the 27th.

Nariman House, a Jewish center, was also attacked and taken over by two terrorists on the evening of the 26th. Just before the center was attacked, a nearby gas station blew up, causing the people in the center to look out of their windows, making them targets for the terrorists who shot at them. Nine hostages were rescued on the 27th, but a rabbi and his pregnant wife, along with several other hostages, were killed by the terrorists. Late on the 28th the center was stormed by National Security Guard (NSG) commandos, who descended by ropes down onto the roof from helicopters.

John Giduck said the Lubavitch or Jewish center was the only place where hostages were held for a period of time. The other targets were nothing more than active-killer situations.

"But when the Indian forces arrived, they treated them all — it was like Columbine all over again — as though they were in mass-hostage situations rather than active-killer. And so they slowed down, and they took their time, and a lot of people died because of it."

On the 29th NSG commandos, accompanied by Marine Commandos and members of the Rapid Action Force, fought their way into the Taj Mahal and Oberoi-Trident hotels, killing the remaining terrorists and ending the attacks.

Giduck said he visited India shortly after the attack and met several of the military commanders involved in responding to the attacks.

"Just by mixing up their tactics, five two-man teams running around an enormous city of fifteen million people had the Indian authorities believing they had somewhere between a hundred and two hundred terrorists."

During the three-day Active Shooter/Killer Course for Civilians at Tactical Defense Institute, Ed Lovette, the retired CIA officer, gave us some more details about the Mumbai attack — what to watch for and how to respond. The Mumbai terrorist attack is the "worst case active-shooter situation that you might find yourself in," Lovette said. "Right now all the law-enforcement agencies are using this as a model to see what we would do here if something like this happened."

Law-enforcement agencies are finding out that they do not have the resources to cope with a Mumbai-style attack. The people who pulled off this attack were well-organized, well-trained, and professional, he said.

"These folks had their act together."

This group was sponsored, controlled, and equipped by the Pakistani intelligence service, known as ISI. "It's just like the Hezbollah, Iran, Syrian connection — a state-sponsored group."

This is a problem, because these terrorists are prepared and extensively trained for each mission they undertake. They had very competent two-year surveillance of their targets.

Each terrorist carried a Chinese AK-56 with a thirty-round magazine; a 9mm pistol; two spare magazines; eight-to-ten hand grenades; and Improvised Explosive Devices (IEDs) containing RDX, an explosive more powerful than TNT. Each of them carried all their equipment in a backpack.

When you go about your daily life with your handgun and perhaps one spare magazine, "is this something you want to take on head on?" asked Lovette.

The point of the Active Shooter/Killer Course was to rethink our tactics. There may be something we could do here. "The last thing we want to do is get into a confrontation with someone armed with an AK," Lovette said.

When we talk of moving from cover to cover, remember that cover that will stop a pistol bullet may not stop an AK or AR round. "A lot of the things that we do are impacted by what we are up against here. We need to understand that. What do we do about people throwing hand grenades at us?"

Global Positioning System handsets and satellite phones helped the attackers orient themselves and find their targets after landing on a beach in the dark. These guys had no problems and went to where they were supposed to go. They were also in direct contact with their controllers in Pakistan. "This is the masterstroke."

"Their handlers were these guys in a safe-house in Karachi watching the event real-time on TV and then talking to these guys on the ground telling them what to do next," Lovette said.

In October 2009 in Chicago the FBI arrested an American citizen born in Pakistan and charged him with providing material support in the Mumbai attack. He had anglicized his name and traveled to Mumbai. Lovette described him as a jet-setting sort of guy, who took notes of everything while he was over there scoping out the targets.

The organizers of the attack used the symphonic model. "They rely on small, highly mobile, heavily armed teams to attack several locations at once."

The tactics included armed assaults, car-jackings, drive-by shootings, prefabricated IEDs they left at different places and that worked, building takeovers, barricades, and hostages.

If you see someone with a long gun, and particularly if it is an AK, look for the other guy. They tend to work in pairs or small groups, Lovette said.

When you hear about terrorist organizations, assess what the organizations are capable of. If you look at the successful terrorist operations, there is usually a mastermind behind them. In the case of Mumbai, the handler is manipulating these guys on the telephone.

Terrorists tend to carry their weapons, explosives, and other supplies in backpacks. They did this in Madrid and London as well as Mumbai.

Three of these shooters came to the Leopold Café. They all had backpacks. They sat down and had a beer. After they finished their beers, they pulled AKs from their backpacks and opened fire, killing ten people in the café. A lot of people, particularly young people, have backpacks they carry with them. If somebody picks up a backpack holding an AK, multiple magazines, grenades, etc., it is going to look heavy. However, that is not much to go on. When they pull the AKs out of those backpacks, you will know for sure.

"Those are the kinds of things, and that may be all you get. Don't sit there and let it happen and not respond to those little indicators that show up."

"Do you think the U.S. is prepared for this type of attack? Do you think your community is ready for this type of attack? Do you think you are ready for this type of attack?" Lovette asked.

John Benner said this kind of attack could work in New York or Chicago.

How do we respond if we are caught up in one of these attacks? If we can't escape, we have to fight. We have no choice because we will be killed anyway. Adult males will be tortured and killed; females will be raped and killed.

If the attack is by Muslim terrorists, they are likely to shout: "Allahu Akbar," which translates from Arabic as "God is Great," the war-cry of radical Islamic terrorists.

Benner quoted one of the "9/11" terrorists: "When the confrontation begins, strike like champions who do not want to go back to this world. Shout 'Allahu Akbar' because this strikes fear in the hearts of non-believers."

Highly organized attacks can also involve the taking, holding, and murder of hostages, designed to hold media attention over an extended period. The attack September 1, 2004, by several dozen Islamic militants, mostly Chechens, of a school at Beslan in South Russia is an example. According to news reports, the terrorists took more than eleven hundred hostages, including 777 children. The attack took place on the first day of the new school year.

It ended after three days with an attack by Russian special forces, prompted by an explosion in the school's gymnasium where many of the hostages were imprisoned. The cause of the explosion is disputed but may have been accidental. Russian official casualty figures have varied with the passage of time. However, according to Giduck, 314 civilians died at the Beslan school, including 186 children. In addition, thirty-one of the forty-nine terrorists were killed, one was captured alive, and seventeen escaped. Ten members of the elite Alpha and Vympel counter-terror units were killed along with three other troops. According to John Giduck in his excellent book, *Terror at Beslan* (see Bibliography), the terrorists appear to have followed an Al Qaeda play book, separating and killing the young men early on and wiring the building with explosives.

Giduck states: "There was to be no Stockholm Syndrome inside the Beslan School. The vicious, feral brutality of the terrorists saw to that."

The Mumbai attack of 2008 is the type of escalation most likely to happen in the United States. It will involve small groups of terrorists attacking in several locations at once. They are likely to be U.S. citizens trained in the Middle East or Middle Eastern nationals here illegally or as a result of an incompetent vetting system.

Giduck says it is unlikely that radical Muslims will pull off an attack similar to Beslan with dozens of attackers. It would be too difficult to orchestrate, and because of the numbers involved, it would likely come to the attention of the authorities before it happened.

"I would simply say that the symphonic attack has become the preferred means of attack for most of these terrorist groups now. It just wreaks havoc on a society, and it actually instills complete terror on an entire population. It's not just like the population is terrorized because they know there are terrorists holding a school, or a hospital, or a theater, or what have you, and there are other attacks going on all over your city. And that has, as they have seen up to this point, the most dramatic effect."

He thinks rather than fifty terrorists taking over a school here in the U.S., they are more likely to do it with ten or fifteen. They have been working hard to reduce the number of terrorists in mass-hostage seizures, while they increase the number of hostages.

He mentioned the Nord-Ost Dubrovka theater attack in October of 2002 in Moscow. Forty terrorists took over the theater, but they kept on average twenty-five of their number inside the theater to control 979 people. But in Beslan, they had twelve hundred hostages, with about eight to nine hundred kept in the gym, where they had between three and five terrorists to control them.

"What they've gotten better at is the placement and configuration of explosives to control the hostages for them. And so that allows greater numbers of the terrorists to be out about the building in fortified positions."

However, in terms of numbers, the terrorists won't have to beat any records in terms of hostages taken or killed.

"Because we won't have ever seen it before, and in the U.S., of course, we live very comfortably with horrors that happen to other people around the world, but my God, when it happens to us, that's different. Now it's real," Giduck says.

334 ⌐ Surviving a Mass Killer Rampage

Paris Attack

In late 2015 ISIS demonstrated its ability to conduct attacks on a more global scale. On the morning of Friday, November 13, 2015, President Obama claimed that the Islamic State was "contained." Hours later ISIS terrorists launched a symphonic attack against several soft targets in Paris, killing 100 people and wounding about 350. Eight terrorists, divided into three teams, attacked a sports stadium, several cafes and restaurants, and a theater where an American band was playing.

According to news reports, shortly after 9 p.m. a terrorist wearing a suicide bomb vest attempted to enter the Stade de France, where France and Germany were playing a friendly soccer game. A security guard stopped him and discovered the bomb vest. The terrorist backed off and moments later triggered the vest, killing himself and one other person. Police speculate that the terrorist planned to blow himself up inside the stadium, causing a panic with spectators running out into the street, where two other suicide bombers waited. The other two blew themselves up in the street some minutes later. Total killed was four — three terrorists and one victim.

There was no panic inside the stadium, though French President Francois Hollande, who was watching the game with the German foreign minister, was evacuated at halftime. The game continued to the end.

The bomb vests used by the terrorists contained triacetone triperoxide (TATP), an easy-to-make but unstable explosive containing peroxide.

Shortly after the first explosion outside the soccer game, at least two terrorists armed with Kalashnikovs shot up several bars, cafes, and restaurants killing about thirty-nine Friday-evening patrons. It appears one of the attackers blew himself up at another café. While he was the only fatality in the explosion, he injured about fifteen others.

The last target was the deadliest. About fifteen hundred people were crowded into the Bataclan theater to hear the American rock band "Eagles of Death Metal," when three men armed with AK-47s entered and started shooting members of the audience. Witnesses said the men shouted "Allahu Akbar."

The trio took dozens of hostages before an elite tactical team of the French National Police rescued them. Two of the terrorists deliberately activated their bomb vests, while the third was hit with a hail of bullets. His vest went off as he hit the ground. The death toll at the theater was put at eighty-nine, not including the terrorists. Seven of the eight terrorists who carried out these attacks died, but one escaped. Another man suspected of organizing the attacks was killed in a police raid in Paris a few days later. Investigators found a cell phone that gave them leads about others connected to the attacks. It appears they were organized in Belgium. After threats of more attacks, Brussels was virtually shut down for several days while authorities reported an imminent threat of terrorist attacks there. Brussels police also searched for more suspects in the Paris attack. Schools, the subway, and many stores were closed as people were advised to stay at home. Police and soldiers armed with sub-machine guns patrolled the streets.

ISIS also claimed responsibility for two suicide bombings in Beirut, which killed forty-four people on November 12, the day before the Paris attacks.

The terrorist organization also announced it was responsible for downing a Russian airliner in Egypt on October 31. According to news reports, examination of the debris led Russia to announce that a small bomb had been placed aboard the Airbus A321-200. The bomb exploded twenty-two minutes after the plane left the airport at Sharm el-Sheikh in the Sinai heading for St. Petersburg. All 224 people aboard were killed. Most of the passengers were tourists returning to Russia.

According to the *Times of India*, intelligence officials in Europe and the U.S. say these three attacks were centrally planned, but the details were left to operatives on the ground. They also call for reassessment of the Islamic State's ability to hit targets outside the Middle East.

Prior to the rise of the ISIS, the main terror threat was Al Qaeda, the radical Muslim organization that was responsible for the terror attacks of September 11, 2001, that killed almost three thousand people, described earlier. Since then, the United States has not been subjected to the type of highly organized strategic attacks like the Paris incidents or the attacks in Mumbai, India, in November 2008.

San Bernardino

The attack on a county social-services facility in San Bernardino, California, on December 2, 2015, appears to be a good example of a lone-wolf type of attack, even though two terrorists carried it out. A Christmas party, attended by about seventy-five people, was going on when a husband and wife team entered and began shooting. The two Muslim fanatics killed fourteen and wounded twenty-one, mostly county employees. The husband, a twenty-eight-year-old U.S.-born citizen of Pakistani parents, was an inspector of the county public-health department and knew many of the victims. His wife, 27, was a Pakistani citizen with a green card. News reports stated the husband had found his wife on-line and met her in Saudi Arabia in 2014 before bringing her back to the U.S. on a fiancé visa.

When they attacked the social-services party, both were wearing masks and tactical vests stuffed with loaded magazines. They used a DPMS AR-15 and a Smith & Wesson M&P 15, both in .223 caliber. They also carried

9mm-caliber handguns, one a Smith & Wesson, the other a Llama. Police said they fired between sixty-five and seventy-five rounds at the victims. Investigators found three unexploded pipe bombs.

Police Lieutenant Mike Madden was the first officer on the scene. He had been going to lunch when he heard the call on his radio and immediately drove to the social-services center. The twenty-four-year police-department veteran spoke in a firm voice touched by emotion at a news conference the day after the shooting.

"It was something that, although we train for it, it's something that you're never actually prepared for," he said.

When he arrived at the scene, he believed active killers were still inside the building shooting people.

"My goal was to assemble an entry team and enter into the building to engage the active shooter. This mindset and this type of training became indoctrinated in us after the Columbine incident, and that was the goal. We wanted to get in there, and we wanted to stop any further innocent people from being injured and possibly killed. Three officers arrived; there was an approximate two-minute time lapse from the time that I got there until we had a team assembled of our four initial responding officers."

Madden said, as the team went around the south side of the building, it was clear that the initial reports of the seriousness of the situation were true. Victims that were obviously dead were lying outside the conference room. He reported over the radio what they found and asked for more assistance.

"As we entered into the conference room, the situation was surreal. It was something that, again, we prepare for and at active-shooter [training] we talk about sensory overload: they just try to throw everything at you to prepare you for dealing with that — what you're seeing; what you're hearing; what you're smelling — and it was all of that and more. It was unspeakable: the carnage that we were seeing;

the number of people who were injured or unfortunately already dead; and the pure panic on the faces of the individuals that were needing to be safe."

They went further into the building, searching for the shooters and passing many people who needed medical attention. But they had to find and stop the active killers. Medical assistance had to come later.

In waiting two minutes for an entry team of four, the officers did what they had been trained to do. They were following the protocol of their department. However, the question needs to be asked: should Madden have gone in immediately? He said he believed the shooting was still going on when he arrived. If the average active killer wounds or murders between four and five people a minute and there were two killers.... Could more people have been saved? This is no criticism of Lieutenant Madden, but it is a question that should be talked about in police departments around the country. If Officer Justin Garner at the Pinelake Health and Rehabilitation Nursing Home had waited for backup, more elderly patients and staff would almost certainly have died. (See Chapter 11.)

After a search of the area, they realized the killers had escaped. Later they were spotted in a black SUV in a residential area. They shot it out with police and were killed. They shot seventy-six rounds with the rifles at the law-enforcement officers, who fired at them 380 times, according to San Bernardino Police Chief Jarrod Burguan.

The terrorists had fourteen hundred rounds of .223-caliber rifle ammunition and two hundred pistol rounds in 9mm caliber on them and in their vehicle when they were killed. When investigators searched their home in Redland, they found twenty-five hundred rounds for the rifles and two thousand for the pistols, as well as twelve pipe bombs and the tools for making them, police said. The guns were bought in 2011 and 2012.

Based on the amount of bombs and ammunition, investigators think the pair had planned other attacks.

Two weeks after the attack, a former neighbor of the two terrorists was charged with conspiracy to support terrorism. He is accused of planning in 2011 and 2012 with the male terrorist to attack Riverside City College with pipe bombs and rifles. According to prosecutors, the pair also planned to attack a local freeway with pipe bombs to stop traffic then shoot people in the stopped vehicles. The neighbor was also accused of buying the two rifles that were used in the 2015 attacks. He lied about buying them for himself, but sold them to the U.S.-born terrorist, which is a federal crime. The attacks were called off after members of another plot were arrested. There was no evidence that the neighbor knew about the 2015 attack, according to officials.

Since September 11, 2001, these are the types of attacks that have been experienced in the United States.

However, there are some officials who acknowledge the possibility of symphonic attacks in the U.S. In a CBS News *60 Minutes* segment that ran on November 22, 2015, Anderson Cooper interviewed New York City Police Commissioner William Bratton. Bratton said the New York Police Department has been preparing for a group of simultaneous attacks since Mumbai. He believes that a Mumbai-type incident is very likely to happen in the U.S.

"That's why we prepare for it," he said.

Bratton said at Mumbai the terrorists went for soft targets without much security, such as hotels, a railway station, and taxi cabs. Police have learned that terrorists take hostages to get more media attention.

"They are going to kill them. They're not interested in negotiating to surrender."

So far what we have seen are the lone-wolf attacks by Muslim extremists at Fort Hood and at a military base and a recruiting office in Chattanooga.

Fort Hood Attack

Fort Hood is the largest U.S. Military base in the country in terms of population. Near the city of Killeen in central Texas, the base covers more than two hundred thousand acres and has a population of more than fifty thousand soldiers and civilian employees.

On November 5, 2009, a radicalized Muslim, who was also an Army major and psychiatrist, shot and killed thirteen soldiers and wounded more than thirty. About 1:20 p.m. at the Soldier Readiness Processing Center (SRP), where hundreds of soldiers were being processed for deployment to Afghanistan, the major started his rampage. The SRP was crowded with offices and cubicles, a large briefing room, and a waiting area.

According to news reports, the major was also being processed for Afghanistan. He was sitting alone at a table with his head bowed as though praying. He stood up, yelled "Allahu Akbar," pulled a handgun, and started shooting at his fellow soldiers.

The handgun was an FN Herstal Five-seven semi-automatic, which fires 5.7mm or .224-caliber bullets at a muzzle velocity of more than two thousand feet per second. Its standard magazine holds twenty rounds. The pistol was equipped with red and green laser sights.

The major started shooting at soldiers sitting in the waiting area. As they tried to get away, he followed them, shooting many multiple times. Initially some of the soldiers thought the sound of firing was some kind of exercise. They soon realized what was going on. Several witnesses said there was pandemonium, with people running to get outside and others screaming.

Several of the unarmed people in the center tried to fight back. Captain John Gaffaney charged the shooter, but was gunned down before he could reach him. Michael Cahill, a civilian physician's assistant, picked up a chair and tried to charge the gunman with it. The major shot and killed him also. Specialist Logan Burnett threw a folding table at the gunman and was wounded in the hip, but managed to crawl into a cubicle.

Witnesses said the major appeared calm and deliberate as he gunned down the soldiers. He apparently passed up opportunities to shoot civilians, preferring to concentrate on soldiers in uniform.

The area where the Muslim terrorist started shooting was covered with the bodies of soldiers — dead, dying, and wounded. The floor was so slippery with blood that nurses and other responders had trouble keeping their footing. There were screams and cries for help from the wounded and dying. One witness heard a woman crying: "My baby, my baby; don't shoot, please don't shoot." It is possible that it was Private First Class Francheska Velez, who was pregnant when she was killed.

The gunman ran outside the SRP following some of the soldiers who were trying to escape him. He continued shooting and efficiently changing magazines as he needed.

Meanwhile, Fort Hood civilian police officers, Sergeants Kimberly Munley and Mark Todd, responded to the 9-1-1 call by driving their patrol cars to the shooting scene. When Munley arrived she got out of her car and drew her duty pistol, a 9mm-caliber Beretta M9. A soldier pointed the gunman out to her.

She was about fifteen yards from him while he was shooting at Sergeant Todd. The suspect ducked behind a building, so she headed around the building in the other direction hoping to cut him off from other soldiers. When he came into sight they fired at each other. She used the corner of the building for cover, while the major was shooting as he came towards her.

"He rounded the corner, and within eight feet or so we began to blindly exchange fire," Munley later testified.

She was hit in the hand, knee, and thigh, then her pistol malfunctioned. The gunman stood over her and tried to shoot her, but his pistol wasn't working either. The major kicked her gun out of her hand, she said.

Todd yelled at the major to drop his gun, but he turned and started shooting at the sergeant. Todd returned fire. He said that the gunman was still standing at this point. Todd saw him flinch a couple of times as though his bullets were hitting him. The major was hit four times. It is not clear whether Sergeant Munley hit him, but it was fire from Todd that brought him down.

In an interview with *NBC News*, Todd said that while he was shooting at the gunman he was conscious of his training. "I remember my firearms instructor, he was in my ear the whole time, he was saying: 'Mark, relax, shoot, take your time, you know what you're doing, take your time, shoot,' and that was it."

This is not unusual. Two police firearms instructors have told me that officers they taught who were involved in gunfights have told them they were conscious of their presence during the incidents, telling them to slow down, watch the front sight, and press the trigger straight back.

Sergeant Todd rushed the major, kicked the gun away from him, and put him in handcuffs. The rampage lasted for about ten minutes.

The major was hit four times, with one bullet hitting him in the spine making him a paraplegic.

After the shooting, investigators recovered 146 shell casings from inside the SRP, all fired by the killer, and an additional sixty-eight outside fired by the gunman and the two police sergeants who took him on. The terrorist had

177 more unfired rounds on him, mostly in twenty- and thirty-round magazines.

The major bought the FN Hershal Five-seven pistol from Guns Galore, a gun store in Killeen, at the beginning of August. He said he wanted the most high-tech handgun with the largest magazine capacity. The gun came with a standard twenty-round magazine, but a thirty-round extended magazine was available. He was a regular visitor to a shooting range in nearby Florence, Texas, where he practiced head and chest shots at a range of one hundred yards.

Before his transfer to Fort Hood, the terrorist major gave plenty of clues to his radicalization, but they were ignored. No one in the Army wanted to be accused of religious discrimination, it appears. He was stationed at Walter Reed Medical Center, where officials were concerned about his behavior. While speaking to other psychiatrists, he spoke about Islam and the Koran. He said unbelievers would be decapitated, set on fire, and sent to hell. He also justified suicide bombings.

The gunman had significant email communications in 2008 and 2009 with a New Mexico-born imam of Yemeni parents. The imam was a recruiter for Al Qaeda and was killed by a drone strike in 2011 in Yemen.

For years the Obama administration refused to call the Fort Hood shooting terrorism, insisting that it was merely workplace violence. Even while the gunman was on trial in 2013, it was not called terrorism. It was not until 2015 that the Army belatedly labeled it as terrorism and allowed the victims to receive the Purple Heart medal and receive benefits available to those wounded in combat.

A Department of Defense directive issued during the George H.W. Bush administration forbids military personnel or anyone else from carrying guns on military bases. The only people who can carry side-arms on military installations in the U.S. are military police and civilian police employed by the military, like Sergeants Todd and Munley. Even military personnel with state-issued concealed-handgun licenses cannot carry their guns on base. This is another misguided policy that probably cost lives at Fort Hood and indicates how the generals and politicians do not trust the soldiers, sailors, and airmen who put their lives on the line for their country.

It seems ludicrous that American warriors who are never far from their personal weapons when stationed in the world's hot spots, should be disarmed when they arrive back in the U.S. Fort Hood was another "gun-free zone."

After the Fort Hood shooting, an editorial in the *Washington Times* erroneously blamed the Clinton administration for the rule. However it accurately stated that "terrorists would face more return fire if they attacked a Texas Walmart than the gunman faced at Fort Hood."

No changes were made to the policy after the Fort Hood shooting or even after two more shootings at military installations. The Washington Navy Yard shooting, described in Chapter 11, took place on September 16, 2013.

On April 2, 2014, a second shooting took place at Fort Hood in which three people were killed and a dozen wounded by an Army specialist who then committed suicide.

Despite these attacks, no one in authority in government or the military was prepared to think outside the box and allow military members the same ability to fight back that civilians with concealed-carry permits have.

Chattanooga Attack

Another attack on a military gun-free zone by a radical Muslim terrorist happened more recently on July 16, 2015, in Chattanooga, Tennessee. The attacker was a twenty-four-year-old naturalized U.S. citizen, born in Kuwait to

Palestinian parents. His family migrated to the U.S. in 1996, and he became a citizen in 2003.

About 10:30 a.m. the gunman pulled up in front of the glass doors of a military recruiting office in a strip center located on Lee Highway. He was driving a rented silver Ford Mustang convertible. Without getting out of the car, he opened fire with an AK-47-style semi-automatic rifle, pock-marking the glass doors with bullet holes. The gunman fired between thirty and forty-five rounds into the recruiting office. The glass doors had a sign announcing it as a gun-free zone.

According to a report on the attack, four Marines, two potential recruits, and the young daughter of the non-commissioned officer in charge, Gunnery Sergeant Camden Meyer, were in the recruiting center. Meyer was in his office with his daughter and another Marine. He yelled to the other Marine to get down and hugged the floor himself, while protecting his daughter with his body. When there was a pause in the gunfire, all the occupants of the center ran out of the back door, with Meyer carrying his daughter over his shoulder. Sergeant DeMonte Cheeley was shot in the leg. Everyone else was unhurt. Once outside one of them called 9-1-1.

Meanwhile the gunman sped off, heading northwest to a Naval Operational Support Center about seven miles away on Amnicola Highway. Responding to the 9-1-1 call, several Chattanooga police officers followed him there. The gunman rammed his car through the gates and stopped in front of the headquarters building. He got out of the car with his AK and a 9mm handgun and started shooting at pursuing police officers with the rifle. At least one military officer shot at the gunman, who then returned fire, shooting into the building with the rifle. The Naval officer who shot at the gunman was Lieutenant Commander Timothy White, the commander of the facility. It was not clear whether he hit the terrorist.

The gunman ran into the building, where he shot and mortally wounded Navy logistics specialist Randall Smith, 26. He ran through the building and out the back entrance, where he entered the motor-pool area. There he shot and killed four Marines, before being shot down and killed by five Chattanooga police officers. Several unarmed Marines ran to the scene and tried to distract the gunman.

Chattanooga Police Chief Fred Fletcher said that Officer Dennis Pedigo, 39, was wounded in the ankle in the exchange of fire and was dragged to safety by other officers, including a female police sergeant. He commended all the officers who put themselves at risk during the incident.

"They are heroes, but that is the last thing they like to hear themselves called," he added.

Reports indicate that the whole incident at the Navy center took between three and five minutes.

FBI Director James Comey later announced: "We have concluded that the Chattanooga killer was inspired by a foreign terrorist organization's propaganda." He said that, as with the San Bernardino case, it is difficult to untangle which terrorist organization was responsible, because "there is competing foreign terrorist poison out there."

After the shootings, governors in many states authorized the arming of personnel at their National Guard recruiting offices. It started with the governors of Texas, Florida, and Indiana, but by December 2015 the Associated Press reported that nineteen other states had followed suit.

Texas Governor Greg Abbott issued a news release that said: "It has become clear that our military personnel must have the ability to defend themselves against these types of attacks on our own soil."

In many states armed civilian volunteers started showing up at storefront military recruiting offices to protect the unarmed personnel inside.

On a national level the mighty bureaucracy of the Department of Defense was immovable. In September 2015 the *Marine Corps Times* reported that, according to Lieutenant General Mark Brilakis, commanding general of the Marine Corps Recruiting Command, none of the armed services wanted to arm their personnel.

"Whichever way you stand on the Second Amendment, recruiters showing up armed is not going to make either educators or parents comfortable," he said.

These people are recruiting young men and women for the armed services. If they or their parents are scared of guns, perhaps they should apply to the Environmental Protection Agency or the federal Office of Personnel Management.

Brilakis praised the Marines at the recruiting office for getting out of the building in less than a minute. They followed their training, he said. So Marines are being trained to flee rather than stand and fight. What sort of message is that sending to troops who may be deployed to some of the most dangerous places on earth? Perhaps if those troops had been armed and able to fight back, the terrorist would not have been able to go on to the Naval installation and kill some of their colleagues.

On April 7, 2016, Army Chief of Staff General Mark Milley testified in front of U.S. senators that it was unnecessary to allow soldiers to carry privately-owned weapons on military bases in the U.S. as they have adequate police protection. Referring to a second shooting at Fort Hood in Texas in April 2014 in which three soldiers were killed and a dozen wounded, Milley said: "Those police responded within eight minutes, and that guy was dead. So, that's pretty quick, and a lot of people died in the process of that, but that was a very fast evolving event, and I am not convinced, from what I know, that carrying privately-owned weapons would've stopped that individual."

In fact, the individual concerned was not stopped by police, but committed suicide.

After terrorist attacks at Fort Hood, the Washington Navy Yard, Chattanooga, and other military installations, one has to wonder whether the generals and admirals prefer a few dead troops to trusting them to be armed — provided of course that the casualties are not above the rank of lieutenant colonel or commander.

CHAPTER 14

RADICAL ISLAMIC JIHAD: THE SOLUTIONS

"Victory at all costs, victory in spite of all terror, victory however long and hard the road may be; for without victory there is no survival." — Winston Churchill

The solution to terrorist attacks is to fight back. Run, hide, fight is the current mantra that governments are promoting to their citizens, with fight being the last resort. However, running or hiding will not stop the attacks, and they leave others to die. The attack will be ended only when the terrorists are confronted with force. The best people to do this are people who are on the scene of the attack and have the means to fight back.

Ron Borsch, the police trainer who has amassed much information about active-killer incidents, says the most important factor in stopping these attacks is "already on-site, armed good guys."

But it is unlikely that law-enforcement officers will be on the scene. Unfortunately, most terrorist attacks are likely to happen in "gun-free zones" where citizens with guns are unlikely to be present.

In this chapter there are three stories of people fighting back and stopping lone-wolf-type terrorist attacks. The first involves three unarmed "good guys" fighting back against an armed terrorist.

The Paris Train

On Friday, August 21, 2015, just after 3 p.m., three young Americans boarded a fast train in Amsterdam bound for

Paris. They had known each other since they had attended a Christian middle school in Sacramento. Recently they had not spent as much time with one another as they wanted, so they came up with the idea of a vacation together in France. Anthony Sadler was a student from California; Spencer Stone was a U.S. Airman First Class; and Alek Skarlatos was a Specialist in the Oregon National Guard.

Skarlatos had just returned from deployment in Afghanistan; Stone was serving in the Azores; and Sadler, their friend from middle school, was going to college in the fall. All were in their early twenties.

The trio traveled in style, buying first-class tickets. They moved from one first-class car to another, because the wi-fi in the first car was poor. They expected to reach Paris about 6:30 p.m.

According to news reports and media interviews with the participants, this is what happened.

The express train was in Belgium with about five hundred passengers aboard. Stone and Sadler were asleep when Skarlatos heard a gunshot and breaking glass. Then he saw a train employee sprinting away from the noise. Stone and Sadler woke up and the three saw a man holding an AK-47 semi-automatic rifle.

At a subsequent news conference in Paris, Stone described what happened.

"It looked like it was jammed or wasn't working, and he was trying to charge the weapon. And Alek just hit me on the shoulder and said, 'Let's go.'"

Without hesitating, Stone charged the gunman, knocking him down. Skarlatos told Megyn Kelly on *Fox News* he had tunnel vision and was staring at the gunman, so he didn't realize Stone was charging at him until his friend crossed his line of sight. He got up and ran towards the gunman followed by Sadler.

Stone slammed into the gunman and tried to grab the AK, but the gunman pulled it away from him, so he got behind him and put him in a choke-hold.

"It seemed like he just kept pulling more weapons left and right, pulled out a handgun. Alek took that. Took out a box-cutter, started jabbing at me with that. We let go, all three of us started punching him while he was in the middle of us. And I was able to grab him again and choke him unconscious, while Alek was hitting him in the head," Stone said at the news conference.

When Skarlatos reached them, the AK was on the floor. He saw the gunman draw a Luger semi-automatic pistol and managed to wrestle it away from him. He tried to shoot the gunman twice with his own gun, but it was empty. Sadler started hitting the gunman, and that was when he pulled out the box-cutter. The gunman slashed Stone with the box-cutter, slicing him on the back of the neck and almost severing his left thumb. The box-cutter also ended up on the floor, while Skarlatos was trying to shoot the terrorist with the AK but couldn't. Initially Skarlatos thought the safety was on.

The shot Skarlatos heard at the beginning of the incident was fired by the gunman from his handgun after he had come out of the car's restroom. A twenty-eight-year-old French banker, who wanted to remain anonymous, became suspicious when the gunman dragged his suitcase into the restroom. He was the first man to tackle the terrorist when he emerged. They stared at each other briefly, then got into a scuffle. A train employee who thought they were just having a fight separated them. The gunman, still clutching the AK-47, entered the car, where another man tried to disarm him.

Mark Moogalian, 51, a French-American professor at the Sorbonne, told his wife to hide behind a seat, then he attacked the terrorist and managed to wrestle the rifle from him. The gunman pulled a handgun, and in the struggle the magazine was ejected from the pistol. The terrorist then shot

Moogalian in the neck, using the last round in the handgun, and retrieved the AK-47.

It was then that the three Americans swarmed him. Initially Stone didn't realize the gunman had cut him with the box-cutter, but Skarlatos noticed it when he crawled over to Moogalian, whose neck was squirting blood. Stone was an EMT and so had medical training. He said he stuck two fingers in the bullet hole and applied pressure to an artery damaged by the bullet. It stopped the bleeding.

Sadler found a first aid kit and Stone told him what he needed out of it while still treating Moogalian's neck. The professor's wife thought he had been shot in the chest, so they cut Mark's shirt off to check for other wounds but found none.

Chris Norman, 62, a British businessman and consultant joined the three Americans. Norman tied up the gunman with scarves and zip ties provided by other passengers. He and Sadler guarded the terrorist, while Skarlatos grabbed the AK and went searching for any other gunmen. When Skarlatos examined the rifle, he cycled another round into the chamber and found the round that had been in the gun had not fired, though it had a firing pin mark on its primer. That was why it didn't fire when Skarlatos tried to shoot the gunman. He said he didn't expect to find any other gunmen, but he asked the passengers if there were any others or whether anybody else was injured. The passengers told him there weren't.

Norman interpreted between the Americans and the train crew. One train employee told Stone to stop choking the shooter and told Skarlatos to put the AK down. They said they were military and told the guy to "get lost."

After it was all over, most of the passengers seemed shocked and quiet. They were on the train for about thirty-five minutes after they subdued the shooter until the train stopped at Arras. By the time they arrived, Skarlatos had cleared all the weapons and put them by the door. Stone was providing medical care to Moogalian and likely saved his life.

Police and paramedics met the train. After some initial questioning on the platform, the police realized the four had saved a lot of lives, and they were taken to the police station for about five hours of questioning.

The gunman was a twenty-five-year-old Moroccan, who had been radicalized and had connections to the organizer of the later attacks in Paris.

A couple of days later, the three Americans held a news conference at the U.S. Embassy in Paris, moderated by Ambassador Jane Hartley.

"I know these young men sitting with me won't like it, because in the brief period we have known each other, they are so humble, but they truly are heroes," Hartley said.

After telling their story, Anthony Sadler said of the gunman: "He never said a word. The second he came in and when he entered the car, we saw him cocking the AK-47. So at that time it was either do something or die."

At the end of the news conference, Sadler had some words of advice: "I would want it to be learned that basically to do something. Hiding or sitting back is not going to accomplish anything. And the gunman would have been successful if my friend Spencer had not gotten up. I just want that lesson to be learned going forward. In times of terror like that, to please do something, don't just stand by and watch."

During a media interview, Chris Norman also had some advice: "We're very, very, very lucky to be alive, and I think from my point of view, I wanted to say thanks to my team members — Alek, Spence, Anthony — and I think that one way or another we're going to be facing this kind of problem quite a few times in the future. And I would advise you all to think about what would I do in that situation. Act if the opportunity presents itself. Obviously you don't want to throw yourself at a situation that is hopeless, but act if you can."

Before they left Paris, Stone, Skarlatos, Sadler, and Norman were each presented with the Legion D'honneur, France's highest award, by French President Francois Hollande.

On September 17 the three Americans were invited to the White House where President Obama praised their actions.

"Because of their courage, because of their quick thinking, because of their teamwork, it's fair to say that a lot of people were saved, and a real calamity was averted," he said.

As Norman said, all of them are lucky to be alive. It is likely that if the gunman were better trained in the use of his weapons and had better ammunition, they might all have been killed. The other passengers on the train were also lucky because the gunman was carrying nine magazines and unless stopped would have killed until he ran out of ammunition.

Oklahoma Attack, Mark Vaughan

The second story is about an employer who gets a rifle from his vehicle and stops a man armed with a knife, who is attacking other employees.

Vaughan Foods was a fresh-food processing company in the City of Moore, a suburb on the south side of Oklahoma City. Mark Vaughan, 49, was the chief operating officer of the company that was started by his parents in 1961. He had sold the company in 2011 to a competitor, but had remained with the company. At the time it employed about 450 people, mostly workers who cut and packaged vegetables. This did not include truck drivers and off-site personnel.

On Thursday, September 25, 2014, Vaughan was sitting at his desk on the second floor in the administration area of the building just after 4 p.m. As usual, he was wearing casual slacks and a dress shirt with long sleeves. He had arrived at work between 6 a.m. and 6:30 and his normal work-day was coming to an end. He was answering emails when the black phone on his desk rang. He picked it up to find his director of safety and security, Dan Vreeland, on the line. Vreeland said someone was attacking people with a knife in the customer-service area.

"There was no question he was agitated and very serious about what he was saying."

Vaughan immediately ran out of his office, down the stairs to where his tan-colored Subaru Outback was parked.

Vaughan wears two hats. He was the company's chief operating officer, which employees at the company knew. What most of them didn't know was that he was also a reserve deputy sheriff in Oklahoma County. He lives in Oklahoma County, although the plant is in Cleveland County about a mile south of the Oklahoma County line.

"I was not carrying a handgun that particular day," Vaughan said.

As well as being a reserve deputy, he had been a long time NRA firearms instructor. As a reserve deputy he was expected to maintain the same standards and training as full-time deputies.

"We've been through active-shooter training. We have the same qualification standards for firearms and defensive tactics and all those things a full-time deputy has to comply with."

One of the things he learned from active-shooter training was he needed to have a way to identify himself. So he bought a vest with the word "Sheriff" on the front and back and kept it in his car. It had pouches for extra magazines, a first-aid kit, a flashlight, and a few other essentials in it. He

Mark Vaughan wears two hats: chief operating officer
of Vaughan Foods and reserve deputy sheriff
in Oklahoma County.

had a couple of magazines in the vest. Also in his car he kept his CAR-15, semi-automatic carbine in .223 caliber, with a collapsible stock. He opened the Subaru's hatchback and took out the vest and the carbine.

"So I donned the vest, loaded the rifle, and ran the hundred yards or so to the customer-service area."

As he ran from his vehicle to the customer-service area, about thirty people were milling about outside the building. Shipping coordinator Bryan Aylor was one of them. Aylor was very distraught and said something to Vaughan as he sprinted past. It was something to the effect that the man was killing people.

"That whole run over there, I was running full speed, it was being reinforced that something really bad was happening," Vaughan said.

When he reached the entrance to the processing plant adjacent to the customer service area, he was met by Vreeland, who was armed only with an expandable metal baton.

They entered a hallway inside the building. Forty or fifty feet along the corridor, there was an intersection with a hallway that led to the employee-facilities area. People were running out of the hallway, and several were pointing down the hallway as they ran. It was shift change, so many people were leaving the lunchroom and the locker rooms.

"There were people screaming; it was very chaotic, and there was already a crowd gathered outside customer service, crying and screaming, very distraught, many people, because they had already seen a bunch of what had already gone on. And down at the end of this hallway, there was a black man with a knife who was actively attacking someone. I couldn't see the person he was attacking because they were a little bit around the corner. I could see most of him and the knife and a partially obscured person, but I couldn't really make out the person."

The attacker was holding a large butcher knife like a hammer rather than like an icepick. He was making downward slashing motions at somebody with the knife. Vaughan was about sixty feet from the attacker down the dimly-lit, narrow hallway.

"I yelled, and the black man stopped and came around the corner toward us."

Vreeland was beside Vaughan, but about four steps behind him.

The attacker took a couple of steps towards them, then disappeared around the corner back where he was attacking. Vaughan gave chase, running after him, but before he had gone five or six steps, the attacker came back around the corner, running at Vaughan and Vreeland at full speed, the knife in his hand.

"I yelled a couple of times, but I let him get too close. At about fifteen feet, sixteen feet, I fired one round. He hesitated, but kept coming; then I fired two more rounds."

Vaughan said that according to the investigation, the first round hit the attacker when his chest was at a sideways angle to him. The bullet cut a groove across his chest above the nipple line.

"It was like you took a knife and cut a slice in his chest, maybe a half-inch deep. It was bleeding, but it wasn't incapacitating."

Investigators said Vaughan missed with one of the subsequent rounds, but the other one — either the second or the third — went through the assailant's arm and through his lower abdomen before exiting his body.

"That was the incapacitating round, but he didn't really fall down; he just stopped his forward movement, leaned against the wall of the hallway, and slid to the ground. His feet slid out from under him with his back against the hallway wall, his knife still in his hand. He was probably ten feet from me," Vaughan said.

"I covered him while the security guy with me got his ASP and knocked the knife away from him. He was in considerable pain, and I would say mostly incapacitated, but thank goodness he didn't have a gun, because even at that point he could have shot me, there's no question."

Vaughan's carbine was loaded with full-metal-jacket rounds he used for practice and that tend to over-penetrate. He would normally have the gun loaded with the soft-point rounds issued by the Sheriff's Office that were safer and more effective for defense.

Vaughan kept the assailant covered, while Vreeland and others got the woman he had been attacking to an ambulance.

"The gal he had attacked when I came on the scene was bleeding profusely from the neck," he said. This was Traci Johnson, an employee who had filed a complaint against the other employee who had attacked her and had been shot by Vaughan.

A Moore City police officer armed with a shotgun arrived on the scene about ninety seconds after the attacker was stopped, Vaughan said.

The 9-1-1 operator heard over the phone the shots Vaughan fired and upgraded the call from an assault to a shots-fired call.

Referring to the responding officers, Vaughan said: "They were expecting an active-shooter situation when they got there, so it's a good thing I had my vest on."

When the first officer arrived, Vaughan's back was to him. He was using his rifle to cover the assailant, who was writhing on the ground. The officer was able to see Vaughan's vest with "Sheriff" emblazoned in large letters on the back.

After the assailant had been taken by ambulance to the hospital, Vaughan found out what had led to the incident.

The man with the knife was a thirty-year-old employee, who had just been suspended for three days. He had come to work for Vaughan Foods while at the Carver Center, a halfway house for people released from prison. They are housed at the center and are bussed to work to their different employers. Part of the money they earn goes to pay for their keep and a reintroduction program into society. They get to keep some of what they earn.

"Unfortunately, he did have a violent past. He had an altercation with a female state trooper, where he struck her and escaped from custody."

He was caught and sent to prison. He was later released through the Carver Center, Vaughan said. He transitioned out of that program and remained an employee at the company.

He apparently converted to the Muslim faith while he was in prison and was an active member in a local mosque. The company made accommodation for Muslims and members of other faiths so they could pray, Vaughan said.

"He had been, in recent months leading up to this, trying to convert co-workers and inviting them to the mosque, trying to convert them to his faith."

Traci Johnson was a new employee, who had been at the company for only a week or two. On the day of the incident she was working close to the employee when he made what Vaughan called "racially motivated comments against her."

He was black, and she was white.

"Some comments like women should have their heads covered in public and should not be in the work place. Other things like that," Vaughan said.

Whatever he said to Johnson, it prompted her to lodge a complaint with her manager, who followed company procedure, filling out an incident form and turning it in to Human Resources.

In mid-afternoon, the employee was called down to the Human Resources office, which is in a separate building down the street. An investigation was done with both Johnson and the employee being asked questions. The result was that he was suspended for three days. He turned in his access card, and he left.

"He was agitated when he left, but not so that anyone suspected that he would take this sort of action," Vaughan said.

The employee went home to his apartment, which was less than a mile away. He cut vegetables for a living and was issued a knife, but that was turned in each day. However, at home he picked up a knife of his own.

"He testified that he had the knife stuck in his boot or shoe and his pants leg over it, so it was not obvious," Vaughan said.

"He drove here in, I am assuming, a very agitated state, because he pulled in the parking lot and ran into, with his automobile, a pickup truck that was parked in a parking spot and hit it pretty good."

He timed his return at a period of shift change, when people were coming to work and others were leaving. That was at 4 p.m. They have a shift that starts at 6 a.m. and works to 4 p.m.

He did not have his access card, but with all the people coming and going, he did not have a problem getting into the production area. He was a regular employee, so no one questioned why he was there. Few people would have known he had been suspended.

He entered the shipping office and proceeded into the customer-service room, which contains many cubicles where staff members meet with customers. It probably contained eight to ten people including two managers. The company services food distributors, restaurant chains, grocery stores, and convenience stores with a whole gamut of fresh-food products.

Immediately inside the customer-service area, there is a manager's office, and his first victim, Colleen Hufford, whom he did not know at all, was in the customer-service manager's office. She was standing in the doorway of the office discussing an issue with the manager, Gary Hazelrigg, who was seated at his desk. Her back was to the suspended employee.

"When he came around the corner, she turned and looked at him. He just grabbed the top of her head. His knife was in his hand evidently at this point, and he drew it across her throat. I mean just that quick. According to the customer-service manager, she had no opportunity to resist. Imagine turning and seeing someone and in that instant they're grabbing your head and a knife to your throat. And so he cut her severely at that point, and then, of course, others around, including the customer-service manager got up to fight off, render aid, fight off the attacker."

The employee was a big guy in shape, and had been a football player in high school.

"The customer-service manager hit him with a chair, kicked him. He got up and chased him away with the knife. Of course most of the people in the customer-service area are women, and they ran out of the building screaming. Other men were in the area, mainly in the shipping office and of course were alerted to all this. Our plant manager and a shipping supervisor both went in to render aid, see what was going on, and [the employee] was on the ground in the process of severing Colleen Hufford's head. The operations manager [Mark Vanderpool] kicked him squarely in the chin.

"It is required here to wear steel-toed boots for this class of people — managers and people in the plant — they have to have proper footwear, so he had steel-toed shoes, [the operations manager] hit him very hard in the chin, didn't phase him, and the guy got up and started swinging the knife at the operations manager and ran him out."

Vanderpool testified at a preliminary hearing in early January 2016 that the knife came within two inches of his chest. The man with the knife chased off Vanderpool and Bryan Aylor. He went back to Hufford and finished severing her head.

Vaughan said he had seen the assailant in the plant but had never spoken to him. When he and Vreeland entered the building they stayed in the hallways and did not see the havoc wrought by the assailant in the customer-service area.

When he tackled the attacker he did not know he had already killed someone.

The suspect said Colleen Hufford was not an intended victim.

"He said that he was passing by her or approaching her, and she looked at him in a demeaning manner, and he attacked her," Vaughan said.

However, Traci Johnson, the woman who filed the complaint against him and was being attacked when Vaughan arrived, was an intended target. In addition, on his list of intended victims were his supervisor, Tim Bluford, and the person in the human-relations department who suspended him.

Interviewed in February 2016, Vaughan said the suspect has been remanded for trial but is not co-operating with his own defense.

"What we're hearing is that he is wanting to die in the name of Allah."

Vaughan doesn't believe this was completely an act of terrorism.

"I do believe that his belief did play a role. Severing someone's head is an unusual act, I think everyone would agree."

However, he said, there is no evidence that he had any direct contact with any terrorist organization, but he was a follower of ISIS to some degree. He kept up-to-date on ISIS, infamous for its beheadings. The FBI ruled the incident a case of workplace violence.

John Whetsel, sheriff of Oklahoma County, and Vaughan's boss as a law-enforcement officer, was pleased with his deputy's response.

"I think he did awesome. He reacted based upon his training, and he reacted based upon another human being in trouble. And I think you put those two together, and he was prepared to meet the challenge when he walked in that building."

Whetsel said, based on his training, when he put on the vest that said "Sheriff" front and back, Vaughan knew law enforcement would be coming, and he knew he would be holding a weapon.

"When they walked in the door, he wanted to make sure they knew who he was and that he wasn't the object of any mistakes."

The vest had a second purpose: it transmitted to the attacker that Vaughan was an authority figure.

Whetsel said that his office's policy is to train every deputy, whether reserve or full-time, in dealing with active shooters.

"Our policy is for the first deputy on the scene to make entry and to continually feed back information to various additional responding officers. The issue becomes the first officer, the first deputy in, has the potential for saving lives."

When Vaughan owned Vaughan Foods, he did not prevent people with concealed-carry licenses from carrying at work, but since he sold the company the policy has changed, and employees are no longer allowed to carry. He knew several of the management staff who used to carry.

"We did not prevent licensed concealed carry on the premises."

Vaughan said as a peace officer and COO, he is a part of the security team.

"I wasn't specifically prohibited, I guess would be the way to put it. I was adhering to company policy at that time as I did not have a handgun."

In April 2015 he was named NRA Law Enforcement Officer of the year.

Vaughan believes strongly in the right for citizens to be able to defend themselves.

"We are a country that firearms are very much a part of how we got to where we are as a nation, and I believe that protecting ourselves from folks like [the attacker] and these people in San Bernardino is something that can't be given up, not even a little bit. It's mental health, there's a whole lot of other things that are contributing to this, but gun ownership and the availability of guns is something that needs to continue.

"I mean here's a great case, this guy did not even have a gun, so this is not a gun-violence situation. A gun was used to stop a threat, and they're very effective for that. When you need a tool you need a tool, and a gun was the only tool that would solve this."

He is not impressed with gun-free zones.

"Gun-free zones are really a joke. It is silly to think that it deters anyone who is criminally motivated one bit. A gun-free zone is not even a consideration; all it does is it restricts law-abiding citizens. It doesn't do a darn thing for the criminal element."

The Garland Attack

The third story is about police officers who anticipated an attack and took down two armed terrorists.

When Pamela Geller and the American Freedom Defense Initiative rented the Curtis Culver Center in Garland, Texas, to hold a Mohammed Art Exhibit and Contest, the Garland Police Department knew it could expect trouble. The center belongs to the Garland Independent School District, which rents it out for special events. Garland is a suburban city of 235,000 people just east of Dallas and is part of the Dallas-Fort Worth Metroplex.

The event included a cartoon contest of the Prophet Mohammed and a speech by a controversial Dutch politician. Geert Wilders was put on an Al Qaeda death list after releasing a film critical of Islam and the Quran. He is an outspoken opponent of his country's acceptance of asylum seekers from the Middle East.

The event organizers solicited artists to submit cartoons portraying Mohammed. Many Muslims consider depicting the Prophet as blasphemy. The Culver Center was picked as the location for what was advertised as a free-speech event, because in January 2015 the center hosted an anti-Islamophobia event.

The event was scheduled for Sunday, May 3, 2015, but preparations started several months before. As soon as the event was made known to Garland police, the department began planning and coordinating with other local, state, and federal law-enforcement agencies, including Garland

Independent School District, according to Police Chief Mitch Bates.

"Normally for that size of event, the police security detail would consist of only two to four police officers, in addition to the Garland ISD security personnel. However, due to the nature of this event and the security concerns surrounding several of the attendees, our police department security detail was increased to forty police personnel, including numerous members of our SWAT team and the Garland Police Department bomb unit, in addition to Garland ISD security personnel, the Texas Department of Public Safety, the ATF, and the FBI," Bates said.

The extra security cost the organizers $10,000 in addition to their own security arrangements.

The police department was concerned because of previous attacks earlier in the year in France and Denmark. On January 7 in Paris two masked gunmen armed with Kalashnikov semi-automatic rifles attacked the offices of Charlie Hebdo, a satirical weekly news magazine that had published cartoons of Mohammed. They stormed into a news meeting and shot several of the editorial staff and contributors. In total, twelve people were killed, including two police officers.

In Copenhagen, Denmark, on February 14 a radical Islamic terrorist, armed with an AR-15-type semi-automatic rifle, attacked an event called "Art, Blasphemy, and the Freedom of Expression." One civilian was killed and three police officers were wounded. The target of the attack was believed to be Lars Vilks, a Swedish cartoonist, who in 2007 had drawn pictures of Mohammed that had infuriated radical Muslims. Vilks was unhurt, and the gunman was killed later by police.

The Garland event, with about 150 people attending, was proceeding peacefully and was due to end at 7 p.m. About 6:50 p.m. a black sedan pulled up to the west entrance parking lot.

What happened next was described by Officer Joe Harn, the spokesman for Garland Police Department, and by Chief Bates at separate news conferences. Some additional information came from contemporary news reports.

A police car and a barricade blocked the parking lot entrance. A Garland traffic officer, about sixty-years-old, and an unarmed school-district security officer were standing near the police vehicle. Two men, wearing body armor, got out of the black sedan carrying military-style semi-automatic rifles, came around the back of the car, and opened up on the police officer and the security guard. The police officer was reportedly armed with a .45-caliber Glock.

"The Garland police officer returned fire with his duty pistol and wounded both suspects. Within seconds, four members of the SWAT Tactical Response Team responded and also engaged both of the suspects, who continued their efforts to attack those at the location by retrieving additional weapons and ammunition. The SWAT team members responded to these actions by firing their duty weapons, consisting of assault rifles and duty pistols. Both suspects were killed at the scene. Dozens of rounds were fired by the suspects and the officers," Bates said.

The security officer, Bruce Joiner, was shot in the lower leg. He was taken to a local hospital, treated, and released the same day.

The two shooters, aged about thirty and thirty-four, had driven a thousand miles from Phoenix, Arizona, where they lived, to carry out the attack. Both were connected to radical Islam.

Bates said: "The Garland Police Department bomb unit, with the assistance of the ATF, the FBI bomb unit, the Plano Police Department bomb unit, and the DFW Airport bomb unit spent several hours clearing the scene for possible explosive devices both within the vehicle and on the two suspects. No explosive devices were found. However, several weapons — a total of three assault rifles and three pistols — in addition to hundreds of rounds of ammunition, were found on the suspects' bodies and in the vehicle."

The suspects were stopped before they could get past the outer security perimeter, though they obviously intended to get into the center and shoot as many of the attendees as they could.

Bates said the police department has not released the names of the five officers who engaged the terrorists due to direct and indirect threats to their safety and the safety of their families. Their identities are being withheld indefinitely. Garland police, the FBI, Texas DPS, and other agencies are continuing to monitor and investigate any potential threats on social media or elsewhere, he added.

Bates thanked all the federal, state, and local law-enforcement agencies that assisted Garland before, during, and after the incident. He also praised the members of his own department, adding: "Most deserving of our praise, are the five Garland police officers and the Garland ISD security officer who put their own lives at great risk by responding to this attack by engaging the enemy in defense of our community of Garland, our great state of Texas, and our great nation."

He said there had been reports that Garland police may have had information prior to the event occurring that the two suspects might be planning to attack the event.

"These reports are not accurate. No one, not the Garland Police Department, the FBI, the Texas DPS, nor any other agency had any information prior to the event that either suspect may target this event. No information was missed or ignored."

Bates said, on the day of the event an FBI analyst sent an email containing a general information bulletin to the local FBI Joint Terrorism Task Force regarding one of the suspects. That email and general information bulletin was one of many emails sent on that day. It did not contain any information that listed the suspect as a potential threat, and even if it had it would not have changed the law-enforcement response.

Terrorist Surveillance Detection

At the Active Shooter/Killer Course for Civilians at Tactical Defense Institute, former CIA officer Ed Lovette described how to detect terrorist surveillance. The terrorists come out of the shadows when they are in the preparation phase of an attack. They will be conducting surveillance as part of their planning.

"Our government has done a miserable job of informing you about things that you can do to help our government."

It doesn't matter what your job or profession is, everyone has an opportunity to see something that is part of a hostile operation. Lovette gave an example of several Middle-Eastern-looking men who turned up at a major city hospital about 3 a.m. and said they were hospital inspectors. When the staff made a phone call to check them out, they left. This was possibly a pre-operational act, he said.

You are as likely to see indicators of attack planning as police or the security services. The IDF (Israeli Defense Force) credits the civilian population with finding about 80 percent of terrorist bombs in public places.

On March 30, 2008, General Hayden, then CIA director, announced that Al Qaeda is training "western appearing" operatives "you wouldn't pay attention to if you were going through Customs at Dulles."

On September 7, 2007, Hayden said analysts assessed with high confidence that Al Qaeda leadership was planning high-impact plots against the U.S. homeland; that the organization had regenerated key elements of its homeland-attack capability; and that Al Qaeda was focusing on targets that would produce mass casualties, dramatic destruction, and considerable economic aftershocks.

Generation Two terrorism is anything after "9-11." Home-grown jihadis, such as the Fort Hood shooter, are an increasing threat.

Lovette, speaking before the rise of ISIS, didn't think that Al Qaeda was the biggest terrorist threat, as it was not the organization it used to be, particularly since the death of Usama Bin Laden.

"The Unholy Trinity is part of everything that is going on down in Mexico."

It is composed of the drug cartels; the Latino free gangs like MS-13 and M-18 that provide security and which are working in the U.S.; and terrorists, most notably Hezbollah.

At safe houses provided by Muslim businessmen in Mexico, "special interest aliens" (AKA PIIOs — Persons of Interest of Islamic Origin) received Spanish-language training and guidance regarding fitting in with the local culture. They also received state-of-the-art documents. In exchange they provide training in explosives (example: car bombs in Juarez, cell-phone trigger). After training they are taken across the border by gang members using the same routes the cartels use.

They may well have settled into Latino communities, but we don't know who they are, why they are here, how many have crossed into the U.S., and how many cities they are in.

Despite the rise of ISIS, Hezbollah is still a major concern, Lovette said.

It is believed by many to be more dangerous than Al Qaeda. It is backed by Iran and Syria and will have had first-rate training. It has conducted bombings in South America and fought the Israelis to a standstill.

Rep. Sue Myrick, a member of the House Intelligence Committee, sent a letter to DHS Secretary Janet Napolitano dated June 23, 2010, asking that she "form a Homeland Security task force to engage U.S. and Mexican law-enforcement and border-patrol officials about Hezbollah's presence, activities, and connections to gangs and drug cartels."

The DHS response, provided to the *Charlotte Observer* on August 24, 2010, by DHS spokeswoman Amy Kudwa, was: "At this time, DHS does not have any credible information on terrorist groups operating along the Southwest Border."

Lovette said it was an unbelievable statement, especially in light of the following information, which was documented by two different sources: "Operation Cazando Anguilas," a study contracted out by the Office of the Secretary of Defense to develop some ground truth in South and Central America on the issue, March 2009. There is also a thesis titled *The Relationship Between Criminal and Terrorist Organizations and Human Smuggling* by Joseph Lanzante, the Naval Postgraduate School, December 2009.

According to intelligence reports, gang members of MS-13 and M-18 serve as couriers, escorts, and protection for drugs, special interest aliens, money, and weapons for drug-trafficking organizations. They eliminate competition and enforce discipline for the drug traffickers.

The National Gang Intelligence Center has information that documents U.S.-based gang members crossing the U.S.-Mexico border for the express purpose of smuggling drugs and aliens from Mexico into the U.S.

The people who smuggle narcotics are the same people, or associates of, those who smuggle aliens. The routes used to smuggle narcotics are the same routes used to smuggle people.

If you are a human smuggler, you are going to have the ability and infrastructure established in Mexico to keep the subjects hidden; that is why Al Qaeda on its own cannot smuggle terrorists or weapons of mass destruction into the country; they have to rely on local talent.

In order to secure those routes into the U.S. and to keep those lines going, the trafficking organizations are employing the gangs. Gangs are already in the community; they have lookouts and the infrastructure to move things clandestinely.

The National Gang Intelligence Center claims that MS-13 are experts at gaining illegal entry into the U.S. Schools set up by Muslim businessmen to train special-interest aliens to blend into the local communities.

Hezbollah relies on the same criminal weapons smugglers, document traffickers, and transportation experts as the drug cartels. The terrorists know if they pay the cartels money, they are going to get the job done. They are going to get the cell across the border.

If You See Something, Say Something

Look for suspicious activity or suspicious interest, regardless of gender, race, or ethnicity.

"One of the things people have a problem with is saying something to the authorities about anything you are not sure of — you're not absolutely certain about."

If you are not sure about what you are seeing, consider the following. Think outside the box — could these activities be pre-attack planning and preparation? For example, "I just need to know how to take off, I am not concerned with landing." Or, "I only need to rent this apartment for a couple of months." Coupled with paying in cash.

Is critical infrastructure involved? Today this can be anything from a bridge to a school to your place of business. (Communications, transportation, financial, government, etc.) It is normal for people on vacation to take photographs, but if they are taking pictures of bridges, government buildings, and such, this is probably worth passing on.

Trust your common sense and instincts. Does it pass the smell test? Look at the totality of the activity or interest. For example, two men are staying in a motel room during the winter. Despite the cold they insist on keeping the windows open.

They refuse maid service, although they are there for several days. (For example, the Millennium Bomber preparing his explosives to blow up the Los Angeles International Airport.)

If you do see something that appears suspicious, you have options, Lovette said. You can call local law enforcement, the FBI, or the fusion center. Local law enforcement may be your best bet. Bear in mind that if you call the Bureau, you will never get any feedback, he added.

Bombs

The Active Shooter/Killer Course for Civilians at Tactical Defense Institute included a session on recognizing and coping with bombs. This was taught by Greg Ellifritz, a police-training officer from Columbus, Ohio. He said bombs are the trend with terrorists.

"It's the cool thing for active shooters to do now. They've got to get a bigger and better body count, and how do they get bigger and better body counts? High explosives."

Ellifritz told us to shoot in the head anyone wearing a bomb. A shot to the body might set off the bomb.

At Columbine, the two killers had more than ninety improvised explosive devices. Even though they were fairly unsophisticated, it is fortunate that the ones that did explode did not do much damage. At Mumbai, the terrorists were using some serious bombs — RDX and hand-grenades.

"If you are dealing with an active shooter, I think you have to be prepared to deal with bombs as well.

"My goal is for you to be able to recognize some of the common explosives that terrorists or active shooters may be using and figure out what to do with them or what to do with yourself."

He did not suggest disarming a bomb, but recognizing it and getting out of harm's way. He wanted us to be able to recognize what a bomb looks like and the capabilities of a bomb, so we know where we have to be to be safe, then how to isolate it and report it to the proper authorities.

He went through types of explosives we might encounter, such as dynamite. Dynamite is used by farmers, road-construction crews, and miners. You need a federal license, but it is not that hard to get, or you can steal dynamite. Dynamite is a very unstable explosive.

Some of the more stable explosives require a booster charge, which is often set off by a detonator.

"In most of your big booms, it is really a series of very little booms strung together with almost no time in between." You need other explosives, booster charges, to set off bigger explosives. Booster charges often look like batteries, but may be a little bigger. They are set off by something smaller, such as a blasting cap or detonating cord, which in turn is set off by an electrical spark or a model-rocket engine. "There is an entire chain that goes into the big boom."

Some more powerful bombs are made from ammonium nitrate (as in fertilizer) and fuel oil. The fertilizer has time-release capsules so it doesn't burn your grass. They are ground up and mixed with diesel, kerosene, or gasoline — the result is a bomb. Of the three numbers on fertilizer bags, the first relates to nitrogen. The higher the nitrogen number, the better for bombs. If someone orders bags of 35-0-0, that might be suspicious. It would rarely be used as fertilizer. The bomb at Oklahoma City was nine thousand pounds.

Other explosives used to make bombs include:
- ANFO — ammonium nitrate and diesel.
- C4 — usually white, but can come in other colors.
- Concentrated hydrogen peroxide — containers of 30 percent hydrogen peroxide should trigger alarm bells.
- Potassium chlorate and Vaseline.

Ellifritz said there are many ways of setting off explosives, so don't mess with them. They can be set off by motion detectors or other movement. Terrorists may set off bombs with cell phones or pagers.

Before they blow themselves up, terrorists often give warning signals. They may become especially emotional. They may start giving away their possessions as the Fort Hood killer did. Their clothing may not be right for the conditions, because they may be trying to hide weapons or explosives. They may be carrying heavy backpacks stuffed with guns and explosives. Patting the upper body indicates they are hiding something they don't want exposed. Homicide bombers and other active killers tend to have emotionless eyes and walk robotically, as though they are in a trance.

They may wear heavy cologne to cover up the smell of chemicals used in making explosives. They may also be wearing uniforms of police officers, phone company employees, or delivery staff.

"Just because someone is wearing a police or fire uniform, don't automatically assume they are police or fire. There've been lots of uniforms stolen."

Terrorists often set off one bomb and, when the emergency responders arrive, they set off another strategically placed device. The first bomb concentrates all the first responders in one place. If evacuating people from the scene of a bomb, don't usher them into the obvious area where there may be a second bomb.

"The strategy is you set off a bomb. It could be a small bomb; it doesn't even have to kill anybody, but what does that do? It concentrates our emergency responders in one place. Then you come in with a bigger bomb and blow them all up. Now in the entire town, when 90 percent of its police and fire personnel are blown up, who's going to respond to the active shooter that is the second wave of the attack?"

Ellifritz said that was what happened in Mumbai. To get a bomb in amongst a bunch of cops, they dressed like cops, walked right in, and blew themselves up.

"As an individual, your prime job is to not get yourself blown up. If you get blown up, you can't do anything to help anybody else. Therefore, if you see a bomb, the number one rule is: do not touch it. We don't know how it's set to blow up. So move people away from it. Mostly there will be a secondary device, so don't move people to a parking lot where a car could be a bomb. Search the potential evacuation area for secondary bombs. Check for anything out of place.

Rule of thumb: if you can see the bomb, you are too close. Beware of the bomber's handlers or lookouts. Handlers who will not draw attention to themselves are just as dangerous as the bombers. In some cases the handler has a way of setting off the bomb in case the bomber gets cold feet.

"Not everyone who is recruited for suicide bombing thinks it's a real good idea. They might get right up to it and decide: 'Hey, I really don't want to blow myself up today.' But the buddy who is five hundred feet away has another way to set off the bomb."

For a small car bomb, the pressure wave of the bomb is one hundred feet; the evacuation distance is five hundred yards. For a backpack or suicide bomb, the evacuation distance is between two-hundred and four-hundred yards. Shielding is another solution if we have something that stops the blast pressure wave, such as a wall — but not between two walls. The safest place in a room with a window on the side towards the blast is under the window. The pressure wave of plastic explosives travels at thirty thousand feet per second. A rifle bullet may travel at three thousand feet per second. Some people think they can duck a bomb blast.

Remember, if you engage a suicide bomber, you may be signing your own death warrant.

If you are an armed citizen, and you are not in the immediate line of fire, should you go in and try to stop a terrorist incident?

Terrorism expert and author John Giduck says: "My question would be: Why not? It comes down to the personality, the psychological makeup of that person, and the training and the weapons of that person. If you've got somebody with a Walther PPK/S and a single magazine, you're talking eight rounds. I don't know that I would advise that — some woman pulls that PPK/S out of her purse, but she's only got eight little bullets, I don't know that I would advise her to apply these tactics. On the other hand, I've got a lot of friends and professional colleagues, they go everywhere with two, three high-cap mags — they're nine mil — and they'd probably be in a far better position to actually attempt to engage some people and survive and have a positive effect."

He says even one person can slow up a group of terrorists intent on taking over a building, be it a school, a mall, or a hotel. If you can prevent them from completing their plan, they will have to deal with you first, and that gives law enforcement time to reach the scene.

"If it's a mass-hostage siege, they've got to collect those hostages, they've got to secure them, they've got to start fortifying, none of which they can do, or certainly none of which they can do on the time-line that they've developed in their plan, so long as they are deviating from that complete attack plan. And they also know that they are under the gun, literally under the gun, because they know responding forces are on the way."

More than ever, we ordinary civilians are the foot soldiers in the war on terrorism. If you are lawfully armed, wear your gun and get training in its use. Don't just leave it at home or in the car. Yes, I know it's awkward and heavy but, as they say, it is better to have it and not need it than to need it and not have it. And even if your state allows open carry, keep your gun concealed. If you wear it openly, it is like having a target on your back; you will be the first to be shot.

Chapter 15

THE IRREGULAR FIRST RESPONDERS

Irregular forces: armed individuals or groups not members
of the regular armed forces, police, or other
internal security forces. — New Webster's Dictionary

One of the things that tends to get ignored in any study of mass shootings is the number of incidents where intervention by an armed or unarmed civilian stops them before the toll of dead and wounded rises to qualify the incident as a mass killing.

The three young Americans on the Amsterdam to Paris train and Mark Vaughan's timely intervention in Moore, Oklahoma, are examples. Both of these incidents received national publicity. However, many receive little or no publicity, particularly if the civilian used a gun. One such incident that received no national publicity occurred in 2012 between the shooting at the movie theater in Aurora, Colorado, and killings at a Sikh temple near Milwaukee, Wisconsin.

Vic Stacy Intervenes

July 29, 2012, was a normal hot summer day with the temperature crowding one hundred degrees. It was the sort of day when tempers can be short and sometimes violent.

But Vic Stacy was in his trailer, relaxing in the air conditioning. He was watching a Rambo movie — *First Blood*. He'd seen the movie before but this time he wouldn't see it through to the end.

About 1:30 p.m. he heard several shots.

"I looked out to see what was going on, but I didn't see anything," Stacy said.

He thought somebody was engaging in a little recreational shooting. But a few moments later he got a call from a neighbor, Phil Brown, who told him: "Get over here quick, and bring your gun."

Brown said there was a dead body lying in the road. So Stacy picked up his revolver, a Colt Python with a six-inch barrel. The revolver was loaded with six rounds of Remington .357 Magnum hollow-points. He slid the holstered gun into his waistband, under his T-shirt, and headed for Brown's motor home.

The Peach House RV Park is a few miles north of Brownwood in central Texas. There were half a dozen trailers and recreational vehicles in the park at the time. Stacy had lived there in his trailer for about a year.

Vic Stacy was a tall sixty-six-year-old welder with a weathered face and an easy-going attitude. He was a Brown County resident and a Texan from the top of his hat to the heels of his boots. Although he had no military or law-enforcement experience, he had been shooting all his life.

As Stacy rounded the corner of his own trailer, he looked to his left and saw another neighbor, a fifty-eight-year-old man with a reputation for being cantankerous, coming out of his trailer carrying a lever-action .30-30-caliber Marlin rifle with a scope on it. When he saw the man with the rifle, Stacy knew he had done the shooting. He'd had a couple of arguments with the man himself.

The man had an ongoing dispute with a couple who lived in a trailer near Brown's RV. David Michael House, 58, and Iris Valentina (Tina) Calaci, 53, had two dogs, a small white poodle mix and a black-and-white Border-collie mix. The cantankerous neighbor became angry with the couple because their dogs had been defecating around his trailer.

After arguing with House and Calaci, the man shot and killed the couple and one of their dogs, wounding the other, with a 9mm-caliber SIG Sauer semi-automatic pistol. That was the shooting Stacy heard. A witness later told investigators the gunman chased Calaci twice around her pickup then shot her in the head at pointblank range. The witness saw the killer return to his trailer and emerge with the rifle. That was when Stacy saw him.

Phil Brown said he was napping with his blinds down and his air conditioner running full blast. It was noisy and he did not hear the shots that killed House and hit the dogs. He said he awoke when Calaci bumped into his RV. Brown heard her scream: "No, not my dogs you're not."

When he heard the woman's voice, he raised his blinds and looked out. "I seen him, David, laying over there about like in the fetal position, and I seen the dogs both and the one dog was still alive."

That's when Brown called Vic Stacy. Then he called 9-1-1.

When Stacy arrived at the motor home, Brown told him that House was lying in the driveway near his trailer, apparently dead from a gunshot wound to the head. Stacy could see House and the dogs. They then noticed Tina Calaci lying dead in front of Brown's vehicle.

The bodies of Tina Calaci, David House, and their dogs after they were shot. The pickup and trailer are behind them. (Crime scene photo.)

The door to Brown's motor home was on the side away from where the killer's trailer was parked. Stacy edged carefully to the front of Brown's motor home and looked for the gunman.

Brown, who didn't have any firearms, followed Stacy. About that time Stacy heard the first police siren from a patrol car speeding north from Early. Although the RV park is outside the city limits of Early by several miles, the first officer to arrive was Sergeant Steven Means, 29, of the Early Police Department.

Means was on radar-traffic-enforcement duty in Early when he heard the call on his radio that there had been a shooting at Peach House RV Park. Means pulled into the park and stopped his patrol car about forty yards from the killer's white Dodge pickup. The dash camera on Means's vehicle recorded the action. It shows the gunman moving behind a tree for cover. He apparently fired two shots at Means who grabbed his .223-caliber Smith & Wesson M&P-15 semi-automatic rifle and took cover at the rear of his patrol car.

Stacy saw Sergeant Means pull into the park and stop. The gunman started shooting at the officer as he was getting out of his patrol car. Stacy said he could see the killer shooting and working the lever of his hunting rifle.

"At that time I had made up my mind I was going to see if I could hit him," Stacy said.

At the time the killer was using an oak tree with a trunk about a foot thick as cover from Means. However, Stacy was at right angles to the line of fire between the gunman and the police officer. The gunman was standing with his right side exposed to Stacy's line of fire.

Stacy cocked the revolver and took aim at the gunman, bracing his arms on the hood of Brown's motor home. The range was fifty-seven yards.

"I shot the first shot and it hit him in the thigh," Stacy said.

Stacy shows how he shot the killer from Brown's motor home. He is using the author's Smith & Wesson .41 Magnum revolver because his Colt Python was seized for evidence. It was later returned.

The dash camera record shows the gunman stumbling forward to the ground.

"He went to scrambling around on the ground there trying to get turned around. I saw him throw another shell in that rifle. He swung it around and shot at me. It hit underneath the RV there and scattered rocks. Some of those hit me on the leg. He got pretty close, but he didn't get close enough," Stacy said with a chuckle.

"I returned four more shots and hit him in the abdomen so he rolled over, and he never fired another shot."

According to the autopsy, Stacy's second hit went through the gunman's left arm into his chest cavity and was recovered from the upper left lung.

Means also returned fire shooting seven times with his rifle from the rear of his patrol car. He hit the gunman three times. One round entered just below the left shoulder blade and severely damaged the liver and left lung, according to the Texas Ranger report of the incident. A second bullet severed the spinal column and jugular vein. The third hit severely damaged the right lung.

"These wounds were consistent with angles of fire from Stacy and Sergeant Means at the scene," the report states.

"Pretty much the gun battle was over after that," Stacy said.

More law-enforcement officers arrived from Early, the Brown County Sheriff's Office, and the Texas Department of Public Safety. A couple of other officers and a DPS trooper armed with an AR-15 rifle and approached Stacy and Brown. The dash camera recorded the officers yelling repeatedly: "Put the gun on the ground; put the gun on the ground," and "Step away from the gun; step away from the gun."

In his statement, Means said Stacy had a stainless revolver in his hand and was slow to drop it. The DPS Trooper with the rifle "came over to where we was at, and I still had the gun in my hand. The officer said: 'Get rid of the gun and get on the ground.' So I did," Stacy said.

The trooper was pointing the rifle at him. Once Stacy was lying on the ground, the officer cuffed his hands behind his back. Brown was also on the ground, but they didn't handcuff him, Stacy said.

The rocks he was lying on were hot on his chest from the sun, Stacy said. After talking among themselves the police came over and helped him to his feet, but it was another fifteen minutes or so before they took the cuffs off.

It is wise to holster a gun or put it down when police arrive on the scene of a shooting. They do not know that you are the good guy or gal. We have seen teachers and other civilians being taught about this at Tactical Defense Institute.

While coming to the assistance of a law-enforcement officer may be a dream of some who carry concealed weapons, it comes with its own set of problems. If a police officer requests your assistance, that is one thing, but voluntarily involving yourself in a gunfight between police and bad guys can be hazardous to your health. The biggest uncertainty is: does the officer know you are on his side? Or does he see you as another enemy? This is no criticism of Vic Stacy's actions that July afternoon. However, it is something to bear in mind.

Brown County Sheriff Bobby Grubbs, a former Texas Ranger, is very pro the Second Amendment and against gun control. "Had this citizen not had a gun, this could have been a whole lot worse," he said.

Sergeant Means was not injured. However, the Border collie was still alive but badly injured and had to be shot by a game warden.

Grubbs asked the Texas Rangers to lead the investigation. This is common practice in officer-involved shootings, particularly in rural areas. Ranger Danny Crawford coordinated the investigation and wrote the final report.

Stacy's Colt Python was taken by investigators for testing and evidence. When you use your gun defending yourself or others, your gun will be taken for evidence. It was more than three months before he got it back. If your shooting results in a trial it could be years before your gun is returned, so it is as well to have a spare, preferably a twin to your carry gun.

Stacy said he did what he thought was necessary. When the gunman was shooting at Means, he feared for the officer's life if he didn't do something to help. "I could see a vision of him getting killed and him having three or four kids at home and a wife. And when I met the officer, sure enough that was true: he had three kids and a wife at home. And if he had gotten killed he would never have knew his kids, and his kids would never have knew him. So it all worked out for the best."

The following day, Sheriff Grubbs issued a statement that read in part: "It has been determined that [Stacy] acted valiantly and perhaps saved the lives of Sergeant Means and responding deputies. His actions may also have saved the lives of other citizens who could have innocently walked into the situation. Thus far, it appears that law enforcement and the citizens of Brown County owe a debt of gratitude toward this man for his courage to act."

Stacy said Ranger Crawford called him and told him they were not planning to file any charges on him or Means.

"Before I hung up, he said: 'By the way, I don't want you shooting at me. You're a better shot than I am.' That made me feel good in that respect."

On October 24 a grand jury in Brownwood no-billed Vic Stacy and Sergeant Steven Means, in effect exonerating them in the shooting death of the killer. Ranger Crawford returned Stacy's Colt Python revolver to him.

In March 2013 at Brown County Courthouse, Sheriff Grubbs presented Stacy with a plaque in appreciation for what he did. Grubbs praised Stacy for his courage in becoming involved in the incident.

"He did a fantastic job. We will never know how many lives Vic may have saved that day."

Texas Governor Rick Perry presents Stacy with a LaRue Tactical .308-caliber semi-automatic rifle.

Two days later, Stacy was called to Governor Rick Perry's office at the Capitol in Austin. The governor also praised Stacy for his courage. "Vic Stacy is a great example of Texas and what people both intuitively think about Texas and what is real about Texas. That is, when neighbors are in need, Vic is there to help his neighbors."

Perry presented him with what some people would describe as an assault rifle. It was a .308-caliber semi-automatic military-style rifle built by LaRue Tactical. It is the rifle carried by Texas Rangers.

The Irregular First Responders

In this incident, Vic Stacy was the first person on the scene to take the action that probably saved Sergeant Means's life. Stacy was not a trained police officer, had never been in the military, and was not a paramedic. But he knew about guns, and he was the first person to respond to the scene, and he stopped the killer. As such he was the first responder. In most cases, law-enforcement officers are the first responders. They are trained to respond first and usually when a crime, such as hostage taking, kidnapping, murder, or robbery, is committed they are. However, rapid mass murders are different. The killer is trying to slay as many people as possible before the Stopwatch of Death runs out, often when law enforcement arrives. According to statistics I've mentioned earlier, more of these killings are stopped by ordinary, "unqualified" citizens who either are in harm's way or put themselves there. To differentiate them from the trained first responders, I have dubbed these citizens the "Irregular First Responders."

They include Jon Lane at Moses Lake, Washington, 1996; Joel Myrick at Pearl, Mississippi, 1997; Jake Ryker, Springfield, Oregon, 1998; the three unarmed Americans who took down the terrorist on the Amsterdam to Paris fast train, 2015; and many others.

These people — be they teachers, worshipers, shoppers, off-duty cops, or just ordinary citizens who happen to be in the wrong place at the right time — they are the answer to the problem of active killers indulging in rapid mass murder.

Time is the enemy. Again and again we have seen how these active killers have been able to run up shocking totals of dead and wounded in the time before law-enforcement officers with their own military-style semi-automatic rifles, shotguns, and semi-automatic pistols can reach the scene and engage them.

Although these Irregular First Responders are usually unarmed, don't they deserve to be allowed to carry the best weapons they are able to to even the contest? Suzanna Hupp was there when her parents were killed in the Luby's Cafeteria in Killeen in 1991. Her words echo through every mass killing since: "I can't begin to get across to you or anybody else what it's like to sit there and wait for it to be your turn. I get very angry right now even thinking about that. Can you imagine not being able to fight back?"

Her father did try to fight back and was gunned down in front of her. If only somebody in there had had a gun....

Heroes Will Take on the Risk

Having a gun is not always a guarantee of success. On February 24, 2005, Mark Wilson was in his apartment overlooking the courthouse square in Tyler, Texas. Wilson, 52, was a Navy veteran and former owner of a shooting range who had a concealed-handgun license. He watched as a forty-three-year-old Mexican legal immigrant ambushed his recently divorced wife and twenty-one-year-old son as they were about to ascend the courthouse steps. The gunman was shooting a MAK-90, a Chinese-made semi-automatic AK-47-style rifle, and he was wearing body armor. He hit and killed his former wife and wounded his son, then he started shooting at law-enforcement officers coming out of the courthouse, wounding one badly.

Wilson grabbed his Colt .45-caliber semi-automatic pistol and headed downstairs. The lightweight Tactical Officer's Model contained a magazine holding eight Hydra-Shok hollow-point rounds plus one in the chamber for a total of nine.

A witness said he saw Mark Wilson wearing a red shirt taking cover behind the gunman's pickup. As he watched, Wilson took aim at the gunman, who had his back to him while still loosing off rounds in the direction of the courthouse. The killer was backing up towards the open driver's-side door but was still close to the tailgate. Wilson aimed over the truck bed using a two-hand hold. He fired several fast shots at the gunman knocking him down. Wilson turned away and started to walk towards the sidewalk. He could not see the shooter because he was on the other side of the truck. Wilson was probably trying to go around the front of

From his apartment window, Mark Wilson had a clear view of Spring Avenue, the east entrance to the courthouse, and the place where he would eventually lose his life to the killer's bullets. (Photo by Robert Langham.)

Mark Wilson, when he owned On Target Indoor Shooting Range. (Photo courtesy of Lock & Load Indoor Shooting Range.)

the pickup where he could check on the gunman while using the engine block as cover.

Unaware of the gunman's body armor, Wilson may well have thought he had killed the gunman or badly wounded him. But as he turned away, the witness watched in horror as the killer scrambled up and fired at Wilson hitting him in the back on the right side. Wilson fell face down alongside the pickup with his head against the curb. The gunman stepped around the back of the pickup and fired another shot hitting Wilson in the back of the head, killing him.

The gunman was later killed by police. Mark Wilson was called a hero and a plaque was erected to him on the courthouse square where he fell. He was as much a hero as any law-enforcement officer or soldier defending the country. What he tried to do was what any warrior would have done. (See a full account in *Thank God I Had a Gun.*)

But have we lost our warrior ethos? Have we become a nation of cowards? Have we become brainwashed by big government, big media, and big academia into believing that personal risk is unacceptable in a civilized society — that dignity and self-respect must bow to safety at all costs? Jeffrey Snyder in his excellent 1993 article, "A Nation of Cowards," certainly thought so.

As he pointed out, if we do not fight crime on a personal level we are abdicating our personal responsibilities as citizens and condoning evil. And yet for decades, we have been told by big city police departments to give the criminal what he wants. "Do not resist because you might get hurt." We have allowed our schools to demonize firearms, which are the most effective weapons for personal defense. With zero-tolerance policies, we have brainwashed our kids that violence, even in self defense, is wrong. We have been encouraged to rely on authority to protect us.

Cathy Lanier, police chief in Washington, D.C., was interviewed by Anderson Cooper on a *60 Minutes* segment that ran on November 22, 2015.

"Your options are run, hide, or fight," Lanier said.

As mentioned in the ALICE instructor course (Chapter 8), this is the new mantra of many federal, state, and local law-enforcement agencies: run, hide, or fight.

Lanier said that most active killers shoot most of the victims in ten minutes or less. Referring to her own department, Lanier said, "the best police department in the country is going to be about a five to seven minute response," she added.

Ron Borsch estimates that active killers wound or murder between four and five victims a minute. (See Chapter 6.) This means that somewhere between twenty and thirty-five victims would be killed or wounded before the Washington, D.C., police arrived.

Now law-enforcement agencies around the country are trying to teach people how to survive before law enforcement arrives, Lanier acknowledges.

"If you're in a position to try and take the gunman down, to take the gunman out, it's the best option for saving lives before police can get there. And that's kind of counterintuitive to what cops always tell people, right? We always tell people, 'Don't take action. Call 9-1-1. Don't intervene in the robbery.' We've never told people, 'Take Action.' This is a different scenario."

Unfortunately, Lanier's hypocritical slip is showing. Despite her call for ordinary citizens to take down an active killer, she has deliberately deprived those citizens of the best weapon to do that. According to *Fox News*, since October 2014 requests for 233 concealed-handgun permits have been received by the Metropolitan Police Department and 185 of them have been denied. This is an 80 percent rejection record. Lanier has final say on which permits are approved.

Despite confirmation by the Supreme Court in 2008 that the District of Columbia's gun laws were unconstitutional, the politicians and bureaucrats in the nation's capital have made it as difficult for residents to own handguns, let alone carry them, as it is for a camel to pass through the eye of a needle.

In the case of *District of Columbia versus Heller*, the court affirmed that the Second Amendment to the Constitution guarantees, with some restrictions, individuals the right to keep and bear arms.

Starting in October of 2011, Emily Miller, an editor with *The Washington Times* and a district resident, tried to get government permission to own a handgun. It took four months and $435 in fees for her to take home a SIG Sauer P229, and even then she could not carry it outside her home. Miller wrote a series of columns for the newspaper which resulted in a slight easing of the process. She also wrote a book: *Emily Gets Her Gun* (see Bibliography). This is how the District of Columbia defies the Supreme Court of the United States.

"Gun-Free" Zones

We have to get rid of the so-called gun-free zones. Why is it that people who have qualified to get concealed-handgun licenses can walk down the street wearing handguns, but if they turn into a courthouse, a bar, a sporting event, or a school, suddenly they are committing a crime and could go to prison? For that matter, why should anybody who is qualified to buy a gun be deprived of the best means of self defense when they enter certain areas?

The biggest problem with gun-free zones is that they aren't free of guns. They are the places of choice for killers and terrorists to rack up their totals of killed and wounded in places like Columbine, Virginia Tech, Fort Hood, and the Charleston AME Church. They are killing zones.

In 2015 the Texas Legislature passed a law opening up colleges and universities to people with concealed-handgun licenses to carry on the premises. Unfortunately they dirtied up the bill with language that allows campus administrators to designate gun-free zones. When the law goes into effect for public universities August 1, 2016, it is likely that campuses will be littered with gun-free zone signs thus defeating the object of the law. Other states, such as Utah and Idaho, where students with concealed-handgun permits are allowed to carry on university campuses, appear to have had no problems.

We have to recognize that the country is at war with radical Islamic terrorists and, unlike World War II and Vietnam, the foot soldiers are not just those in uniform but every man and woman in the country. It is in the nature of government officials not to trust members of the public, but because this war is being fought in our towns and cities, they have to trust ordinary people. Remember the cries of gloom and doom when concealed-carry laws were being passed by state legislatures? The predictions of blood in the streets and every traffic accident turning into a gunfight did not happen. Why? Because the men and women with the permits turned out to be much more responsible than the media and many of the politicians gave them credit for. So far gun-free zones have not worked. The definition of insanity is doing the same thing and expecting a different result. Let's try something different. The government should be encouraging the people to get concealed-handgun permits and to get training in how to cope with rapid mass murder. Law-enforcement agencies should be holding training courses instructing ordinary citizens in how to cope with active killers. Give them the tools and the training and let them do the job.

Law-Enforcement Attitudes

Attitudes in law enforcement are changing, but they need to go further. Faced with a high violent-crime rate in 2013, Detroit Police Chief James Craig urged his residents to get concealed-pistol licenses and carry guns. More than fourteen thousand Detroit residents got their licenses in 2013 and 2014. Violent crime went down. After the attacks in Paris, Craig said he believes armed residents are a good deterrent against terrorist attacks, because terrorists, like ordinary criminals, like their victims to be unarmed.

Senior law-enforcement officials are slowly starting to realize they are seldom going to arrive in time to affect an active-killer incident. For decades, big-city police departments have routinely told their citizens, "don't fight back; give the criminals what they want." How well has this worked for active-killer events?

But habits and traditions die hard. Police in general and their managers in particular are very reluctant to admit that there is an area of public safety that is beyond their control.

They have to admit that the Irregular First Responders are going to have the responsibility of stopping the killer.

Generally speaking, sheriffs tend to be more amenable to concealed carry by their citizens than are police chiefs. Sheriffs have to be elected by the people, while police chiefs have only to pander to members of city government, which in large cities tend to distrust armed citizens. They are harder to control.

Law-enforcement also has to change their training so the first officer on the scene goes in and tackles the active killer. Officer Justin Garner of the Carthage Police Department in North Carolina is an excellent example. True, eight people died, and three more were wounded, but if Garner had waited for backup the casualties could have been double that.

After Columbine, law enforcement realized that waiting for the SWAT team wasn't going to do a thing for the victims. They went to *ad hoc* four-man teams composed of the first officers on the scene, but even that took too long. At Sandy Hook the shooting was still going on in the school while officers were outside assessing the situation. Ron Borsch, in his inimitable way, refers to it as Tactical Loitering. Law-enforcement officers have to realize that it is their duty to go in as soon as they arrive to have any chance of cutting down on the carnage.

Terrorism expert John Giduck says the average law-enforcement officer has enough training and equipment to tackle an active killer immediately he or she arrives on the scene.

"I always go back to this same recognition of the reality, which is huddled inside there are a bunch of innocent people who have no guns, no weapons, no body armor, no training whatsoever, and often, as we know in the majority of incidents in the U.S., they are children. They don't stand a chance. You are a grownup, you've got body armor, you've got firearms, you've got training, maybe you die, maybe you don't, but at least you have a chance. And at least if that person has to deviate what he's doing to deal with you, these innocent people live. I think it all just boils down to that one simple reality. And I honestly believe if you're not the person to ever go into that situation, for those reasons alone, I think law enforcement should not be your chosen field."

Political Correctness and Zero Tolerance

In 2010 when news analyst Juan Williams commented on Fox that he felt worried and nervous flying on the same plane as Muslims in traditional garb, he got fired by National Public Radio, essentially for voicing politically incorrect thoughts.

But when fear of being branded racist caused neighbors of the San Bernardino shooters not to report suspicions to police, they essentially shared some of the blame for the murders caused by the radical Muslim killers.

The most dreaded accusation for white liberals and politicians is that of racism. They will shy from that accusation as an unbroken horse will shy from the catch rope. With prompting from the professional racemongers like Al Sharpton and Jesse Jackson, they will deplore the shooting of black criminals by white cops, but ignore that the vast majority of black murder victims are killed by black criminals. The result is that people will neglect their civic duty and will not report reasonable suspicions to law enforcement, particularly if the suspect is of another race or religion. The only way for evil to triumph is for good men and women to do nothing.

And then we have zero tolerance. Since the mid-1990s schools have enacted zero-tolerance policies about guns, real or imaginary, in reaction to some mass shootings. This has resulted in our children being taught that all guns are bad and anyone who has a gun is probably a criminal. It is as stupid to blame guns for shootings as it is to blame cars for traffic accidents.

While the Second Amendment has come under attack as a result of these policies, so has the free-speech guarantee of the First Amendment. In April 2013 Jared Marcum, 14, went to Logan County Middle School wearing a T-shirt that proclaimed "NRA: Protect Your Right," accompanied by a picture of a scoped hunting rifle. While lining up for lunch, a teacher told Marcum to turn his T-shirt inside out. He refused, saying he was doing nothing wrong. The teacher sent him to the administration office where he was again told to reverse the shirt. When he again refused, the administrators called police. While sitting down Marcum interrupted the officer to tell his side of the story and was promptly arrested for obstructing a police officer. A judge eventually threw out the case.

In another incident of bureaucratic stupidity, nine-year-old Vincent Olivarez was almost suspended from Telfair Elementary School in the Los Angeles Unified School District when he was caught with what administrators called "extremely disturbing and offensive" photos. Are we talking "porn" shots here? No, they were photos of him and his brother shooting guns at a shooting range under the supervision of their aunt, who happened to be a police firearms instructor.

John Giduck says that years ago he was preaching fighting back against active killers in schools. "I was one of the first people advocating publicly for people in schools, kids, teachers, to all know there are some times when you just have to fight. I would get excoriated for ever suggesting such a thing. My attitude was every teacher should know what weapon they've got in their classroom. I don't care if it is an umbrella, a big pair of scissors, a stapler.

"The point is to get them to look around their classrooms today and to know what their weapons are, and what the

"Gun-Free" Zone sign outside Castle Hills Elementary School in San Antonio, Texas.

series of weapons they can default to are, even if it comes to arming some of the larger teenage male students. If it's that or die, arm people and fight. It was not well received at all."

While defending oneself from a physical attack is legal in one's home or on the street, it is not permitted in schools with a zero-tolerance policy for violence. If a child defends him- or herself against a bully, he or she is in as much trouble as the perpetrator. Like many school policies, this is very convenient for teachers and administrators who do not have to decide who is right and who is wrong, but it is grossly unfair to students. They are being brainwashed into believing that violence is never the answer.

Excuse me. If violence is never acceptable, why do we have a military whose members are trained to fight and kill? And why do police officers have guns? If we do not abandon some of these corrosive policies, we will be become a nation of wimps unwilling to fight for our own survival.

BIBLIOGRAPHY

Artwohl, Dr. Alexis, and Loren W. Christensen. 1997. *Deadly Force Encounters: What Cops Need to Know to Mentally and Physically Prepare for and Survive a Gunfight.* Boulder, Colo.: Paladin Press.

Assam, Jeanne. 2010. *God, the Gunman and Me.* Colorado Springs, Colo.: Jeanne Assam Publishing.

Ayoob, Massad. 2014. *Deadly Force: Understanding Your Right to Self Defense.* Iola, Wisc.: Krause Publications.

Bird, Chris. 2011. *The Concealed Handgun Manual: How to Choose, Carry, and Shoot a Gun in Self Defense,* 6th ed. San Antonio, Texas: Privateer Publications.

———. 2014. *Thank God I Had a Gun: True Accounts of Self-Defense,* 2nd ed. San Antonio, Texas: Privateer Publications.

Duew, Grant. 2007. *Mass Murder in the United States: a History.* Jefferson, NC: McFarland & Company, Inc.

Giduck, John. 2005. *Terror at Beslan: A Russian Tragedy with Lessons for America's Schools.* Golden, Colo.: Archangel Group.

———. 2011. *Shooter Down: The Dramatic, Untold Story of the Police Response to the Virginia Tech Massacre.* Golden, Colo.: Archangel Group.

———. 2011. *When Terror Returns: The History and Future of Terrorist Mass-Hostage Sieges.* Golden, Colo.: Archangel Group.

Grossman, Lt. Col. Dave. 1996. *On Killing: The Psychological Cost of Learning to Kill in War and Society.* New York: Little, Brown & Company.

———, and Loren W. Christensen. 2008. *On Combat: The Psychology and Physiology of Deadly Conflict in War and in Peace.* Opelousas, Louisiana: Warrior Science Publications.

Hupp, Suzanna Gratia. 2010. *From Luby's to the Legislature: One Woman's Fight Against Gun Control*. San Antonio, Texas: Privateer Publications.

Korwin, Alan., and David B. Kopel. 2008. *The Heller Case: Gun Rights Affirmed*. Scottsdale, Arizona: Bloomfield Press.

Lavergne, Gary M. 1997. *A Sniper in the Tower*. Denton, Texas: University of North Texas Press.

Lott, John R. Jr. 2010. *More Guns Less Crime: Understanding Crime and Gun Control Laws*, 3rd ed. Chicago: University of Chicago Press.

Lovette, Ed, and Dave Spaulding. 2005. *Defensive Living: Preserving Your Personal Safety Through Awareness, Attitude & Armed Action*. Flushing, NY: Looseleaf Law Publications, Inc.

Lysiak, Matthew. 2013. *Newtown: An American Tragedy*. New York: Gallery Books.

Martinez, Ramiro. 2005. *They Call Me Ranger Ray*. New Braunfels, Texas: Rio Bravo Publishing.

Miller, Emily. 2013. *Emily Gets Her Gun: But Obama Wants to Take Yours*. Washington D.C.: Regnery Publishing.

New Webster's Dictionary and Thesaurus of the English Language. 1992. Bernard S. Cayne. Danbury, Connecticut: Lexicon Publications, Inc.

Newman, Katherine S., Cybelle Fox, David J. Harding, Jal Mehta, and Wendy Roth. 2004. *Rampage: The Social Roots of School Shootings*. New York: Basic Books.

Phillips, Melanie. 2007. *Londonistan*. London, New York: Encounter Books.

Porterfield, Anita Belles, and John Porterfield. 2015. *Death on Base: The Fort Hood Massacre*. Denton, Texas: University of North Texas Press.

INDEX